PATIENCE AND THANKFULNESS

Kitāb al-ṣabr wa'l-shukr

Book xxxii of the
Revival of the Religious Sciences
Iḥyā' ʿulūm al-dīn

OTHER TITLES IN THE ISLAMIC TEXTS SOCIETY
AL-GHAZĀLĪ SERIES

FROM THE *Iḥyāʾ ʿulūm al-dīn*

Al-Ghazālī on Invocations & Supplications

Al-Ghazālī on the Manners Relating to Eating

Al-Ghazālī on the Lawful & the Unlawful

Al-Ghazālī on Conduct in Travel

Al-Ghazālī on Disciplining the Soul & Breaking the Two Desires

Al-Ghazālī on Love, Longing, Intimacy & Contentment

Al-Ghazālī on Intention, Sincerity & Truthfulness

Al-Ghazālī on Vigilance & Self-examination

Al-Ghazālī on the Remembrance of Death & the Afterlife

OTHER WORKS

Al-Ghazālī on the Ninety-Nine Beautiful Names of God

(*al-Maqṣad al-Asnā fī Sharḥ Asmāʾ Allāh al-Ḥusnā*)

Al-Ghazālī Letter to a Disciple

(*Ayyuhāʾl-walad*)

AL-GHAZĀLĪ
ON PATIENCE AND THANKFULNESS
Kitāb al-ṣabr wa'l-shukr
·BOOK XXXII· of
THE REVIVAL OF THE RELIGIOUS SCIENCES
Iḥyā' ᶜulūm al-dīn · translated with INTRODUCTION & Notes by H. T. LITTLEJOHN

2nd Ed. with al-Ghāzalī's Introduction to the *Revival of the Religious Sciences* •

First edition published 2011 by The Islamic Texts Society

This second edition published 2016 by
THE ISLAMIC TEXTS SOCIETY
MILLER'S HOUSE
KINGS MILL LANE
GREAT SHELFORD
CAMBRIDGE CB22 5EN, U.K.

British Library Cataloguing-in-Publication Data.
A catalogue record for this book is
available from the British Library.

ISBN 978 1911141 31 0 paper

CONTENTS

ON PATIENCE AND THANKFULNESS

Al-Ghazālī's Introduction to the *Revival of the Religious Sciences*

The importance of Imam Ghazālī's Introduction to the Revival of the Religious Sciences *cannot be overstated; it outlines the reasons and motives for the writing of the* Revival *and it explains the structure of the work as a whole. The Islamic Texts Society has decided to include this Introduction at the beginning of all its translations from the* Revival, *including in revised editions of earlier translations. In the list of the forty chapters below, the choice of translation for the titles of the not-yet-published chapters is not restrictive; the final translations will be left to the individual translators and the list below will be periodically updated with the latest chapter headings.*

In the Name of God, the Compassionate, the Merciful

FIRSTLY, I PRAISE GOD with many continuous praises; though the praise of those who praise is meagre in front of what is due to His majesty.

Secondly, I invoke blessings and peace upon His Messenger—blessings that encompass along with the leader of mankind (*sayyid al-bashar*)[A] all other prophets.

Thirdly, I ask for His guidance (Gloried and Exalted is He) as I resolve to write a book for the revival of the religious sciences.

Fourthly, I hasten to put a stop to your censure O critic who—among those who reject [what we say]—has gone to extremes in his criticism, and who—among those who deny [us] and are heedless—is immoderate in his chiding and rejection.[B]

[A] The Prophet Muḥammad.

[B] It is not clear if Ghazālī had a particular person in mind when he penned

My tongue has been set loose, and the responsibility to speak out and to discourse have become incumbent on me due to your persistent blindness to the obvious truth, your obstinacy in backing falsehood and in embellishing ignorance, and your stirring up hostility against him who has given preference to stepping somewhat aside from social conventions and who has verged slightly from formality. [He does this] for the sake of acting according to the dictates of knowledge and in eagerness to gain what God (Great and Glorious is He) has commanded in purifying the soul and rectifying the heart, thus somewhat redeeming a life wasted and in the hope of escaping complete rack and ruin. Hence, he seeks to avoid the risk of being associated with those about whom the Law giver (may God bless him and grant him peace) has said, 'The one who will be most severely punished on the Day of Judgement is he who was granted knowledge (*ʿālim*)[A] and whom God (glory be to Him) did not make benefit from his knowledge.'[B]

By my life, there is no reason for the persistence of your opposition except for the malady that has encompassed the vast majority—indeed the multitudes. [The malady of] the inability to discern the weight of the matter, the ignorance of how grave the situation is and how crucial the issue, that the Hereafter is approaching and that this life is departing, that the end of life is near and the journey still far, that the provision is scanty and the danger immense, that the way is blocked, that for the discerning critic the knowledge and the acts that are purely for God are what avail, and that to pursue the path of the Hereafter—with all its many dangers and without a guide or companion—is exhausting and arduous.

this very severe and direct criticism here and below. Its personal nature does suggest that he did have someone in mind, but he could equally have used this form as a general accusation against a specific group.

[A] The term *ʿālim* (pl. *ʿulamāʾ*) has been translated both as 'he who has been granted or who possesses knowledge' and as 'scholar' according to the context.

[B] Ṭabarānī, *al-Muʿjam al-ṣaghīr*, 1.182.

The guides of the way are those who possess knowledge (*ᶜulamā'*) who are the heirs of the prophets.[A] This age is devoid of them and those who remain are impersonators; most have been overpowered by the devil and been led astray by iniquity. Each one is engrossed with his earthly gain; he sees what is right objectionable and what is objectionable right; thus the banner of religion has been pulled down and the beacon of guidance all over the world is extinguished.

[These impersonators] deceive people into thinking that knowledge is only decrees of the state (*fatāwā ḥukūma*) that judges use in order to resolve disputes when there is disturbance by the rabble, or a form of debating which a person seeking to show off equips himself with in order to gain superiority and the upper hand, or ornate language which a preacher uses to lure in the common people. These three [means] are all they could find to snare illegal gain and to net the vanities [of the world].

Now the knowledge of the path to the Hereafter (*ᶜilm ṭarīq al-ākhira*)—which was followed by the pious predecessors and which was called by God (Glorified is He) in His Book: law (*fiqh*), wisdom (*ḥikma*), knowledge (*ᶜilm*), luminescence (*ḍiyā'*), light (*nūr*), guidance (*hidāya*), right-direction (*rushd*)—has become among people a thing hidden and forgotten.

As this [situation] is a calamitous fissure in religion and as the times are dark, I concluded that it is crucial to undertake the composition of this book in order to revive the religious sciences, to seek out the methods of the previous leaders [of religion], and to clarify what the prophets and the pious predecessors considered beneficial knowledge (may God grant them all peace).

I divided it into four quarters: the Quarter of the Acts of Worship (*rubᶜ al-ᶜibādāt*), the Quarter of the Norms of Daily Life (*rubᶜ al-ᶜādāt*), the Quarter of the Moral Vices (*rubᶜ al-muhlikāt*) and the Quarter of the Saving Virtues (*rubᶜ al-munjiyāt*).

[A] ᶜIrāqī, I.6 says this is in Abū Dā'ūd, Tirmidhī, Ibn Māja and in *Ṣaḥīḥ* Ibn Ḥibbān on the authority of Abū al-Dardā'.

I began the whole [of the work] with 'The Book of Knowledge'[A] (*Kitāb al-ʿilm*) because [knowledge] is of the utmost importance. Firstly, I reveal the knowledge that God (Great and Glorious is He) ordered the elite (*aʿyān*) to seek in the words of His Prophet (may God bless him and grant him peace) when he said, 'Seeking knowledge is a legal obligation (*farīḍa*) for every Muslim';[B] then, I differentiate [in the book] between knowledge that is beneficial and [knowledge] that is harmful, for may God bless him and grant him peace said, 'We seek refuge in You from knowledge that does not benefit';[C] and I illustrate how far the people of this age have departed from right conduct, and how deceived they are by glossy illusions[D] and by their contentment with the husk rather than the kernel of knowledge.

The Quarter of the Acts of Worship is made up of ten Books:

1 The Book of Knowledge
2 The Book of the Foundations of the Articles of Faith
3 The Book of the Mysteries of Purity
4 The Book of the Mysteries of the Prayer
5 The Book of the Mysteries of Almsgiving
6 The Book of the Mysteries of Fasting
7 The Book of the Mysteries of the Pilgrimage
8 The Book of Ways of Reciting of the Qur'ān
9 The Book of Invocations and Supplications
10 The Book of Classification of Litanies and the Division of the Night Vigil

The Quarter of the Norms of Daily Life is made up of ten Books:

11 The Book of the Manners Related to Eating
12 The Book of Conduct in Marriage
13 The Book of Ways of Earning and Making a Living

A We have retained Book for the titles of the chapters of the *Revival*.

B Ibn Mājā 224.

C Muslim 2722.

D Lit. 'mirage' (*sarāb*).

14 The Book of the Lawful and the Unlawful
15 The Book of Ways of Friendship, Brotherhood and Companionship
16 The Book of Conduct in Seclusion
17 The Book of Conduct in Travel
18 The Book of Conduct in Audition and Ecstasy
19 The Book of Enjoining the Good and Prohibiting Evil
20 The Book of Conduct of Living and the Qualities of Prophethood

The Quarter of the Moral Vices is made up of ten Books:

21 The Book of Expounding the Wonders of the Heart
22 The Book of Disciplining the Soul
23 The Book of Breaking the Two Desires
24 The Book of the Vices of the Tongue
25 The Book of Condemnation of Anger, Rancour and Envy
26 The Book of Condemnation of the World
27 The Book of Condemnation of Avarice and Love of Wealth
28 The Book of Condemnation of Status and Ostentation
29 The Book of Condemnation of Pride and Conceit
30 The Book of Condemnation of Self-delusion

The Quarter of the Saving Virtues is made up of ten Books:

31 The Book of Repentance
32 The Book of Patience and Thankfulness
33 The Book of Fear and Hope
34 The Book of Poverty and Abstinence
35 The Book of Unity of God and Reliance upon Him
36 The Book of Love, Longing, Intimacy and Contentment
37 The Book of Intention, Truthfulness and Sincerity
38 The Book of Vigilance and Self-examination
39 The Book of Reflection
40 The Book of the Remembrance of Death and the Afterlife

As to the Quarter of the Acts of Worship, I mention in it the mysteries of their conduct, the subtleties of their ways, the secrets of their meanings, and what the practicing scholar (*al-ʿālim al-ʿāmil*) cannot do without; he would not be among the scholars of the Hereafter if he were not versed in these. Much of this has been neglected in the studies of jurisprudence.

In the Quarter of the Norms of Daily Life, I discuss the secrets of the [various] relations that take place between people (*muʿāmalāt*),[A] their deeper meanings, the subtleties of their ways, and the mysteries of the piety (*waraʿ*) that should run through them. [All] these are what no religious person (*mutadayyin*) can do without.

In the Quarter of the Moral Vices, I list every reprehensible character trait (*khuluq madhmūm*) that the Qur'ān commanded to be uprooted, and the soul to be cleansed and the heart to be purified thereof. I include for each of these character traits its definition (*ḥadd*) and its reality (*ḥaqīqa*), then the cause from which it derives, the evils that result from it, the signs by which it can be recognised, and the different remedies that can be used to eliminate it.

Accompanying all this are proofs from Qur'ānic verses, Prophetic reports (*akhbār*) and narratives (*āthār*).

As to the Quarter of the Saving Virtues, I mention every laudable character trait and every desirable quality of those near [to God] (*muqarrabūn*) and of the righteous (*ṣiddīqūn*) through which the servant can gain proximity to the Lord of the worlds. For every quality I give its definition and its reality, the means by which it can be attained, the fruits that are derived from it, the signs by which it can be recognised, the merits which make it desirable, and the ways that it has been affirmed by the Law (*sharʿ*) and by the intellect (*ʿaql*).

[A] The plural *muʿāmalāt* (sing. *muʿāmala*) does not have the same meaning as *ʿilm al-muʿāmala* below and therefore they have been translated differently according to Ghazālī's intention for each.

Other titles have been written about some of these topics,[A] but this [present] work is distinguished from them in five ways:

Firstly, it clarifies what is complicated in them and elucidates what they have mentioned in passing.

Secondly, it organises what is scattered in them and systematises what is disparate in them.

Thirdly, it summarises what they have overly discussed and gives precision to what they have affirmed.

Fourthly, it deletes what they have repeated and corroborates what they have formulated.

Fifthly, it clarifies ambiguous matters that are difficult to understand and that have never even been the subject of books. For though all [who write] may follow a single method, this does not preclude each one who pursues [this method] from paying special attention to a matter that concerns him and which his colleagues may not know about, or may be aware of it but overlooked it in writing, or may not have overlooked it but something caused them to turn away from it.

While it includes all the [above mentioned] sciences, these are the [five] specific attributes of this work.

Two things prompted me to compose this book in four quarters. The first and primary motive is that this arrangement is indispensable when researching and elaborating [on a subject], given that the knowledge by which we approach the Hereafter is divided into 'the knowledge of contingent actions' (*ʿilm al-muʿāmala*)[B] and 'direct knowledge' (*ʿilm al-mukāshafa*).[C]

[A] In writing the *Revival*, Ghazālī was fully aware of the religious literature of his time and, in the *Revival*, he both draws on a number of titles (for example, Makkī's *Qūt al-qulūb*) and takes this literature a step further.

[B] *Muʿāmala* (pl. *muʿāmalāt*) is usually translated as 'transaction', 'procedure', 'treatment'. But for Ghazālī, there is a return to the root of the term in *ʿamala*, 'to act'. In translating *ʿilm al-muʿāmala* as 'the knowledge of contingent actions', we have taken both Ghazālī's own definition and the root of the term into consideration.

[C] In Sufism, *mukāshafa* is a technical term meaning 'unveiling' and 'direct

By direct knowledge, I mean [the knowledge] whose only requirement is to reveal the object of knowledge (*maʿlūm*) and nothing else.

By the knowledge of contingent actions, I mean [the knowledge] of the actions that necessarily accompany direct knowledge.[A]

The aim of this book is exclusively the knowledge of contingent actions and not direct knowledge which—despite it being the goal of those who seek and the aspiration for the vision of the righteous—is beyond being documented in books. The knowledge of contingent actions is a means to it. The prophets (may God bless them and grant them peace) only spoke to people about the knowledge of the path (*ʿilm al-ṭarīq*) and about guidance to it. As to direct knowledge, they only mentioned it through symbol and allusion, and by way of comparison and in a general fashion, knowing that people's understanding falls short of comprehending it. Now, those who possess knowledge are the heirs of the prophets and thus they cannot verge from the method of emulating and imitating [the prophets].

Knowledge of contingent actions is divided into outer knowledge (*ʿilm ẓāhir*), by which I mean the knowledge of the actions for bodily parts; and inner knowledge (*ʿilm bāṭin*), by which I mean the knowledge of the actions of the heart.

or experiential knowledge'; it is linked with *dhawq* 'tasting'. The term has been translated as 'revelation' (Nabih Amin Faris, *The Book of Knowledge*, p. xiv), but it is clear from Ghazālī's definition that it is not revelation as *waḥy*, but is direct spiritual knowledge of immutable truths.

[A] It should not be understood from this very concise definition that Ghazālī intends each individual to act exclusively on his or her own direct knowledge. The actions referred to here are those derived from the Qur'ān, the *Sunna* of the Prophet, and the example of the pious predecessors and the saints; thus actions based in revelation and in the direct knowledge of the Prophet and the saintly. Each of the chapters of the *Revival* invariably starts with reference to Qur'anic verses, the traditions of the Prophet and the narratives of the Companions and the saints, making them the example to be followed.

What applies to the bodily parts is either worship (*ʿibāda*) or norms of daily life (*ʿāda*).[A]

What occurs in the heart—which by dint of being veiled from the senses is part of the heavenly realm (*malakūt*)—is either commendable (*maḥmūd*) or reprehensible (*madhmūm*).[B]

Thus, this knowledge [of contingent actions] by necessity divides into two halves: outer and inner. The outer half, which is connected to the bodily parts, is itself divided into worship and norms of daily life; while the inner half, which is connected to the states of the heart and the attributes of the soul, is divided into either what is reprehensible or what is commendable. Therefore, the result is four parts and no examination of the knowledge of contingent actions can go beyond these divisions.

The secondary motive [for composing this book]: I have found that—[despite jurisprudence] being exploited by those who do not fear God to boast, and their making use of its prestige and standing in competing [with each other]—there is a genuine desire for knowledge on behalf of the students of jurisprudence. [Thus, in imitation of the works of jurisprudence,] it is divided into four quarters; for he who takes on the garb of the beloved becomes beloved. I believe that styling the book in the form of [books of] jurisprudence will gently lead hearts [to it]. This was the reason why one of those who wanted to draw the attention of persons in authority to [the science of] medicine structured it in the form of an astrological almanac, arranged it into tables and numbers, and called it 'The Almanac of Health', that their familiarity with this kind [of science] may draw them to reading [his title].

Gently leading hearts to the knowledge that benefits everlasting life is more important than leading them to medicine that

[A] Elaborated in the Quarter of Acts of Worship and the Quarter of Norms of Daily Life.

[B] Elaborated in the Quarter of the Moral Vices and the Quarter of the Saving Virtues.

only benefits the health of the body. The fruit of this knowledge is the health of hearts and souls and the arrival through it to life that never ends. How can the medicine that is used to heal bodies, necessarily destined before long to corruption, compare with this!

We ask God (glory be to Him) guidance to what is right and just, for He is the Generous, the Munificent.

The Islamic Texts Society
Rabīʿ al-thanī 1436/February 2015

ABBREVIATIONS

ʿAṭṭār	:	Arberry (tr.), *Muslim Saints and Mystics*
EI²	:	*Encyclopaedia of Islam* (Second edition)
GAL	:	Brockelmann, *Geschichte der arabischen Literatur*
GALS	:	Brockelmann, *Geschichte* (Supplement)
Ḥākim	:	al-Ḥākim al-Nīsābūrī, *al-Mustadrak*
al-Ḥakīm al-Tirmidhī	:	al-Ḥakīm al-Tirmidhī, *Nawādir al-uṣūl*
Hujwīrī	:	Nicholson (tr.), *Kashf al-maḥjūb*
Lane	:	Lane, *An Arabic-English Lexicon*
Lumaʿ	:	Sarrāj, *K. al-Lumaʿ*
Maʿārif	:	Ibn Qutayba, *al-Maʿārif*
Ma'thūr	:	Daylamī, *al-Firdaws bi-ma'thūr*
Qushayrī	:	al-Qushayrī, *al-Risāla fī ʿilm al-taṣawwuf*
Qūt	:	Makkī, *Qūt al-qulūb*
Shawkānī	:	al-Shawkānī, *al-Fawā'id al-majmūʿa*
SEI	:	*Shorter Encyclopaedia of Islam*
Sulamī	:	al-Sulamī, *Ṭabaqāt al-ṣūfīya*
Ṭabarānī, *Ṣaghīr*	:	al-Ṭabarānī, *al-Muʿjam al-ṣaghīr*
Tahdhīb al-tahdhīb	:	Ibn Ḥajar, *Tahdhīb al-tahdhīb*
Ṭayālisī	:	al-Ṭayālisī, *al-Musnad*
ʿUqaylī	:	al-ʿUqaylī, *al-Ḍuʿafā' al-kabīr*
Zabīdī	:	al-Zabīdī, *Itḥāf al-sādat al-muttaqīn*

PREFACE

What first drew me to *Kitāb al-ṣabr wa'l-shukr* (the Book of Patience and Thankfulness) from *Iḥyā' ʿulūm al-dīn* (The Revival of the Religious Sciences) is the extent to which it lends itself to the area of inter-faith studies; the moral and spiritual concerns of patience and thankfulness are not the exclusive possession of any one religious community. What Ghazālī wrote for Muslim readers of his own generation has many notes useful for our contemporary generation, Muslim and non-Muslim alike. He expressed in deep earnestness what he felt a living faith in God should be. His espousal of Sufism is very evident, but it was qualified and modified by his previous juristic training, teaching and authorship in traditional Shāfiʿī Sunnism. He casts his thought in legalistic terms but with Sufi aspirations and he remains 'sober' in every sense of the term. He was not afraid to quote non-Muslim sources occasionally and use them to buttress his arguments. There is a steady 'no-nonsense' drive in his discussion, which is occasionally relieved by his sense of humour. His pictorial imagery and Sufi anecdotes keep his commentary fresh and lively so that he remains in touch with the common man. At the same time, it is laced with the authority of Qur'ānic quotations and traditions of the Prophet, thus he remains faithful to the Islamic origins. Yet through it all the originality of the reflective thinker comes through and we can appreciate him as one of the truly great minds of medieval times.

This project of an annotated translation of Ghazālī's *Kitāb al-ṣabr wa'l-shukr* has been underway for a number of years. It began at the suggestion of the late Dr. Nabih Faris of the American University in Beirut, who was noted for his English translations of Ghazālī's books. Upon the death of Dr. Faris, it was providential that I found myself living in the same building in Beirut with another scholar of Ghazālī, Dr. Ali Othman, who was generous in giving his time to review my work of translation. The translation was first commenced under the supervision of Dr. Charles J. Adams, director of the Institute of Islamic Studies, McGill University, Montreal, with Dr. Faris and then Dr. Othman as field consultants. Some time later, another opportunity came to resume this project. Dr. Ralph Winter of the U.S. Center for World Mission invited me to take it up again in the programme for Cross-Cultural Communication Studies at the William Carey International University, Pasadena, California. The work was supervised by a committee composed of Dr. J. Dudley Woodberry, of the Fuller Seminary, Pasadena, Dr. Sabri Kawash of Sunnyvale, California and Dr. Nicholas Heer of the University of Washington, Seattle, all of whom have made contributions to Islamic studies. The doctoral programme within the general field of International Development was under the guidance of Dr. James O. Buswell III, Dean of Graduate Studies, William Carey International University.

I want to express my sincere thanks to each of these scholars who gave me their guidance and counsel; and to thank Dr Lamin Sanneh of Yale for his encouragement that this study 'should see the light of day.' I am grateful to Dorothy, my wife, for her encouragement in this work; and to our daughter, Carol Johnson, who reviewed the text and made many suggestions in editing and proof-reading. My gratitude also goes to Teresa, Mrs. John Kirk, who remained steadfast in the matters of correction and improvement that went into the initial manuscript. At the Islamic Texts Society, I would like to thank Valerie Turner for her help with editing, Uwais Namaji for his expertise with *ḥadīth*, and Fatima Azzam for her care and companionship in the whole journey from manuscript to published book.

Henry T. Littlejohn
Seattle, March 2010

INTRODUCTION

THE ISLAMIC COMMUNITY often recalls the great figures of its past. Among these, few have rivalled the renown and influence of Abū Ḥāmid al-Ghazālī, who has been called 'the most original thinker that Islam has produced.'[1] His brilliance in the Islamic sciences[2] has been universally recognised. His wide learning, perceptive mind and moderating spirit enabled Ghazālī to make a lasting contribution to Muslim thought. A. J. Wensinck summarised his role as follows,

> Ghazālī succeeded in assuring the mystical or introspective attitude a place within official Islam side by side with the legalism of the lawyers and the intellectualism of the theologians.[3]

The range of his scholarship and its enduring influence on later generations make Ghazālī an intellectual giant. He is commonly referred to as *Ḥujjat al-Islām*,[4] an honorific title that gives credence to the general acknowledgment of his achievements. Whether in agreement or not, every Muslim thinker has had to reckon with the breadth of Ghazālī's thought. His writings and work have left their imprint on Muslim culture and are as relevant today as they ever were before. Moreover, he is now of considerable importance in the field of cross-cultural studies.[5]

In his autobiography, *al-Munqidh min al-ḍalāl*, Ghazālī describes his spiritual journey through the different religious sciences to Sufism. But it is in his masterpiece, *Iḥyā' ʿulūm al-dīn* (Revival of the Religious Sciences), that we find the breadth and depth of his learning and his spirituality. Henri Laoust describes the *Iḥyā'* as a 'profession of faith, a manual of introduction to the life of meditation, a treatise on social ethics, a tract of political ethic, a handbook of manners and a textbook of religious and political indoctrination.'[6] This is a good description of many aspects of the *Iḥyā'*'s contents.

In the *Revival of the Religious Sciences*, Ghazālī sets out his thought concerning the faith and practice of the Muslim. The work is composed of four quarters, ten books each: the first is the quarter [of the acts] of worship (*rubʿ al-ʿibādāt*); the second is the quarter of customs (*rubʿ al-ʿādāt*); the third is the quarter of mortal vices (*rubʿ al-muhlikāt*); and the fourth is the quarter of saving virtues (*rubʿ al-munjiyāt*). The *Book of Patience and Thankfulness* is the second book in this final quarter (the thirty-second book of the *Revival*).

Structure and Development of Ghazālī's Thought in the Book of Patience and Thankfulness

Ghazālī's passion for order in thought is present throughout the *Iḥyā'* and is especially well-illustrated in *The Book of Patience and Thankfulness*. From the point of view of structure and development, this book mirrors many of the other books of the *Revival*. In it, Ghazālī, though digressing at one point or another, particularly with examples, never loses sight of his intended goal. This can be seen in his habit of concise introductions to each of the books in which he projects for his readers the general topics he intends to cover. In the *Book of Patience and Thankfulness*, this is his introduction to the section on patience,

> The first part [will include] An Exposition of the Merit of Patience, An Exposition of the Nature and Meaning of Patience, An Exposition of How Patience is Half of Faith, An Exposition of the Terms Used for Patience in Addition to the Term Patience Itself, An Exposition of the Divisions of Patience According to Variations of Strength and Weakness, An Exposition of the Assumed Need for Patience and that the Servant Cannot Dispense with it Under any Condition, and

> An Exposition of Patience as a Remedy and What is Gained by Resorting to It. These are seven sections (*fuṣūl*), which, God willing, will present all the objectives [of patience].[7]

In the introduction to the section on thankfulness, Ghazālī is more concise,

> It is made up of three sections. The first is on the merit of thankfulness: its reality, its divisions, and its rules. The second is on the nature of blessings and their specific and general divisions. The third is an exposition of what is best; patience or thankfulness.[8]

This approach of defining the subject to be discussed in advance and dividing it into its constituent parts is repeated again and again throughout the *Book of Patience and Thankfulness.*

Furthermore, this systematic approach is sometimes even applied within a single chapter, for example, Chapter Twelve, 'An Exposition of the Nature of the Blessings and Their Divisions.' In using this method, our author becomes like a fisherman who uses ever finer nets as his 'catch' moves down in scale.

Once the constituent parts of the subject are outlined, Ghazālī then follows with detailed discussions and illustrations of the individual parts. Thus, structure moves on to development. Ghazālī's method here is to examine a proposition, produce evidence and argument, and draw one or more conclusions. And in applying this method, our author shows a breadth and range of skill almost peerless in his eastern Islamic culture. For Ghazālī knew that structure alone was insufficient. The skeleton needed the flesh of understanding; it could not remain a mere recitation of religious law. Verbal pictures to illumine the mind and to stir the spirit of the reader to positive action must be integral to the exposition. These he continually sought to supply and, for the most part, he was successful in placing them effectively within context. There are some topics that he deals with less effectively than others; Chapter Fifteen is a case in point. In this discussion of the relationship between patience and thankfulness, Ghazālī is so enthralled with his illustrations that he lets his conclusion slip away from him. However, we must weigh this against the many chapters where Ghazālī brings his arguments to a satisfactory close.

Finally, despite the similarity in the structure of the discussions of patience and thankfulness, the *Book of Patience and Thankfulness* is not divided equally between the two parts. In fact, the *Book of Thankfulness* is several times the length of the *Book of Patience*; approximately sixty pages and nineteen pages respectively of Arabic text.

THE MAJOR TERMS OF THE BOOK OF PATIENCE AND THANKFULNESS

We would like to draw the attention of the reader to the five most important terms that appear in the *Book of Patience and Thankfulness*. But before we proceed to these terms, we need to consider briefly one of Ghazālī's favourite strategies of exposition. This strategy is to harness two subjects together in a diptych in which the author regards them either as two matters that complement each other or as two contrasting phenomena that need to be treated together in the same unit of the *Revival*. If we take the work as a whole, we will find that there are several occurrences of two subjects discussed together: there is one book in the First Quarter;[9] five books in the second Quarter;[10] four books in the Third Quarter;[11] and finally, the *Book of Patience and Thankfulness* is the first of eight in the Fourth Quarter.[12] It must be noted here that this is not the first time that these two virtues have been paired together. They first appeared in a work with which Ghazālī was familiar, Abū Ṭālib al-Makkī's *Qūt al-qulūb*.[13]

In the *Book of Patience and Thankfulness*, the five most important terms are: patience (*ṣabr*); thankfulness (*shukr*); blessing (*niʿma*); the affirmation of unity (*tawḥīd*); and 'knowledge by unveiling' (*ʿilm al-mukāshafa*).

Patience

Aside from agreeing with Makkī in placing patience and thankfulness together, Ghazālī also agrees with him in placing them low on the ladder of the Sufi stations (*maqāmāt*), coming right after repentance (*tawba*), in the ascent of those travelling the Sufi path (*sālikūn*).[14] This is not dissimilar to Kalābādhī's arrangement, in which he only places abstinence or asceticism (*zuhd*) between them.[15] Qushayrī, an older contemporary of Ghazālī, places patience surprisingly high on his list of the stations, but he also begins with patience.[16] Massignon notes that the importance of patience coupled with thankfulness goes back to the Prophet Muḥammad and has remained important in the life of the Muslim community sustained by the schools of law and the earlier Sufi counsels of Muḥāsibī and Makkī.[17]

If we retrace Ghazālī's exposition of patience in the seven chapters that he allots to the subject, we observe how carefully the author grounds this quality in Qur'ānic and traditional references. It is here also that he places the one quotation of Christ's words from a canonical gospel. Citations are also given from various Sufi men of piety (all of Ghazālī's sources are discussed below).

The four main discussions of patience are the following: the necessity of patience for the arduous intellectual task of dealing with matters of doctrine; the necessity of patience for fulfilling the religious requirements imposed upon the Muslim; the need for patience in refraining from forbidden activities; and, patience as resignation in calamity.

Thankfulness

Before we discuss the term *shukr*, a word needs to be said here about the choice of 'gratitude' or 'thankfulness' as the most suitable translation into English. In this, the scholars are not unanimous.

Both Ali Othman and Mohamed Sherif are Ghazālian scholars who opt for 'gratitude,'[18] as do A. J. Arberry and William McKane.[19] However, Dwight Donaldson prefers 'thankfulness,'[20] and Duncan Macdonald 'thankful praise.'[21] We have chosen 'thankfulness' because, in our opinion, it conveys the aura of reverence and worship more consistently than does 'gratitude'.

Ghazālī's discussion of thankfulness is similar to that of patience, in that he places the concept squarely within the Qur'ānic, traditional and Sufi arguments. However, Ghazālī does link this virtue with two other concepts: remembrance (*dhikr*) and blessing (*niʿma*). As Islamic teaching understands forgetfulness rather than rebellion as the basic defect in man's nature, remembrance becomes the antidote. Many of the passages in the section of the book dealing with thankfulness include elements of warning, caution and admonishment against the forgetfulness of thankfulness.

Then as Ghazālī develops his thoughts on thankfulness, he explains how it functions and he begins to relate it to the affirmation of the unity of God (*tawḥīd*). These are both accomplished by receiving a blessing from God (*niʿma*) and lead to 'knowledge by unveiling' (*ʿilm al-mukāshafa*).

Finally, Ghazālī closes the *Book of Patience and Thankfulness* by bringing together the two virtues, patience and thankfulness, in relation to the experience of trials (*balā'*). The believer must bear them patiently and yet be thankful he has received them because they can potentially cause moral and spiritual growth.

Blessing

Niʿma is the third most important term that Ghazālī uses in the *Book of Patience and Thankfulness.* Aside from its numerous appearances in the text, he uses the singular form three times and the plural form (*niʿam*) six times in chapters twelve and thirteen and their subheadings.

Wehr suggests seven possible English renderings of *niʿma*: 'benefit', 'blessing', 'boon', 'benefaction', 'favour', 'grace' and 'kindness'.[22] Othman, in his discussion of the *Revival*, adds 'bounties' for the plural *niʿam*.[23] Among medieval authorities the author of the *Lisān al-ʿArab* gives *faḍīla* as a synonym of its verbal root, *naʿima*, the first meaning 'to have a surplus', and the second, 'to live in comfort', 'be glad' and 'take pleasure'.[24]

But for Ghazālī, the term is synonymous with the multiple blessings that God bestows on man and for which man must be constantly thankful.

Affirmation of Unity

For Ghazālī, the affirmation of the unity of God (*tawḥīd*) that every Muslim must make is open to multiple interpretations starting from a simple affirmation of divine Oneness to the experience of 'union' with God. Given that the concept is the very basis of Islam, it is no wonder that it counts as one of the most important terms that occur in the *Revival*. In the *Book of Patience and Thankfulness* it becomes a central concept at certain junctures in both the section on patience and the section on thankfulness, for the affirmation of unity is indispensable in understanding Ghazālī's conception of proximity to God (*qurb*).[25]

Knowledge by Unveiling

The final term that we will include here is *ʿilm al-mukāshafa*. It seems to be a comprehensive term that relates to many others. In his expositions, Ghazālī uses this term to mean 'the knowledge by unveiling of the divine mystery' in the personal experience of the seeker. Although not all scholars of Ghazālī will agree, it is our opinion that the following terms appear to be subsumed under its heading: knowledge of God (*maʿrifa*); 'tasting' or the 'immediate experience' (*dhawq*); 'annihilation' (*fanā'*); possessing certainty about or of God (*yaqīn*); inspiration from God (*waḥy* or *ilhām*); nearness to God (*qurb*); and finally, 'union' with God (*tawḥīd*). These terms all have a kinship in Ghazālī's understanding and can hardly be separated from each other. This complexity of terms may also explain why Ghazālī does not always make a clear distinction between *ʿilm*, usually denoting 'formal knowledge' and *maʿrifa*, knowledge [of God], which, in certain contexts, we have chosen to translate as gnosis, to agree with the translation of *ʿārifūn* as gnostics.[26]

Analysis of the Quoted Sources of the Book of Patience and Thankfulness

Although the *Iḥyā'* is not a commentary on the Qur'ān, Ghazālī may justly be called a Qur'ānic theologian. Early in each of the books of the *Iḥyā'*, our author lays down the Qur'ānic foundations of his argument. The *Book of Patience and Thankfulness* is typical in this respect.

ʿAbd al-Bāqī's concordance of the Qur'ān shows a listing of ninety-six verses where the verbal and noun forms of *ṣabara* and *ṣabr* occur one hundred and five times.[27] In the section dealing with patience, Ghazālī chooses eight of these verses as representative of the Qur'ānic teaching on patience: Q.xxxii.34; vii.137; xvi.97; xxviii.54; xxxix.10; viii.46; iii.125 and ii.157. And while he quotes many other verses, Ghazālī makes three of the above verses the main focus of his discussion on patience, *Surely We shall recompense those who were patient with their reward, according to the best of what they did* (xvi.97);[28] *Surely the patient shall be given their reward in full without reckoning* (xxxix.10); *Upon these rest blessings and mercy from their Lord, and they are truly guided* (ii.157).

We should also observe that in addition to direct quotations from the Qur'ān there are at least twenty-two verses to which the author makes allusion through a phrase or divine name. Notable are those passages that are descriptive or speak of natural catastrophe. Ghazālī demonstrates his skill as an expositor by employing scattered references, arranging them in a logical sequence and then 'personalising' them to fit human experience for the purpose of illustration.[29]

The use of Qur'ānic verses is continued in the section of the book dealing with thankfulness. In the introduction to this section alone, there are sixteen references to Qur'ānic verses: XXIX.44; II.152; IV.147; III.135; VII.16; VII.17; XXXIV.13; XIV.7; IX.28; VI.41; II.207; IV.48; IX.15; LXIV.17; XXXIX.74; and X.10. However, 'thankfulness' and the 'thankful ones' occur only in seven of these initial references with 'praise' (*ḥamd*) as a synonym in two more. The remaining seven are really admonitions. Ghazālī is thus setting up a Qur'ānic basis for judgement on disobedience and failure to express thankfulness. In addition, the author links patience and thankfulness each to a second virtue akin to it. With patience it is certainty (*yaqīn*), a deepening of faith through struggle; with thankfulness it is remembrance (*dhikr*) of God to sustain loyalty to Him.

Throughout the *Book of Patience and Thankfulness*, as indeed throughout the entire *Iḥyā'*, Ghazālī does not conclude any argument simply on the strength of his own reasoning. He invokes the authority of the Qur'ān to persuade his reader that his logic is sound and in harmony with the truth of the Qur'ān. An example, in Chapter Six, 'An Exposition of the Assumed Need for Patience and that the Servant Cannot Dispense with it Under any Condition,' our author analyses the kinds of situations in which the servant of God must exercise patience. Several problem areas are discussed. One is when the Muslim believer is assaulted by temptation and he can choose to repel it. In this area, there is the question of forbearance with regard to a requital (*mukāfa'a*). Ghazālī goes on to affirm that 'God commended those who forego their rights to retaliation (*qiṣāṣ*) and other matters,' and cites three authorities: the Qur'ān, a Prophetic tradition (*ḥadīth*) and an Islamic version of a canonical statement of Christ from the Gospel of Matthew (5:38–41). The order of the Qur'ān, then the *ḥadīth*, then a previous scriptural authority, prophet or Sufi tradition, is usually Ghazālī's sequence of support for his arguments, though it is not uniformly so.

In conclusion, Ghazālī refers to the Qur'ān as his principal source of spiritual and moral authority, although there are chapters in which other sources dominate his discussion or no authority is used at all. Each section of the *Book of Patience and Thankfulness* is introduced with a series of Qur'ānic passages that relate to patience and then thankfulness. While other Muslim sources of authority are frequently used, a particular point of discussion is often sustained or summarised by a passage or several passages from the Qur'ān. While many of the passages that Ghazālī selects function in a particular context, they also sometimes support his Ashʿarī determinism or Sufi predilections.

Tradition Literature

After the Qur'ān, the next most authoritative documentation that Ghazālī employs is the tradition literature attributed to the Prophet Muḥammad, the *ḥadīth*. Ghazālī makes use of both the 'prophetic traditions' (*ḥadīth nabawī*) and the 'sacred traditions' (*ḥadīth qudsī*) in which the Prophet speaks in the words of God. An example of this can be found in Chapter Six,

> The Prophet (may God bless him and grant him peace) said, 'The period of waiting patiently for release from suffering is an act of worship.'[30]

and

> The Prophet (may God bless him and grant him peace) said, 'God, Almighty and Glorious, said, "If I put my servant to the test with a trial [of illness], and he endures it and does not express distrust of Me before those who come to visit him, I shall give him flesh better than his flesh and blood better than his blood. If I grant him health, he [rises] without sin; and if I decree his death, it is to My mercy [he returns]."'[31]

Consistent with his method of exposition in many other books of the *Iḥyāʾ*, Ghazālī proceeds directly from the Qurʾānic references to the tradition literature in laying a foundation for what he teaches about patience and thankfulness. Here, Ghazālī's method in using the *ḥadīth* can be divided into three: the first is to put forward a series of topical *ḥadīth* at the beginning of the discourse. These *ḥadīth* are mostly aphoristic or descriptive of the subject. For example, 'Patience is half of faith,' and 'Among the lesser [gifts of God] that you have been granted are certainty (*yaqīn*) and resolute patience (*ʿazīmat al-ṣabr*).'[32] The second is the use of the *ḥadīth* in order to illustrate the failure of many to practice faith and to obey God. Ignorance (*jahl*) and heedlessness (*ghafla*) are named as the primary reasons and Ghazālī considers them symptoms of spiritual disease that can manifest itself in different ways. The main *ḥadīth* here is,

> About this, he (may God bless him and grant him peace) said, 'He who looks in this world to who is below him and looks in his religion to who is above, God will record that he is patient and thankful. He who looks in this world to who is above him and looks in his religion to who is below him, God will not record that he is patient and thankful.'[33]

The third way Ghazālī uses the *ḥadīth* is in opening or closing an argument or a chapter. For example, in concluding Chapter Five, 'An Exposition of the Divisions of Patience According to Variations of Strength and Weakness,' he quotes the *ḥadīth*,

> Worship God with contentment (*riḍā*). But if you cannot, then there is great benefit in [having] patience with what you dislike.[34]

One final comment must be made here regarding Ghazālī's use of *ḥadīth*. Ghazālī's choice of Prophetic traditions and his placement of them in the text depended on his own judgement of whether the *ḥadīth* is valid and was not dependent on its inclusion or validation by the standard collections of *ḥadīth*. This has opened Ghazālī to some criticism. The Ḥanbalī Ibn al-Jawzī was a severe critic of Ghazālī's selection of weak traditions.[35] Subkī, in his *Ṭabaqāt al-Shāfiʿīyya*, gives a 198-page biographical notice to Ghazālī, but he also wrote one hundred and two pages in criticism of traditions used in the *Iḥyā'*. He comments, 'And in this section I have gathered all the traditions that are in the *Kitāb al-Iḥyā'* for which I found no support at all!'[36] The *Book of Patience and Thankfulness* receives a four-page entry. ʿIrāqī, in the margins of his edition of the *Iḥyā'*, notes that seventy-seven of the one hundred and eighteen traditions are cited as weak or defective.[37] But Ghazālī did not only have critics, Zabīdī goes to great lengths to defend the traditions that Ghazālī uses.[38]

The Person and Teachings of Jesus

A notable element in Ghazālī's use of traditional material in the *Iḥyā'* is his inclusion of citations from or referring to Jesus. Aside from his utilisation of Qur'ānic references to Christ, Ghazālī actually includes full and partial quotations from an Arabic version of the New Testament. When citing the Gospels, Ghazālī usually precedes the quote with, 'I have observed in the Gospel.'[39] Other references to Jesus take the form of Muslim traditions attributing certain sayings to Christ, Gospel events interpreted by the Prophet, and Sufi anecdotes referring to Jesus. In every case, the citation or tradition is used to support the particular argument of the moment.

An example of Ghazālī's use of the story of Jesus in the Qur'ān can be seen in his interpretation of the idea of divine support (*ta'yīd*),

> It is what God intended by, [*When God said, 'Jesus, Son of Mary, remember My blessing upon you and upon your mother,. . . when I confirm you with the Holy Spirit,. . .* '] It draws him near sinlessness (*ʿiṣma*). It is an expression for a divine presence which spreads inwardly, strengthening the person in the pursuit of

good and the avoidance of evil. It resembles an imperceptible preventative in his inner self.[40]

A direct quotation from the Gospel is to be found in Chapter Six, 'An Exposition of the Assumed Need for Patience and that the Servant Cannot Dispense with it Under any Condition,'

> And I have observed in the Gospel that Jesus son of Mary (may the peace of God be upon him) said, 'It has been said to you in the past, "A tooth for a tooth and a nose for a nose," but I say to you, do not oppose evil with evil. Whosoever strikes your right cheek, turn to him the left cheek. Whosoever takes your coat, give your buttoned garment. Whosoever obliges you to go with him a mile, go with him two miles.' All these are commendations for forbearance in harm. Thus, patience with the harm [done] by men is among the highest grades of patience.[41]

A tradition which is attributed directly to Christ can be found in Ghazālī's explanation of the nuances of patience. It suggests an echo to I Corinthians 13, Jesus said, 'You come to understand what you love only through patience with what you abhor.'[42]

Another tradition presents the Prophet Muḥammad responding to a statement regarding a Gospel event,

> Swimming can be learned, but walking on water is not acquired by learning, rather it is acquired by the power of certainty. For this reason, when it was said to the Prophet (may God bless him and grant him peace) that, 'Jesus (peace be upon him) is said to have walked on water,' he (may God bless him and grant him peace) replied, 'Had he increased in certainty, he would surely have walked on air.'[43]

As to the appearance of Jesus in Sufi literature, Ghazālī gives us this anecdote from Sahl al-Tustarī,

> A man said to Sahl [al-Tustarī] (may God be pleased with him), 'A thief entered my house and took my furniture.' Sahl replied,

> 'Be thankful to God (Exalted is He!). Had Satan entered your heart, he would have corrupted your belief in the unity of God. What would you have done then? Likewise, Jesus (may the blessings and peace of God be upon him) sought refuge in his supplication, saying, 'Almighty God, do not cause my misfortune to be in my religion.'[44]

While a quotation from Ḥātim al-Aṣamm is fitting for our transition to discuss Ghazālī's inclusion of other Qur'ānic prophets in the *Book of Patience and Thankfulness*,

> Ḥātim al-Aṣamm said, 'Truly, God, Almighty and Majestic, will judge men on the Day of Resurrection according to four categories related to four persons: Solomon for the rich; Christ for the poor; Joseph for the slaves; and Job for the sick (may God bless them all).'[45]

The Person and Teachings of Other Prophets

Aside from Jesus, seven Qur'ānic prophets are mentioned in the *Book of Patience and Thankfulness*: Joseph, Moses, David, Solomon, Job, Ezra (ᶜUzayr) and Zachariah. Also mentioned is the Qur'ānic Shuᶜayb, who is claimed by a number of Muslim commentators to be Jethro or Reuel. There are no direct Biblical quotations in this set of traditions and not all of the prophets are speakers; some are even addressed by God with words of admonishment.

Two traditions in which God addresses a prophet are to be found at opposite ends of the book. In Chapter One, the word is addressed to David,

> It is said that God (Exalted is He!) revealed to David (peace be upon him), 'Let your character be moulded by Mine, and among My attributes is that I am the Patient.'[46]

Then in Chapter Fifteen, Ghazālī quotes the story of Zachariah taking refuge in a tree,

> It was reported that when Zachariah (peace be upon him) fled from the unbelieving Israelites, he hid in a tree. They knew that and brought a saw. They cut into the tree until the saw reached Zachariah's head. He let out a moan. God (Exalted is He!) revealed to him, saying, 'O Zachariah! if you let out a second moan, surely I will erase you from the register of the prophets.' Thereupon Zachariah (peace be upon him) bit his finger until it was cut in two.[47]

In a tradition attributed to the Prophet Muḥammad, Ghazālī narrates the story of Solomon mourning for the loss of a son. Here Solomon is responding to two visiting angels rather than to God Himself,

> [On the authority of] Abū 'l-Dardā', [the Prophet] (may God bless him and grant him peace) said, 'A son of Solomon, son of David (peace be upon them both), died, and [Solomon] grieved for him intensely. Then, two angels appeared and knelt before him in the guise of two disputants. One of them said, "I sowed seed and when it was ready for harvest, this one passed by and spoiled it." [Solomon] asked the other, "What do you say?" He replied, "I took to the main road and I came to the crop. I looked to the right and to the left but the road passed through it." Solomon (peace be upon him) asked [the first], "Why did you sow seed on the road? Did you not know that people must use the road?" The first replied, "Why did you mourn your son? Did you not know that death is the path of the Hereafter?" Thereupon Solomon turned to his Lord in repentance and did not mourn for any of his children after that.'[48]

A final example is to be found in Chapter Ten, 'An Exposition of How to Raise the Veil on the Thankfulness Due to God.' This is a dialogue between God and Moses,

> Know that this observation occurred to both David and Moses (peace be upon them). For Moses said, 'O Lord, how do I

> thank You when I [can] only thank through a second blessing from Your blessings?' In another version, 'and my thankfulness to You is another blessing from You, which necessitates thankfulness from me.' God (Exalted is He!) revealed to him [Moses], 'If you know this, you are thankful to Me.' In another report, 'When you know the blessing is from Me, I accept this as a form of thanks from you.'[49]

Sufi Resources

After the Qur'ān and traditional material related to the Prophet Muḥammad and to other Qur'ānic prophets, the most important resource that Ghazālī uses in the *Book of Patience and Thankfulness* is the literature of Sufism.

Four centuries had passed from the time of Ḥasan al-Baṣrī and the first stirrings of Sufism to the time of Ghazālī and the writing of the *Iḥyā'*. Sufism had grown from an ascetic ideal practised by the few to a 'sober' or 'intoxicated' religious practice that claimed the adherence of thousands. As a result and as a form of expression, a vast literature had made its appearance.

We have seen above that Ghazālī turned to Sufism at a time of personal crisis. This is his own description of his state before his decision to espouse Sufism,

> It had already become clear to me that I had no hope of the bliss of the world to come save through a God-fearing life and the withdrawal of myself from vain desire. . . . It was clear to me too that the key to all this was to sever the attachment of the heart to worldly things by leaving the mansion of deception and returning to that of eternity, and to advance towards God most high with all earnestness.
>
> Next I considered the circumstances of my life, and realized that I was caught in a veritable thicket of attachments. I also considered my activities, of which the best was my teaching and lecturing, and realized that in them I was dealing with

sciences that were unimportant and contributed nothing to the attainment of eternal life.

After that I examined my motive in my work of teaching, and realized that it was not a pure desire for the things of God. . . I saw for certain that I was on the brink of a crumbling bank of sand and in imminent danger of hell-fire unless I set about to mend my ways.

I reflected on this continuously for a time, while the choice still remained open to me. One day I would form the resolution to quit Baghdad and get rid of these adverse circumstances; the next day I would abandon my resolution. . . Worldly desires were striving to keep me by their chains just where I was, while the voice of faith was calling, 'To the road! to the road! All that keeps you busy, both intellectually and practically, is but hypocrisy and delusion. . . '

Soon, however, Satan would return. 'This is a passing mood,' he would say; 'do not yield to it, for it will quickly disappear. . . '

For nearly six months beginning with Rajab 488 AH [July 1095 CE], I was continuously tossed about between the attractions of worldly desires and the impulses toward eternal life. . . God caused my tongue to dry up so that I was prevented from lecturing. One particular day I would make an effort to lecture in order to gratify the hearts of my following, but my tongue would not utter a single word nor could I accomplish anything at all.

This impediment in my speech produced grief in my heart, and at the same time my power to digest and assimilate food and drink was impaired; I could hardly swallow or digest a single mouthful of food. My powers became so weakened that the doctors gave up all hope of successful treatment. . . .[50]

Ghazālī then goes on to narrate the stages which brought him to a full preoccupation with Sufism, even to the point of severance from his family for a period of time. The notions of perdition (*halāk*) and salvation (*najāt*) come out of his experience as major themes and are dominant in the second half of the *Iḥyā'*. While his studies of the writings of renowned Sufis is reflected in every one of the forty books that make up the *Revival*.

Compared to some of the other books of the *Iḥyā'*, Ghazālī makes use of Sufi materials rather sparingly in the *Book of Patience and Thankfulness*. For example, the *Book of Fear and Hope* (*Kitāb al-khawf wa'l-rajā'*), which directly follows the one on patience, is about half its length but includes more than twice as many citations from Sufi literature.

From his own acknowledgements and from the quotations that are found in the book, it is obvious that Ghazālī had ready access to the major collections of Sufi literature. In his autobiography, Ghazālī says,

> I began to acquaint myself with their (the Sufis) relief by reading their books such as 'The Food of Hearts' (*Qūt al-qulūb*) by Abū Ṭālib al-Makkī, the works of al-Ḥārith al-Muḥāsibī, the various anecdotes about al-Junayd, al-Shiblī and Abū Yazīd al-Bisṭāmī. . . , and other discourses of their leading men.[51]

Zabīdī, in his commentary on the *Revival*, identifies the following sources: Abū Ṭālib al-Makkī's *Qūt al-qulūb* (25 citations), Qushayrī's *Risāla* (18 citations), Abū Nuʿaym's *Ḥilyat al-awliyā'* (10 citations), various works by Ibn Abī Dunyā (6 citations), and Abū Manṣūr Daylamī's *Musnad al-firdaws* (3 citations).

In nineteen of the citations, the individual writer or speaker is named; eighteen male and one female. Interestingly, their lives span 250 years, a period which saw a considerable development in Sufism. The earliest to be quoted is Ḥasan al-Baṣrī and the latest is Ḥallāj. Junayd, Shiblī, Fuḍayl b. ʿIyāḍ and Sahl al-Tustarī are the most quoted.

The aphorisms and teachings of these men and women of Sufism and the anecdotes taken from their lives can readily be found verbatim in the earlier compendiums. While Ghazālī occasionally acknowledged the sources, he also lifted them out of the collections and employed them in any specific context where they would lend support to his argument. Therefore, the use that Ghazālī makes of the anecdotes, aphorisms, etc., is to give a fourth source of authority to his arguments after the Qur'ān, the *ḥadīth* and the references to other prophets. An example of this can be seen in a quotation from the Umayyad caliph ʿUmar b. ʿAbd al-ʿAzīz, who is held in high esteem by Sufis. After the quotation of a series of three traditions from the Prophet Muḥammad and a fourth tradition attributed to the prophet David, Ghazālī quotes,

> ʿUmar b. ʿAbd al-ʿAzīz (may God have mercy upon him) said in a sermon, 'God bestows a blessing upon a servant and then snatches it away from him, replacing it with patience in order to compensate the servant with something better than what He has taken away from him.'[52]

Then ʿUmar b. ʿAbd al-ʿAzīz goes on to quote a passage from the Qur'ān. The Qur'ānic passage is followed by four short Sufi anecdotes, one from the closing days of Shiblī and a second from the life of the wife of Fatḥ al-Mawṣilī, acknowledged by Zabīdī as one of the notable Sufis,[53]

> Fuḍayl was asked about patience and replied, 'It is contentment with the decree of God.' It was then asked, 'How can that be?' He replied, 'The contented one does not desire anything beyond the degree he has attained.'
>
> It was said that when Shiblī was confined to the hospital a group of friends came to visit him. He asked, 'Who are you?' They replied, 'Your beloved friends who have come to visit you.' Whereupon he began to throw stones at them, and they started to run. He said, 'If you were my beloved friends, you would have been patient with me in my tribulation.'
>
> One of the [Sufi] gnostics used to take a note out of his pocket every hour and look at it. These words were written on it, *And be patient under the judgement of your Lord: surely you are before Our eyes.* [Q.LII.48]

> It is said that the wife of Fatḥ al-Mawṣilī stumbled, and her fingernail became detached. She laughed. It was asked of her, 'Do you feel pain?' She replied, 'The delight of its reward caused the bitterness of its pain to vanish from my heart.'[54]

Among the anecdotes that Ghazālī cites are those in which a dialogue takes place between a Sufi and another person. They are some of his most effective illustrations. We shall include two of them as representative of this type of literature. The first one occurs in Chapter Seven, 'An Exposition of Patience as a Remedy and What is Gained by Resorting to It.' Here the anonymous speaker testifies to his self-control in patience,

> One of the kings asked an ascetic, 'Have you any need?' He replied, 'How shall I ask anything of you when my kingdom is greater than your kingdom?' He [the king] asked, 'How is that?' He replied, 'The one to whom you are a slave is my slave!' Then [the king] asked, 'How can that be?' [The ascetic] replied, 'You are a slave to your appetite, wrath, sexual urges and stomach, while I rule over all these! For they are my slaves!'[55]

The second dialogue, one of the most dramatic in the book, occurs in Chapter Fourteen, 'An Exposition of the Causes which Turn People Away from Thankfulness.' Muḥammad b. al-Sammāk, a famous ascetic and preacher, was at court conversing with one of the caliphs; most probably Hārūn al-Rashīd, since he was the reigning caliph during the last decade of Ibn al-Sammāk's life. The episode focuses on God's blessing in the fulfilment of the simplest of needs, and how it becomes a cause for thankfulness,

> Ibn al-Sammāk visited one of the caliphs, [who was] holding in his hand a jug of water and drinking from it. The caliph said to him, 'Give me advice!' He replied, 'If you were not given this drink unless you gave up all your wealth, or you would remain thirsty, would you give it up?' The caliph replied, 'Yes.' Then he asked, 'If you were not given this drink unless [you

gave up] all your kingdom, would you leave it?' The caliph said, 'Yes.' [Ibn al-Sammāk] said, 'Then take no joy in a kingdom that does not equal even a drink of water!'[56]

Finally, it is important to note that though Ghazālī does make use of Sufi sayings and anecdotes, in number they are much fewer than the Qur'ānic verses and the prophetic traditions.

Arabic Poetry

Aside from his use of Sufi literature in the *Revival*, Ghazālī also makes use of Arabic poetry. As with all his sources, the inclusion of the poetry is there to support an argument. The verses are often inserted at a transitional point in the exposition or at the close of an argument. Though Ghazālī does include poetry, he does so sparingly. In the *Book of Patience and Thankfulness*, lines of poetry occur only eleven times in nine of the chapters.

Ghazālī defended the place of poetry and music in the life and practice of Muslims, provided that these arts did not lead to unlawful actions. In her study of Ghazālī, Margaret Smith reminds us that, in addition to all his other achievements, Ghazālī was also a poet and she cites a number of examples of his poetry.[57] It should thus not be surprising that we would find some poetry in the *Book of Patience and Thankfulness*.

In his commentary on the *Iḥyā'*, Zabīdī was not always able to identify the authors of the poetry quoted by Ghazālī. It may be that some of the unidentified verses are from Ghazālī's own pen.

The first use of poetry appears in the fifth chapter, 'An Exposition of the Divisions of Patience According to Variations of Strength and Weakness.' Ghazālī is discussing the struggle the believer (*mu'min*) may experience between the religious impulse (*bāʿith al-dīn*) and the impulse of passion (*bāʿith al-hawā*): he may subdue passion, he may be overcome by it, or he may frequently be in a state of flux in his capacity to resist temptations. The place of patience as a discipline of the soul is very relevant and Ghazālī cites a line from the poetry of Mutanabī (d. 354/965) to alert the reader about the critical nature of making the correct choice,

> I have not seen a fault among men more grave,
> As the failure of those who are capable of perfection.[58]

In the section dealing with patience there is only one more poetic quotation and it falls in Chapter Seven, 'An Exposition of Patience as a Remedy and What is Gained by Resorting to It.' Ghazālī brings this chapter to a close with an anecdote from the life of Abū Bakr al-Shiblī and a few lines of Sufi poetry,

> Patience away from You,
> Blameworthy are its consequences;
> Patience in the rest of things
> Is praiseworthy;
> Patience is beautiful in all its habitations,
> Except away from You;
> Then it does not beautify its possessor.[59]

The next selection of poetry appears in Chapter Nine, 'An Exposition of the Definition and Nature of Thankfulness.' In many ways this chapter is the summit of the whole book. Ghazālī discusses the vision of the 'heart' when the soul is not drowned in sensual experience. The contrast is sharpened by the tart lines of Mutanabī's poetry,

> And he who possesses a bitter mouth is sick,
> And the sweet water he finds bitter.[60]

A large part of Chapter Ten, 'An Exposition of How to Raise the Veil on the Thankfulness Due to God,' is taken up by Ghazālī's demonstration of the meaning of thankfulness and how it relates to two affirmations: first, the affirmation of the unity of God (*tawḥīd*), and second, the affirmation of annihilation in Sufism (*fanāʾ*). These verses strike a warning regarding the failure to persevere, a note earlier sounded in relation to patience,

For all men there are movements toward the highest ambition,
But rare among men are those who persist.[61]

In Chapter Eleven, 'An Exposition of the Distinction Between What God Loves and What He Hates,' Ghazālī links thankfulness to concrete patterns of conduct and attitudes in daily life and commerce. Those who respond to divine guidance through right conduct can take on the attributes of God; here Ghazālī mentions a stanza of poetry,

We drank a good drink in the presence of the Good,
Likewise, the drink of the good is [always] good.
We drank and we poured its excess on the ground,
The ground also receives a portion from the cup of the generous one.[62]

In Chapter Twelve, 'An Exposition of the Nature of the Blessings and Their Divisions,' Ghazālī reflects on the various categories of God's blessings and asserts that none can do without the success which is granted by God (*tawfīq*),

If there is no help from God for the young man,
It is mostly his striving that brings him injury.[63]

The next citation of poetry is in Chapter Fourteen, 'An Exposition of the Causes which Turn People Away from Thankfulness,' the words of a poet again find a place in his counsels,

He who wishes a comfortable living by which to increase his success in religion and in worldly matters
Let him consider those above him in piety, and let him consider those below him in wealth.[64]

In the same chapter, Ghazālī, after having quoted from the Qur'ān and the traditions of the Prophet Muḥammad, includes a couple of verses of poetry,

As food comes to you,
  So come health and security.
Once you become a brother of sorrow,
  Then sorrow will not from you depart.[65]

Ghazālī's next poetic quote is to be found in Chapter Fifteen, 'An Exposition of that which Unites Patience and Thankfulness.' As the title of the chapter indicates, the writer now surveys the complex situations of life where both of the virtues discussed in this book have a bearing on the quality of human action. He treats the problem both from the standpoint of daily life and from its implication for the Hereafter. Ghazālī recalls the condolence visit of a bedouin to ʿAbd Allāh b. ʿAbbās. The visitor so pleased Ibn ʿAbbās with his words of sympathy that he exclaimed, 'Nothing comforted me more than his consolation.' Ghazālī includes the lines of the bedouin poet,

Be patient! And let us be patient with you.
  Truly, the patience of the followers is only after the patience of the leader.
Your reward for separation from him is better than al-ʿAbbās himself.
  And God is better for al-ʿAbbās than you.[66]

In Chapter Sixteen, 'An Exposition of the Merit of Blessing over Tribulation,' Ghazālī seeks to tackle the issue of misfortune (*balāʾ*). He states that it is necessary for us to ask God both for the most complete blessing (*tamām al-niʿma*) in this world and a repulsion of tribulation (*dafʿ al-balāʾ*). However, by quoting the poetry of the Sufi Sumnūn, Ghazālī portrays the Sufi's ideal of commitment to God in whom he trusts. The Sufi is prepared for anything that may cross his path, even though it may mean suffering,

I have no share in anything other than You,
  Then try me in whatever way You wish.[67]

The last passage of poetry is to be found in the next paragraph of the Arabic text. In some respects it is the most important piece of poetry that Ghazālī quotes,

> I desire his union and he desires my parting,
> So, I shall leave what I desire for what he desires.[68]

Here Ghazālī is continuing the idea of the believer as lover and God as the Beloved which was first expressed by the famous woman mystic, Rābiʿa al-ʿAdawiyya and was also used by Muḥāsibī, Bisṭāmī and Junayd.

Editions of the Iḥyā'

In the absence of a critically edited standard text of the *Iḥyā' ʿulūm al-dīn*, the following texts were used for the translation: (1) ʿĪsā 'l-Bābī 'l-Ḥalabī (abbreviated IH), Cairo, n.d., which is a copy of the 4-volume edition published in 1346/1927–1928 with an introduction dated 1377/1957 by Badawī Ṭabbāna, whose text is still the most reliable; (2) the text shown by Zabīdī in his commentary on the *Iḥyā'*, namely, the 10-volume *Itḥāf al-sādat al-muttaqīn bi-sharḥ Iḥyā' ʿulūm al-dīn*, published by al-Maṭbaʿa al-Maymaniyya (Z), Cairo, 1311/1893–1894; (3) the text on the margin of the *Itḥāf* (ZM), which the publisher of the *Itḥāf* has added since the text of Zabīdī is not complete. The pagination in the references to the *Iḥyā'* is that of the Cairo edition of al-Ḥalabi, IH mentioned above. Al-Ḥāfiẓ al-ʿIrāqī's book, *al-Mughnī ʿan ḥaml al-aṣfār*, on the traditions cited by Ghazālī is printed on the margins of the IH edition.

Notes to Introduction

1 Duncan B. Macdonald, 'Al-Ghazzālī,' *SEI*, p. 111.

2 The Islamic sciences are generally recognised to be the following: (1) *tafsīr*, the study and interpretation of the Qur'ān; (2) *ʿilm al-ḥadīth*, the study and exposition of the traditions of the Prophet; (3) *sharīʿa*, the study and interpretation of Islamic law; (4) *fiqh*, the study and exposition of Islamic law as it applies to acts of worship (*ʿibadāt*), practical transactions (*muʿāmalāt*), and conduct (*ādāb*); (5) *ʿilm al-kalām*, theology; and finally (6) *taṣawwuf* or Sufism, the study and practice of mysticism and ethics. Ghazālī was a profound thinker in the first three fields, employing them continually in his writings, and he made major contributions in the last three fields.

3 Quoted from A. J. Arberry, *Sufism: An Account of the Mystics of Islam* (London: George Allen & Unwin Ltd, 1963), pp. 82–83.

4 'The authority of Islam.' It was given in recognition of his memorisation of 300,000 traditions. Philip K. Hitti, *History of the Arabs from the Earliest Times to the Present* (London: Macmillan & Co., Ltd, 1961), p. 412. It is also sometimes rendered 'the proof of Islam,' coming from the verb *ḥājja* which means 'to overcome in a dispute.'

5 Watt comments that in his outlook Ghazālī 'is closer than that of many Muslims to the outlook of modern Europe and America, so that he is more easily comprehensible to us.' (*Muslim Intellectual: A Study of al-Ghazali* [Edinburgh: Edinburgh University Press, 1963], p. vii.)

6 Henri Laoust, *La Politique de Gazālī* (Paris: Librairie Orientaliste Paul Geuthner, 1970), pp. 117–130.

7 Page 5. *Iḥyā'*, IV.60.

8 Page 63. *Iḥyā'*, IV.78.

9 It is the ninth book of the *Revival*, the 'Book of Invocations and Supplications' (*K. al-adhkār wa'l-daʿawāt*), I.301–339.

10 They are the following books of the *Revival*. Book 13: 'On the Manners of Acquisition and Earning a Livelihood' (*K. adāb al-kasb wa'l-maʿāsh*); Book 14: the 'Book of the Lawful and the Unlawful' (*K. al-ḥalāl wa'l-ḥarām*); Book 15: 'On the Duties of Friendship, Brotherhood, Companionship and Association with the Creation' (*K. al-ulfa wa'l-ukhuwwa wa'l-suḥba wa'l-muʿāshara*); Book 18: 'On Music and Singing' (*K. al-samāʿ wa'l-wajd*); and

Book 19: 'On Enjoining the Good and Forbidding Evil' (*K. al-amr bi-maʿrūf wa'l-nahy ʿan al-munkar*).

11 They are the following books of the *Revival*. Book 25: 'On the Condemnation of Anger, Rancour and Envy' (*K. dhamm al-ghaḍab wa'l-ḥiqd wa'l-ḥasad*); Book 27: 'On the Condemnation of Miserliness and Condemnation of the Love of Wealth' (*K. dhamm al-bukhl wa-dhamm ḥubb al-māl*); Book 28: 'On the Condemnation of Status and Ostentation' (*K. dhamm al-jāh wa'l-riyā'*); and Book 29: 'On the Condemnation of Pride and Conceit' (*K. dhamm al-kibr wa'l-ʿujab*).

12 Aside from the 'Book of Patience and Thankfulness,' they are the following books of the *Revival*. Book 33: 'On Fear and Hope' (*K. al-khawf wa'l-rajā'*); Book 34: 'On Poverty and Abstinence' (*K. al-faqr wa'l-zuhd*); Book 35: 'Book of Unity and Trustfulness' (*K. al-tawḥīd wa'l-tawakkul*); Book 36: 'On Love, Longing, Intimacy and Contentment' (*K. al-ḥubb wa'l-shawq wa'l-uns wa'l-riḍā*); Book 37: 'On Intention, Truthfulness and Sincerity' (*K. al-niyya wa'l-ṣidq wa'l-ikhlāṣ*); Book 38: 'On Vigilance and Self-examination' (*K. al-murāqaba wa'l-muḥāsaba*); and finally, Book 40: 'On the Remembrance of Death and the Afterlife' (*K. dhikr al-mawt wa-mā baʿdahu*).

13 Abū Ṭālib al-Makkī, *Qūt al-qulūb fī muʿāmalat al-maḥbūb* (Cairo: Maṭbaʿat Muṣṭafā 'l-Bābī 'l-Ḥalabī, 1961), 1.407.

14 Ibid., 1.394ff.

15 Muḥammad b. Isḥāq al-Kalābādhī, *Kitāb al-taʿarruf*, pp. 94–95; trans. A. J. Arberry, *The Doctrine of the Sufis* (Cambridge: Cambridge University Press, 1935), pp. 93–94.

16 ʿAbd al-Karīm al-Qushayrī, *al-Risāla al-Qushayriyya* (Cairo: Dār al-Kutub al-Ḥadītha, 1385/1966), 1.397ff.

17 Louis Massignon, *Essai sur les origines du lexique technique de la mystique musulmane* (Paris: J. Vrin, 1954), pp. 246–247.

18 Ali Othman, *The Concept of Man in Islam in the Writings of al-Ghazalī* (Cairo: Dār al-Maʿarif, 1960), p. 93; Mohamed Sherif, *Ghazali's Theory of Virtue* (Albany: State University of New York Press, 1975), pp. 129ff.

19 Arberry (trans.), *Doctrine of the Sufis*, p. 100; Ghazālī, *K. al-khawf wa'l- rajā'*, trans. William McKane, *Al-Ghazali's Book of Fear and Hope* (Leiden: E. J. Brill, 1953), p. 11.

20 Dwight M. Donaldson, *Studies in Muslim Ethics* (London: S.P.C.K., 1953), p. 164.

21 Duncan Macdonald, *The Religious Attitude and Life in Islam* (Beirut: Khayat, 1965), p. 260.

22 Hans Wehr, *A Dictionary of Modern Written Arabic* (Wiesbaden: Otto Harrassowitz, 1961), p. 980.

23 Othman, *Concept of Man*, p. 93.

24 Ibn Manẓūr, *Lisān al-ʿArab* (Cairo: Dār al-Maʿārif, n.d.).

25 Cf. Fadlou Shehadi, *Ghazali's Unique Unknowable God* (Leiden: E. J. Brill, 1964), p. 29.

26 Aside from Shehadi, *Ghazali's Unique Unknowable God*, pp. 29–36, 58–59, 68–77, see also Othman, *Concept of Man*, pp. 93–96, 113, 127–132; Sherif, *Ghazali's Theory of Virtue*, pp. 108–113; Farīd Jabre, *Essai sur le lexique de Ghazali* (Beirut: Publications de l'Université Libanaise, 1970), pp. 174–175, 272, 282f.

27 Muḥammad Fu'ād ʿAbd al-Bāqī, *al-Muʿjam al-mufahras lī-alfāẓ al-Qur'ān al-karīm* (Beirut: al-Khayyāt, n.d.), II.399–401.

28 All extracts from the Qur'ān are taken from A. J. Arberry, *The Koran Interpreted* (New York: Macmillan, 1995); Muḥammad Marmaduke Pickthall, *The Meaning of the Glorious Koran* (London: A. A. Knopf, 1930), or ʿAbdullah Yūsuf ʿAlī, *The Meaning of the Holy Qur'ān* (Brentwood, MD: Amana, 1992) with occasional modifications.

29 This is especially noticeable in the 'allegory of the local earthquake,' which is found in Chapter Two, 'An Exposition of the Nature and Meaning of Patience,' *Iḥyā'*, IV.63.

30 Page 41. *Iḥyā'*, IV.71.

31 Page 41. *Iḥyā'*, IV.71.

32 Page 8. *Iḥyā'*, IV.71.

33 Page 183. *Iḥyā'*, IV.122.

34 Page 31. *Iḥyā'*, IV.66–67.

35 Abū 'l-Faraj Ibn al-Jawzī, *Talbīs Iblīs* (Beirut: Dār al-Waʿy al-ʿArabī, n.d.), where Ibn al-Jawzī wrote against Sufism in general, then against Abū Ṭālib al-Makkī, Qushayrī and others, repudiating their terminology, and finally against Abū Ḥāmid al-Ghazālī, particularly for his weak traditions, pp.164–166, 178, 245.

36 ʿAbd al-Wahhāb b. ʿAlī 'l-Subkī, *Ṭabaqāt al-Shāfiʿiyya* (Cairo: Maṭbaʿat ʿĪsā 'l-Bābī 'l-Ḥalabī, 1967), IV.287–389.

37 ʿAbd al-Raḥīm al-ʿIrāqī, *al-Mughnī ʿan ḥaml al-aṣfār fī asfār fī-takhrīj ma fī'l-Iḥyā' min al-akhbār*, 4 vols. (Cairo: Maṭbaʿat al-Bābī 'l-Ḥalabī, 1358/1939).

38 Murtaḍā 'l-Zabīdī, *Itḥāf al-sāda al-muttaqīn bi-sharḥ asrār Iḥyā' ʿulūm al-dīn* (Beirut: Dār Iḥyā' al-Turāth al-ʿArabī, n.d.).

39 Page 39. *Iḥyā'*, IV.70.

40 Page 143. *Iḥyā'*, IV.106.

41 Page 39. *Iḥyā'*, IV.70.

42 Page 9. *Iḥyā'*, IV.61.

43 Page 114.

44 Page 193 *Iḥyā'*, IV.126–127.

45 Page 203. *Iḥyā'*, IV.130.

46 Page 9. *Iḥyā'*, IV.61.

47 Page 203. *Iḥyā'*, IV.130.

48 Page 202. *Iḥyā'*, IV.130.

49 Page 80. *Iḥyā'*, IV.83.

50 Translation by W. Montgomery Watt, *The Faith and Practice of al-Ghazālī* (London: George Allen & Unwin, 1953), pp. 56–57; Arabic text, Ghazālī, *al-Munqidh min al-ḍalāl*, ed. Jamīl Ṣalība and Kāmil ʿIyād (Beirut: Dār al-Andalus, 1967), pp. 103–104.

51 Watt, *Faith and Practice*, p. 54.
52 Page 41. *Iḥyā'*, IV.71.
53 Zabīdī, *Itḥāf*, IX.29.
54 Page 42. *Iḥyā'*, IV.71.
55 Page 59. *Iḥyā'*, IV.77.
56 Page 181. *Iḥyā'*, IV.77.
57 Margaret Smith, *Al-Ghazālī the Mystic*, pp. 36–37, 83–85.
58 Page 30. *Dīwān al-Mutanabbī* (Cairo: Lajnat al-Ta'līf wa'l-Tarjama wa'l-Nashr, 1944), p. 492.
59 Page 61. Zabīdī, *Itḥāf*, IX.42.
60 Page 75. Zabīdī, *Itḥāf*, IX.81.
61 Page 85. Zabīdī, *Itḥāf*, IX.57.
62 Page 113. Zabīdī, *Itḥāf*, IX.74.
63 Page 141. Zabīdī, *Itḥāf*, IX.96.
64 Page 183. Zabīdī, *Itḥāf*, IX.132.
65 Page 184. Zabīdī, *Itḥāf*, IX.133.
66 Page 198. Zabīdī, *Itḥāf*, IX.141–142.
67 Page 206.
68 Page 207. Zabīdī, *Itḥāf*, IX.149.

THE BOOK OF PATIENCE AND THANKFULNESS

Kitāb al-ṣabr wa'l-shukr

BOOK XXXII OF THE REVIVAL OF THE RELIGIOUS SCIENCES

Iḥyā' ʿulūm al-dīn

THE BOOK OF PATIENCE AND THANKFULNESS

Being the Second Book of the Quarter of the Saving Virtues

[PROLOGUE]

In the name of God, Most Compassionate and Merciful

PRAISE BE TO GOD, Who is worthy of praise and glorification, Who alone is robed in majesty, Who is unique in the attributes of glory and exaltation. He is the One Who sustains the select of the saints (*ṣafwat al-awliyā'*) with the power of patience (*ṣabr*) in good fortune and adversity, and with thankfulness (*shukr*) in trial and prosperity.

BLESSINGS, GUARDED ALWAYS FROM EXTINCTION AND PRESERVED through repetition from decrease and expiry, be upon Muḥammad, the lord of the prophets; and upon his Companions, the leaders of the pure, and upon his family, the foremost of the righteous and of the pious.

To proceed. As the 'narratives' (*āthār*)[A] have said and as the 'traditions' (*akhbār*) have borne testimony, 'faith (*īmān*) has two halves. One half is patience and the other is thankfulness.'[1] These are also two of the attributes of God (Exalted is He!) and two of His beautiful names, for He has named Himself the Patient (*al-Ṣabūr*) and the Thankful (*al-Shakūr*).[B] Therefore, ignorance of

[A] *Āthār*, plural of *athar*, are defined as 'all positive teaching having for an author someone other than the Prophet.' Jabre, *Essai*, p. 1. The *akhbār*, plural of *khabar*, are the sayings of the Prophet.

[B] For a discussion of these two divine names, see Ghazālī, *al-Maqṣad al-asnā* the reality of patience and thankfulness is ignorance of the two branches of faith. Furthermore, it constitutes negligence with respect to two of the attributes of the Compassionate. There is no other way of attaining proximity to God (Exalted is He!) except through faith.

Yet, how can following the path of faith be imagined without knowledge of what faith is and the One in Whom there is faith? The lack of knowledge of patience and thankfulness is [both] a lack of knowledge of Him in Whom there is faith and a lack of comprehension of what faith is. How necessary is it then for the two halves [of faith] to have a clear explanation and exposition! By God's will, we shall set forth the two parts in one book because of the relationship of the one to the other.

fī sharḥ maʿānī asmāʾ Allāh al-ḥusnā (Beirut: Dār al-Mashriq, 1971), pp. 114 and 161 (English translation, *The Ninety-nine Beautiful Names of God*, trans. David Burrell and Nazih Daher [Cambridge: Islamic Texts Society, 1992], pp. 148–149 and 101–102). It should be noted that while the name *Shakūr* occurs in the Qur'ān (Q.xxxv.30, xxxv.34, xlii.23, lxiv.17), the name *Ṣabūr* does not. However, it does occur in traditions, for example, in Tirmidhī's *Sunan*, *K. Daʿawāt*.

PART I
ON PATIENCE

The first part [will include]: An Exposition of the Merit of Patience, An Exposition of the Nature and Meaning of Patience, An Exposition of How Patience is Half of Faith, An Exposition of the Terms Used for Patience in Addition to the Term Patience Itself, An Exposition of the Divisions of Patience According to Variations of Strength and Weakness, An Exposition of the Assumed Need for Patience and that the Servant Cannot Dispense with it Under any Condition, and An Exposition of Patience as a Remedy and What is Gained by Resorting to It. These are seven sections (*fuṣūl*), which, God willing, will present all the objectives [of patience].

CHAPTER ONE
An Exposition of the Merit of Patience

GOD (EXALTED IS HE!) has given those who are patient specific characteristics. He has mentioned patience in the Qur'ān in more than seventy places.[1] He has attributed most of the stages (*darajāt*) and the rewards (*khayrāt*) to patience, making them its fruits. God (Exalted is He!) has said, *We appointed from among them leaders who guide by Our command, when they endured patiently.*[2] And He has said, *And perfectly was fulfilled the most fair word of your Lord upon the Children of Israel, for they endured patiently.*[3] And, *Surely We shall recompense those who were patient with their reward, according to the best of what they did.*[4] Again, *These shall be given their reward twice over for they endured patiently.*[5] And He has said, *Surely the patient shall be given their reward in full without reckoning.*[6]

For each action bringing us close [to God] has its reward according to a predetermined measure and calculation, with the exception of patience. It is because fasting pertains to patience, and indeed is half of patience,[7] that God (Exalted is He!) has said, 'Fasting is mine and I shall reward for it;'[8] He specifically related it to Himself, [and set it] apart from the other acts of worship.

He has promised the patient that He will be with them, He (Exalted is He!) has said, *And be patient; surely God is with the patient.*[9] He has made victory conditional upon patience, saying, *If you are patient and God-fearing and the enemy attacks you suddenly, your Lord will reinforce you with five thousand swooping angels.*[10] He has brought together for the patient [certain] things that He did not bring together for others. God (Exalted is He!) has said, *Upon these rest blessings and mercy from their Lord, and they are truly guided.*[11] Therefore, guidance (*hudā*), mercy (*raḥma*) and blessings (*ṣalawāt*) are brought together for the patient. An exhaustive list of all the Qur'ānic passages pertaining to the station (*maqām*)[A] of patience would be lengthy.

The Traditions

As for the traditions, he [the Prophet] (may God bless him and grant him peace) has said, 'Patience is half of faith.'[12] The way in which it is half of faith will be explained later.

He, may God bless him and grant him peace, said, 'Among the lesser [gifts of God] that you have been granted are certainty (*yaqīn*)[B] and resolute patience (*ʿazīmat al-ṣabr*). [However], he who is given his share of these two should not be concerned about what he has missed out on in rising up to pray by night and fasting by day. It means more to me that you bear patiently whatever situation confronts you than that each of you offers me work totalling the capacity of all. But I am concerned that life will be prosperous for you after me. Then you will deny each other and the people of heaven will deny you in turn. He who is patient and who sacrifices in anticipation of God's reward will win the fullness of his reward.'[13] Then the Prophet recited His words, *What is with you comes to an end, but what is with God abides; and surely We shall recompense those who were patient with their reward.*[14]

Jābir relates that the Prophet (may God bless him and grant him peace) was asked about faith (*īmān*) and he replied, '[It is] patience and tolerance (*samāḥa*).'[15]

[A] The first major collection of Sufi thought in which the *maqāmāt* (stations) are discussed is that of Abū Naṣr al-Sarrāj, *Kitāb al-lumaʿ fī'l-taṣawwuf*, trans. R. A. Nicholson (Leiden: E. J. Brill, 1914). In it the meaning of *maqām* is 'the place where the servant stands before God with respect to his acts of worship, strivings, religious devotions and withdrawal toward God.' See Sarrāj, *Lumaʿ*, pp. 12, 41–42.

[B] For a discussion of certainty in Ghazālī's thought, see Farīd Jabre, *La notion de certitude selon Ghazali* (Paris: J. Vrin, 1958).

The Prophet also said, 'Patience is one of the treasures of Paradise.'[16]

He was once asked, 'What is faith?' He replied, 'Patience.'[17] This reply is of similar brevity to his saying, 'The pilgrimage is ʿArafa.'[18] This means that the greater part of the pilgrimage is what occurs at ʿArafa.

[The Prophet] (may God bless him and grant him peace), also said, 'The best actions are those that people are compelled to do.'[19]

It is said that God (Exalted is He!) revealed to David (peace be upon him), 'Let your character be moulded by Mine, and among My attributes is that I am the Patient.'[20]

In a tradition of ʿAṭā', on the authority of Ibn ʿAbbās, when the Messenger of God (may God bless him and grant him peace) met the Helpers (al-Anṣār),[A] he said, 'Are you believers?' They were silent. ʿUmar (may God be pleased with him) replied, 'Yes, O Messenger of God!' Muḥammad asked, 'What is the sign of your faith?' They replied, 'We are thankful for abundance, we are willing to bear grievous trial patiently, and we accept the divine decree (*qaḍā'*).' Whereupon the Prophet (may God bless him and grant him peace) said, 'You are believers, by the Lord of the Kaʿba!'[21]

The Prophet said, 'There is much good in being patient with what you dislike.'[22]

Christ (peace be upon him) said, 'You come to understand what you love only through patience with what you abhor.'[23]

The Messenger of God (may God bless him and grant him peace) said, 'Were patience a man, truly, he would be generous. God loves those who are patient.'[24] The traditions on this matter are countless.

[A] The Medinan followers of Muḥammad who granted him refuge after the migration from Mecca.

The Narratives

As for the narratives (*āthār*), the following is found in a letter of ʿUmar b. al-Khaṭṭāb (may God be pleased with him) to Abū Mūsā ʾl-Ashʿarī,[A] 'It is incumbent upon you to be patient. Know that patience is of two kinds, one is better than the other. Patience in misfortune is good, but preferable to it is patience in relation to what God (Exalted is He!) has forbidden. Know that patience is the foundation of faith and this is because the fear of God (*taqwā*)[B] is the best part of piety (*birr*), and fearing God is [acquired] through patience.'

ʿAlī (may God ennoble his face) said, 'Faith is built upon four pillars: certainty (*yaqīn*), patience (*ṣabr*), striving (*jihād*), and justice (*ʿadl*).'[25] ʿAlī also said, 'Patience is to faith as the head is to the body. No one has a body without a head, and no one has faith without patience.'[26]

ʿUmar (may God be pleased with him) used to say, 'Full[C] are the two saddlebags, and full is the load for those who endure patiently.'[27] By saddlebags he meant blessings and mercy; and by load, guidance. The load is what is carried above the saddlebags on the camel. In this, he is alluding to what God (Exalted is He!) says, *Upon these rest blessings and mercy from their Lord, and they are truly guided.*[28]

Whenever Ḥabīb b. Abī Ḥabīb used to recite the verse, *Surely We found him patient. How excellent a servant he was! He always turned to God,*[29] he wept and said, 'How wonderful it is! He gave and He praised.' That is to say, God is the giver of patience and He praises [for it].

[A] Zabīdī comments that the letter with his admonishment was sent to Abū Mūsā ʾl-Ashʿarī when he was governor of Baṣra (17–23/636–644) (Zabīdī, ix.6).

[B] William Chittick suggests 'god-wariness' as a rendering for *taqwā* (*Faith and Practice: Three Thirteenth-Century Sufi Texts* [Albany: State University of New York Press, 1992], p. 12).

[C] Literally, 'excellent.'

Abū 'l-Dardā' said, 'The pinnacle of faith is patience in the judgement of God (*ḥukm*) and contentment with the divine predestination (*qadar*).'[30]

The above is an exposition of the merit of patience as far as narrated traditions are concerned. From the standpoint of knowledge through the eye of contemplation (*naẓar bi-ʿayn al-iʿtibār*), [the merit of patience] can only be understood when the reality and meaning of patience are understood. To know merit and rank is to know an attribute. This cannot be arrived at without knowledge of the thing described. Let us then discuss its reality and its meaning. May God grant us success.

CHAPTER TWO
An Exposition of the Nature and Meaning of Patience

KNOW that patience is one of the stations of religion (*dīn*) and a way-station (*manzil*) of travellers following the spiritual path. All of the stations of religion are classified according to three things: degrees of knowledge (*maʿārif*),[A] states (*aḥwāl*),[B] and actions (*aʿmāl*).[C] The degrees of knowledge are the source that give rise to the states; and the states bear fruit in actions. The degrees of knowledge, therefore, are like the tree-trunks, the states are like the branches, and the actions are like the fruits. This analogy holds true for all the way-stations of those

[A] *Maʿārif* is the plural of *maʿrifa*. Ghazālī uses the plural form quite frequently. We have mostly chosen to follow Winter's translation of *maʿrifa*, *ʿilm*, and *ḥikma* as gnosis, knowledge, and wisdom. However, where *maʿrifa* is being used as a synonym for *ʿilm* and does not specifically refer to gnosis, we have chosen to translate it as knowledge. Cf. Ghazālī, trans. T. J. Winter, *On Disciplining the Soul* (Cambridge: Islamic Texts Society, 1995), p. 46. Both R. A. Nicholson (*The Mystics of Islam* [London: Routledge and Kegan Paul, 1914], p. 29) and William Chittick (*The Sufi Path of Knowledge* [Albany: State University of New York Press, 1989], p. 149) translate *maʿārif* as 'gnostic sciences.'

[B] Plural of *ḥāl*. Massignon describes them as 'states of mystical consciousness,' *Essai*, p. 305; Arberry holds that *ḥāl* is 'a spiritual mood depending not upon the mystic but upon God,' and quotes Qushayrī's statement that the *maqāmāt* are 'earnings' (*makāsib*) while the *aḥwāl* are 'gifts' (*mawāhib*), *Risāla*, I.193.

[C] Plural of *ʿamal*. Othman defines it as 'behaviour which is concomitant with this knowledge [faith] and this state [*ḥāl*], when the heart possesses faith-knowledge,' and 'conduct peculiar to trust in God [*tawakkul*]' (*Concept of Man*, pp. 121, 131).

who travel towards God (Exalted is He!). Just as we have mentioned before when differentiating between the terms *īmān* and *islām* in the *Book of the Foundations of the Articles of Faith*,[A] the word 'faith' is sometimes limited to the degrees of knowledge, and sometimes is applied to all.[B] Likewise, patience is attained only through an already acquired knowledge and an established state. Consequently, patience is indicative of them both;[C] and action is like the fruit that stems from them.

All this can only be understood through knowledge of the hierarchy between the angels, mankind, and the beasts. For patience is a characteristic of mankind, and it cannot be imagined to occur in beasts or angels. As for the beasts, this is due to their incompleteness. While for the angels, it is due to their perfection.

The explanation is that the beasts are governed by their appetites (*shahawāt*),[D] which dominate them. Consequently, the only factor governing their movement and repose is appetite. They have no power to oppose or turn appetite back from its desired goal. The power to persevere in confronting the desired goal of the appetite is called patience.

As for the angels (peace be upon them), they are ordained to long for the Lordly Presence (*ḥaḍrat al-rubūbiyya*) and to delight in accordance with the degree of nearness to it. No appetite has any authority over them, diverting or obstructing them from the Presence of Majesty (*ḥaḍrat al-jalāl*); and so there is no need for another force to overcome any obstacles.

Man, however, like the beast, is incomplete in infancy. The appetite for the nourishment he needs is created in him. The appetite for amusement and adornment appears in him at a later stage. And finally, [he comes to] the appetite for sexual relations. [Each] follows in succession. [In childhood], he has no power whatever

[A] *K. qawāʿid al-ʿaqāʾid* (*Iḥyāʾ*, 1.2).

[B] That is, applied to knowledge, states and actions.

[C] That is, patience is indicative of knowledge and states.

[D] Plural of *shahwa*.

for patience, which consists of one army standing firm in the face of another army, a struggle having arisen between them due to their contradictory requirements and demands. Like the beasts, childhood has only the power of desire (*hawā*).[A]

However, through His bounty and the breadth of His generosity, God (Exalted is He!) has honoured the children of Adam and has raised their station above that of the beasts. At the point that he nears puberty, God entrusts man to two angels. One of the angels guides him, the other strengthens him. Thus, he is distinguished from the beasts by the help of these two angels. He is favoured with two qualities: one is the knowledge of God and His Messenger, and the other is the knowledge of beneficial deeds that are related to final ends. All this comes about through the angel who is entrusted with guidance and instruction.

The beasts, however, have no knowledge of these matters. They do not proceed towards deeds of eventual benefit, but towards the demands of their immediate appetite. Therefore, they seek only pleasurable delight. As for the effective remedy which is unpleasant in the short term, the beasts do not seek it and do not know it.

Man, by contrast, comes to know, through the light of guidance, that following [one's] appetites can lead to undesirable consequences. However, this guidance would not be sufficient if he did not have the ability to abandon what is harmful. How many are the harmful things man recognises as such, like a disease that afflicts him, but which he has no power to forestall! He is thus in need of a power to slay the appetites. He is able, then, to fight

[A] In the discussion here and below, Ghazālī uses the term *hawā* as synonymous with *shahwa* (appetite). Here it means a basic or instinctual need. However, the term is usually used to denote the motive behind all sinful actions. Toshihiko Izutsu notes that it is 'the principal and immediate cause of *ḍalāl* ("straying"),' and it may be said to mean 'the natural inclination of the human soul, born of lusts and animal appetites' (*Ethico-religious Concepts in the Qur'ān* [Montreal: McGill University Press, 1966], pp. 139–140). The term appears approximately thirty times in the Qur'ān.

them with that power until he brings their hostility against himself to an end.

Now God (Exalted is He!) has also entrusted man to another angel who directs, supports, and strengthens him with unseen forces [lit. armies]. God commands this force to battle the force of the appetite. Sometimes one force weakens and the other strengthens, all in accordance with the help that God (Exalted is He!) extends to his servant in support. Similarly, the light of guidance also varies in strength to an unlimited degree among human beings.

Let us call this quality that makes man different from the beasts in [his] appetites and in their subjugation 'religious impulse' (*bāʿith al-dīn*). Let us call the pursuit of the appetites and their requirements 'impulse of desire' (*bāʿith al-hawā*). Let us understand that the struggle and warfare between the religious impulse and the impulse of desire are alternately successful. The battlefield of this struggle is the heart of the servant. Support for the religious impulse comes from the angels reinforcing the troops of God, while support for the impulse of desire comes from the devils reinforcing the enemies of God. Thus, patience is the steadfastness of the religious impulse in confronting the impulse of desire. If a man remains steadfast until the religious impulse conquers, and endures in opposing the appetites, then the troops of God are victorious and he joins the troops of the patient. But if he slackens and weakens until appetite overcomes him, and he does not persist in repelling it, he joins the followers of the devils.

Thus a state of patience results from abandoning actions arising from desire. [Patience] is the constancy of the religious impulse that opposes the impulse of appetite. The constancy of the religious impulse is a state borne of knowledge of the enmity and the opposition of the appetites to the causes of [true] happiness in this world and in the Hereafter. When a man's certainty is strengthened—I mean by [certainty here] this knowledge that is called faith—[this strengthened certainty is] certainty that the appetite is an enemy, blocking the way to God, then the steadfastness of the religious impulse is strengthened. When his constancy is strengthened, deeds are accomplished in a manner contrary to what appetite demands. The abandonment of the appetite is complete only when the strength of the religious impulse opposes the impulse of the appetite. The power of knowledge and faith also make the evil consequences of the appetite appear odious.

The two angels are entrusted with these two powers by the permission and command of God and they are among the Noble Scribes.[A] They are the angels to whom God has entrusted every human being. Know that the guiding angel is higher in degree than the strengthening angel—[just as] the right side of the seat of honour (*dast*)[B] is more exalted [than the left side]—and that [the strengthening angel] must be subject [to the guiding angel]. He [the guiding angel] is on the right side, the other is on the left.

The servant has [conflicting] states: heedlessness (*ghafla*) and reflection (*fikr*); and lassitude (*istirsāl*) and striving (*mujāhada*). Heedlessness turns the servant away from the angel on the right and offends him, and [the angel] writes it as an evil act. Whereas through reflection, he takes heed in order to benefit from the guidance of the angel, and so he is righteous and [the angel] writes it as a good deed. Likewise, lassitude turns the servant away from the angel on the left and makes him negligent of the support he [the angel] offers, and this is an offence to him [the angel], and he records an evil deed against him. Whereas through striving the servant is fortified by the angel's forces and a good deed is recorded for him.

[A] Angels who record the deeds of men. The theological narrative here has a Qur'ānic basis in Q.LXXXII.11, *There are over you watchers noble, writers who know whatever you do.*

[B] The term is of Persian derivation and means 'upper end of a chamber, which is the most honourable place therein. . . hence, a seat of honour, a seat of office' (Edward W. Lane, *An Arabic-English Lexicon* [London: Williams and Norgate, 1863], I.878). Here the throne refers to a place on a person's back, on which the two angels sit while recording one's deeds.

These good or evil deeds are set down in the records of the two angels. For this reason they are called Noble Scribes: noble, because the servant benefits through their noble natures. Indeed, all the angels are noble and pious. The word 'scribes' is used because they record good and evil deeds. They put them down on pages folded in the innermost heart, and [yet] concealed from the heart so that they are not seen in this world. They [the angels], their records, their writings, their pages, and all that is related to both [angels] are of the unseen world (*ʿālam al-ghayb*) and the world of sovereignty (*ʿālam al-malakūt*), and are not of the visible world (*ʿālam al-shahāda*). Nothing from the world of sovereignty can be seen in this [visible] world.

These pages that are concealed from the servant are made known twice: once at the lesser resurrection and once at the greater resurrection. I mean by the lesser resurrection the state of death, since the Prophet (may God bless him and grant him peace) said, 'He who has died, his resurrection has taken place.'[1] At this resurrection the servant will be alone and then it will be said, *Now you come to Us one by one, as We created you the first time.*[2] It will also be said, *Your soul suffices this day as a reckoner against you.*[3] As for the greater resurrection that includes all created beings, the servant will not be alone, but he may be judged in the presence of a multitude of people. At that time the pious will be led into Paradise and the evil-doers into the Fire in groups, not singly.

The first terror is the terror of the lesser resurrection. For every terror of the greater resurrection, there is a parallel in the lesser resurrection.[A] For example, the Earthquake[B]: in death, your own plot of ground, belonging to you, is shaken. As you know, when an earthquake occurs in a town, it is proper to say, 'their land has been shaken,' although the surrounding countryside may

[A] For Ghazālī's discussion of the events of the Afterlife, see *K. dhikr al-mawt* (*Iḥyā'*, IV.10), trans. T. J. Winter, *The Remembrance of Death and the Afterlife* (Cambridge: Islamic Texts Society, 1995).

[B] One of the events of the greater resurrection.

not have been shaken. Equally, if the dwelling of a man is shaken, the earthquake has taken place with respect to him, because he is harmed by the quaking of the earth through the shaking of his dwelling, but not through the shaking of another's dwelling. Thus, his share of the earthquake is sufficient and lacks nothing.

Know that you are of earthly matter, created from earth. Your particular share of the earth is your own body. As for the body of someone else, it is not your share. The ground upon which you sit is a circumstance of time and place in relation to your body. When the earth quakes, you fear only because your body is shaken. The wind is continually blowing, but you do not fear it because it does not shake your body. Your portion of an earthquake that shakes the entire earth is only the quaking of your own body. Your body is your particular ground and earth; your bones are the mountains of your earth; your head is the sky; your heart is the sun of your earth; your hearing, your sight, and the rest of your senses are the stars of your sky; your sweat glands are the sea of your earth; your hair is the vegetable growth; your limbs are the trees of your earth, and thus it is with all your [other] parts.

When the basic elements of your body collapse in death, the earth has been shaken by its earthquake.[A4] When the bones are separated from the flesh, the earth and the mountains are carried away and they are flattened with one crash.[5] When the bones decay, the mountains are blown out of existence.[6] When your heart darkens at death, the sun will be darkened totally.[7] When your hearing, sight, and the rest of your senses cease to function, the stars shall be scattered completely.[8] When your brain is rent asunder, the heavens are rent asunder fully.[9] When the sweat of your forehead bursts forth from the dread of death, the seas flood over with a great gushing.[10] When your legs become entwined one with the other,[11] and they are your beasts of burden, the she-camel has been abandoned.[12] And when the spirit leaves the body,

[A] In this vivid paragraph, Ghazālī applies some of the events of the greater resurrection mentioned in the Qur'ān to the body at the time of death.

the earth is stretched out and casts forth what is in it and voids itself.[13]

I shall not be exhaustive in comparing all the states and terrors. Nevertheless, I say that this lesser resurrection will come to you at the very moment of death. In the greater resurrection, you cannot escape anything that relates to you specifically, though you might miss that which relates to others. For if the stars continue to exist for others, how will it profit you when the senses by which you saw the stars have disintegrated? Night and day, the eclipse and brightness of the sun, are all the same to the blind person, because all are darkness to him. The sun's darkness is his share of it, and its visibility is the lot of others. [Likewise], he whose head has been rent asunder, his heaven has been rent asunder, since heaven consists of what lies close to the head. He who has no head, has no heaven. Therefore, how can the fact that the heavens continue to exist for others benefit him?

This is the lesser resurrection. But fear, terror, and more evil are yet to come, that is, when the greater calamity occurs; when the specific [resurrections] pass away; when the earth and the heavens cease to be; when the mountains are flattened; and when the terrors grow. Know that this lesser resurrection is of a kind that even were we to dwell on its description we should be unable to give more than a tenth of a tenth of its description.

Furthermore, [the lesser resurrection] in relation to the greater resurrection is as the lesser birth is to the greater birth. For man has two births. One is the exodus from the backbone and ribs[A][14] to the safety of the womb. The womb is then a firm resting-place[15] for a certain fixed time. [Man] has levels and states on the pathway to maturity, beginning from sperm, blood clot, and embryo[16] until he emerges from the stricture of the womb into the vast space of the world. Comparing the generalities of the greater resurrection to the specifics of the lesser resurrection is like comparing the spaciousness of the world's vast expanse to the extent of

[A] That is, the loins.

the womb's space. And comparing the expanse of the world into which a man enters on death is like comparing the spaciousness of the world to the womb; only it is wider and greater.

Therefore, compare the Afterlife (*al-ākhira*) with this life (*al-ūlā*), *for your creation and resurrection are as [the creation and resurrection of] one soul*;[17] and the second birth occurs only to the measure of the first birth. Furthermore, the number of births is not confined to two. There is an indication of this in His saying, *We make you to grow again in a fashion you know not.*[18] Consequently, he who believes in the two resurrections is a believer in the unseen and the visible worlds, and is certain [both] of this world (*mulk*) and the world of sovereignty (*mālakūt*). He who believes in the lesser resurrection and not in the greater is blind in one eye and looks only towards one of the two worlds. To do so is to be ignorant, to err, and to follow the One-eyed Imposter![A] How great, then, is your heedlessness, O pitiful one!

All of us are that pitiful one, and these terrors are before you. If you do not believe in the greater resurrection because of ignorance and error, then is the evidence of the lesser resurrection not sufficient for you? Or have you not heard the saying of the Master of the Prophets (may God bless him and grant him peace), 'Death suffices as an admonisher.'[19] Or have you not heard of his concern at the time of death when he (may God bless him and grant him peace) said, 'Almighty God, ease the agonies of death for Muḥammad.'[20] Or do you not feel ashamed of believing that the assault of death may be delayed, thus following the mob of the heedless *who pay no attention until a single call takes them away while they are still in the midst of disputing? Then they will be unable to make a bequest and they will not return to their people.*[21] Disease comes to them as a warning of death, but they are not disturbed. Old age comes to them as a messenger from death, but they pay no heed. *O woe to the servants! No messenger comes to them but they mock*

[A] Al-Aʿwar al-Dajjāl. This is a reference to the Dajjāl, or Antichrist, who, according to the Islamic traditions, is one-eyed.

him.[22] Do they think themselves eternal in this world? *Or have they not seen how many people We have destroyed in the centuries before them? The dead do not return to them.*[23] Or do they think that the dead have departed from them and that they no longer exist? *But all, without exception, will be brought before Us.*[24] However, *Not a sign of their Lord comes to them, but they turn away from it.*[25] That is because *We have put before them a barrier and behind them a barrier, and We have covered them, so they do not see. It is all the same to them whether you warn them or not, they do not believe.*[26]

Let us return to the objective, for these allusions point to matters that are higher than the sciences of practical transactions (*ʿulūm al-muʿāmala*).[A] We say: it is clear that patience consists of steadfastness in the religious impulse, in opposition to the impulse of desire. This opposition is peculiar to human beings because they are entrusted to Noble Scribes. Neither of the recording angels writes anything against children or the insane. For as we have mentioned, a good deed (*ḥasana*) is based on turning toward the benefit [derived] from them [the angels], and a sin (*sayyiʾa*) is turning away from them. As children and the insane are incapable of benefiting themselves they cannot be said to engage or abstain. The angels only record the turning toward or away of those capable of turning toward and away [from them].

I declare, the beginning of the light of guidance occurs upon the age of discernment[B] and grows gradually to the age of physical maturity, just as the morning becomes clear when the disk of the sun rises. However, it is a limited guidance, which teaches what is detrimental in this life but not what is detrimental to the next life. Therefore a child may be disciplined for abandoning prayers, but is not punished for it in the Hereafter nor is it recorded upon the pages that will be distributed in the Hereafter.

[A] Meaning that we are dealing here with matters that are higher than everyday events.

[B] *Sinn al-tamyīz*. Zabīdī does not suggest an exact age, but he uses the phrase *bulūgh al-ṣaby* (puberty).

Rather, it is incumbent upon the proper guardian and the compassionate righteous protector [of the child], if he is among the pious and if he possesses the qualities of the chosen Noble Scribes, that he instil [the meaning of] evil and good deeds on the pages of the child's heart. He first instils [the necessity for prayer] in his memory; then, he demonstrates it for him; shows him how to go about it; finally, he disciplines the child with a smack [if the child refuses to perform the prayer]. Every guardian who conducts himself thus towards a child has inherited the character traits of the angels, and has used these [traits] for the benefit of the child. Through this, he obtains a level of nearness to the Lord of the worlds, just as the angels have obtained it. He will be among the prophets, the ones brought near, and the righteous. This is alluded to in the Prophet's saying, 'I and the guardian of the orphan are like these two in Paradise,'[27] and he pointed to his two noble fingers.

CHAPTER THREE
An Exposition of How Patience is Half of Faith

KNOW that the term 'faith' (*īmān*) is sometimes applied to beliefs (*taṣdīqāt*)[A] in the fundamentals of religion (*uṣūl al-dīn*); at other times to the good actions they [the beliefs] give rise to; and sometimes to both. There are categories of knowledge (*maʿārif*) and actions (*aʿmāl*), and the term faith includes them all; it has in excess of seventy categories. We have discussed the diversity of these definitions in the *Book of the Foundations of the Articles of Faith* in the Quarter of the Acts of Worship. Still, patience is half of faith, based on two considerations and in conformity with two definitions.

The first consideration is [that faith is] applicable to both beliefs and actions. In this case, it has two foundations: one is certainty, the other is patience. What is intended by certainty is the definite degrees of knowledge that are attained by the servant as a result of God's guiding him in the fundamentals of religion. What is meant by patience is acting according to certainty, for certainty makes one perceive that disobedience is harmful, and obedience is beneficial. Abandoning disobedience and persevering in obedience are only possible through patience. It is the application of the religious impulse to overcome the impulse of desire and sloth.

[A] This term appears twice in the Qur'ān (Q.x.37, xii.111). Nabih Faris translates *taṣdīq* as 'acceptance' and *taṣdīq bi'l-qalb* 'acceptance with the mind' (*Foundations of the Articles of Faith* [Lahore: Sh. Muḥammad Ashraf, 1963], pp. 100, 108); and in Chittick it is 'attesting in the heart and acknowledging with the tongue' (*Sufi Path of Knowledge*, p. 193).

Thus, from this standpoint, patience is half of faith. This is why the Messenger of God (may God bless him and grant him peace) combined them and said, 'Among the lesser [gifts of God] that you have been granted are certainty (*yaqīn*) and resolute patience (*ʿazīmat al-ṣabr*). . . ' and so on.

The second consideration is [that faith] refers to the states that give rise to actions, and not to [degrees of] knowledge. At this point, all that the servant encounters is divided into what benefits him in this world and the Hereafter, and what harms him in both. He is granted the state of patience for what may harm him, and the state of thankfulness for what may benefit him. Thankfulness thus becomes one of the two parts of faith in this respect, just as certainty is one of two parts with respect to the first consideration. Concerning this aspect, Ibn Masʿūd (may God be pleased with him) said, 'Faith has two halves: one half is patience, and the other half is thankfulness.' This statement has also been ascribed to the Messenger of God (may God bless him and grant him peace).

Thus patience is fortitude [against] the impulse of desire with steadfastness in the religious impulse. The impulse of desire is divided into two: one issuing from the direction of appetite, and one issuing from the direction of wrath. The appetite relates to the pursuit of the pleasurable, and wrath with escape from the painful. Fasting is [the exercise of] patience only against the demands of appetite, the appetite of the stomach and loins, not the demands of wrath. The Prophet (may God bless him and grant him peace) said with respect to this consideration that 'fasting is half of patience.' This is because the perfection of patience is in its application to both the appetite and wrath. Accordingly, fasting is a quarter of faith.

Therefore, it is necessary to understand the edicts of canonical law (*al-sharʿ*) and the limitations it places on actions and states, and [to understand] their relationship with faith. The main aim is that you know the multiplicity of the categories of faith, for the term 'faith' applies to various dimensions.

CHAPTER FOUR
An Exposition of the Terms Used for Patience in Addition to the Term Patience Itself

KNOW that patience is of two kinds. One is physical, such as tolerating physical hardships and enduring them with constancy. It occurs either through action, such as arduous actions, whether of worship or other acts; or through endurance, such as bearing a severe beating, a serious illness, or critical wounds. This may be praiseworthy, if it is in harmony with the law. But the patience that is fully praiseworthy is the second kind. It is inner patience (*ṣabr nafsī*)[A] and it applies to matters coveted by [our] nature or the demands of desire. When this kind [of patience] restrains the appetite of the stomach and loins, it is called 'abstinence' (*ʿiffa*). When it is bearing what is hated, people refer to it by different names, according to what patience overcomes. When it is patience in misfortune, then the name 'patience' (*ṣabr*) alone is used, and its opposite is called 'restless anxiety' (*jazʿ*) and a 'violent outburst of grief' (*halaʿ*) and this is giving vent to the motive of the desire [in self-indulgent acts] such as persistently crying aloud, striking the cheeks, rending [one's] garments, and similar acts.[B]

[A] The discussion about the meanings, limitations, and expressions of this kind of patience was underway in the early 'reflective' period of Sufi thought. Abū Naṣr al-Sarrāj cites the statements and stories of Junayd, Khawwāṣ and Shiblī on the subject. See Sarrāj, Nicholson (trans.), *Lumaʿ*, pp. 15 and 42 (Arabic text).

[B] Ghazālī is referring to excessive expressions of sorrow during mourning.

When [patience] refers to withstanding [the temptations of] prosperity (*iḥtimāl al-ghinā*), it is called 'self-control' (*ḍabṭ al-nafs*). The state opposed to it is called 'reckless vanity' (*baṭar*). When it is applied to war and fighting, it is called 'bravery' (*shajāʿa*); its opposite is cowardice (*jubn*). When it refers to suppression of wrath (*ghaḍab*) and anger (*ghayẓ*), it is called 'clemency' (*ḥilm*); complaining (*tadhammur*) is its opposite. If misfortune resulting from the vicissitudes of time proves irksome, [patience] is called 'long-suffering' (*siʿat al-ṣadr*); vexation (*ḍajar*), discontent (*tabarrum*), and depression (*ḍīq al-ṣadr*) are its opposites. When [patience requires] concealing words, it is called the 'keeping of secrets' (*kitmān al-sirr*) and he who exercises it is called discreet. When [patience means renouncing luxuries] beyond the necessities of life, it is called 'asceticism' (*zuhd*); its opposite is covetousness (*ḥirṣ*). When patience means living in proportion to the meagreness of one's fortune, it is called 'contentment' (*qanāʿa*); and greed (*sharah*) is its opposite.

Most of the characteristics of faith, therefore, are included in patience. This is why, when the Prophet (peace be upon him) was once asked about faith, he replied, 'It is patience,' because most of its actions and those most prized [require patience]; just as 'the pilgrimage is ʿArafa.' God (Exalted is He!) has put together the [different] applications and called the whole 'patience'. For He, most High, said, *Those who are patient in misfortune* (ba'sā'), that is, in calamity; *hardship* (ḍarrā'), that is poverty; *peril* (ḥīn al-ba's), that is, in danger; *they are those who have been faithful and they are those who are God-fearing.*[1]

Therefore, these are the different divisions of patience according to its applications. He who concentrates on the different names supposes that the states are different in their essences and in their realities, because he has observed different names. [But] he who walks the straight path and sees through the light of God most High, first observes the meanings and notes their realities, then he looks at the names, for they were laid down as indications to the meanings. Meanings (*maʿānī*) are primary and terms (*alfādh*) secondary. He who wishes to make what is secondary primary will err without question. There is a reference to the two groups in the statement of the Most High, *What, is he who walks prone upon his face better guided than he who walks upright on a straight path?*[2] When the non-believers err, their error is in inversions of this sort. We ask God for success through His generosity and His kindness.

CHAPTER FIVE
An Exposition of the Divisions of Patience According to Variations of Strength and Weakness

KNOW that the religious impulse has three relationships to the impulse of desire. The first subdues the cause of desire so that it can no longer resist; this is attained through continual patience. At this point it is said, 'He who is patient succeeds.'[1] Those who reach this degree are very few in number. Surely they are the righteous, the close companions; *They are those who say 'Our Lord is God,' then they are steadfast.*[2] They are the ones who adhere to and remain firm on the straight and true path. Their souls are at peace because of the religious impulse. It is about them that the herald calls, *O soul at peace, return to your Lord, well-pleased, well-pleasing!*[3]

The second relationship is that in which the motives of desire prevail and the struggle of the religious impulse collapses completely. He surrenders himself to the forces of the devils, and he does not struggle because of his despair of the battle. These are the heedless (*ghāfilūn*) and they are the greatest in number. Their appetites have enslaved them and their difficulties have overcome them. They have made the enemies of God rulers over their hearts, [the very hearts] which are one of the secrets of God and one of His commands. God alludes to them in His statement, *If We had so willed, We could have given every soul its guidance; but now My Word is realised, 'Assuredly, I shall fill Hell with jinn and men all together.'*[4] These are people who exchange the Hereafter for this life; consequently, their bargain results in a loss. It is said to he who seeks to guide them, *Turn away from him who turns away from Our remembrance, and desires only the present life. That is the extent of their knowledge.*[5] This state has its symptoms, which consist of despair (*ya's*), despondency (*qunūṭ*), and deceptive longings (*ghurūr bi'l-amānī*). It is extreme stupidity, as the Prophet (may God bless him and grant him peace) said, 'The wise man is he who judges himself and works for what is after death, while the stupid man is he who lets his soul follow its own passions and presumes upon God!'[6] When exhorted, someone in this state says, 'I am eager to repent, but I find it difficult, so I must be unworthy of it.' Or, while not seeking to repent, he says, 'God is the Great Forgiver, the Compassionate, the Generous, therefore, He does not need my repentance.' The mind of this pitiable person has become a slave to his appetite. For he does not use his mind save in the invention of intricate stratagems for the gratification of his appetite. His mind is possessed by his appetite like a Muslim prisoner in the hands of non-believers, who use him to raise pigs, and to look after and transport intoxicants.[A] His position before God is like one who oppresses a Muslim and hands him over to the non-believers, causing him to become their prisoner. Because of the depravity of his crimes, he subdues that which he has no right to subdue, and he subjugates that which he has no right to subjugate. The Muslim deserves to have mastery because of what he possesses of the knowledge of God and the religious impulse. The non-believer deserves to be subservient because of his ignorance of religion and because of the impulses of the devils. The right of the Muslim to assert control over himself is greater than that of another over the Muslim. Therefore, whenever a noble idea that belongs to the side of God and to the forces of the angels is made subservient to a base idea that belongs to the devils banished from God, it is [analogous] to a person enslaving a Muslim to a non-believer (*kāfir*). This resembles someone to whom a king sought to be gracious, but who takes the king's dearest son and hands him

[A] Acts prohibited to Muslims.

over to the most hateful of the king's enemies. Observe how great is the servant's ingratitude for the king's favour and his response to the king's rancour! For God (Exalted is He!), desire is the most hateful deity on earth; whereas the intellect (ʿ*aql*) is the most precious thing created on the face of the earth.

The third relationship is a war in which success alternates between the two armies. Sometimes the servant has control over the situation, sometimes he is vanquished. He is reckoned among those who strive (*mujāhidīn*) and not among the victors (*ẓāfirīn*). The people of this state are those who *have mixed a righteous deed with a bad one. It may be that God will forgive them,*[7] according to [their] strength and weakness. [This servant] is affected by three states, depending on how patient he is: he either overcomes all the appetites, or overcomes none, or he prevails with some and not with others. The revelation of God's word, *They have mixed a righteous deed with a bad one* applies to someone who lacks resistance against some appetites but not others. Those who put aside resisting the appetites altogether may be compared to cattle, but they are more wayward from the path.[8] Beasts are not created with knowledge and the capacity to struggle against the demands of the appetites. [Rather] these [capacities] were created for man and he neglects them. He is truly remiss, having consciously turned his back [on them]. Thus it was said,

> I have not seen a fault among men more grave,
> As the failure of those who are capable of perfection.[9]

Patience can also be divided according to ease and hardship, into what is so burdensome for the soul that it can only endure it with great effort and intense exertion, this is called 'perseverance in patience' (*taṣabbur*); and into what can be achieved without extreme weariness but can be arrived at with the least effort of the soul, this is called 'patience' (*ṣabr*). With persistence in piety and the strengthening of inner conviction concerning the ultimate good of the Hereafter, patience becomes easier [for the servant]. For this reason, the Exalted said, *As for him who gives and is God-*

fearing and bears witness to goodness, We shall surely make smooth his way to ease.[10] The simile of this division [of patience] is the strength that a wrestler has over others. The strong man is able to fell the weak with minimum effort and little strength, so that weariness and exhaustion do not overtake him in his wrestling. He is not the least bit worried about himself, nor is he breathless. Yet, he is not strong enough to wrestle a stronger man without exertion, exceedingly strenuous effort and perspiration.

Thus is the struggle between the religious impulse and the impulse of desire. In truth, it is a struggle between the forces of the angels and the forces of the devils. Whenever the appetites yield and are overpowered, the religious impulse dominates and gains mastery. Patience becomes easier through long perseverance, and results in the station (*maqām*) of contentment (*riḍā*), as we will explain in the 'Book of Contentment.'[A] For contentment is at a higher [station] than patience. This is why the Prophet (may God bless him and grant him peace) said, 'Worship God with contentment. But if you cannot, then there is great benefit in [having] patience with what you dislike.'[11]

One of the gnostics once said, 'People of patience are divided between three stations: the first [station] is the abandonment of the appetite, this is the level of the repentant (*tā'ibūn*); the second is contentment with what is ordained [by God], this is the level of the ascetics (*zāhidūn*); the third is loving what his Lord does with him, this is the level of the truthful (*ṣiddīqūn*).'

We will make clear in the 'Book of Love'[B] that the station of love is higher than that of contentment, just as the station of contentment is higher than that of patience. This division applies to a particular kind of patience, patience in disasters and tribulations.

Know that patience, according to its legal consequences, is divided into what is obligatory (*farḍ*), what is supererogatory

[A] This is part of the *K. al-maḥabba wa'l-shawq wa'l-uns wa'l-riḍā* (*Iḥyā'*, IV.6)

[B] See above note.

(*nafl*), what is disliked (*makrūh*), and what is prohibited (*muḥarram*).[A] Therefore, patience is obligatory with regard to what is prohibited, and it is supererogatory with regard to what is abhorrent. One is forbidden to be patient with harm [that is] forbidden; for example, to have one's hand cut off or to witness the cutting off of the hand of a son and to remain silently patient. Equally, a man whose women-folk are gazed at with a forbidden lust and his jealousy is stirred up, but who does not disclose his jealousy and keeps his feelings about what is happening to his women-folk to himself—such patience is prohibited. As for patience that is abhorred, it is patience with harm that is abhorred by law. Let the law be the arbiter of patience. Just because patience is half of faith, do not imagine that it is all commendable; what is intended are specific kinds of patience.

[A] The divisions that Ghazālī gives here for patience are based on standard legal definitions that apply to all actions. What is interesting is Ghazālī's 'interiorisation' of the Law in making it equally applicable to inner qualities and virtues. '*Ḥarām* ('forbidden' or 'abominable') expresses the most negative of the five values that judge human behaviour according to Islamic law. The other four are: (1) *farḍ* or *wājib*, that which is commanded either in the Qur'ān or in the Traditions or by *ijmāᶜ* ('consensus'); (2) *mustaḥabb*, *mandūb*, *sunna*, *masnūn*, that which is recommended or desirable; (3) *mubāḥ* or *jā'iz*, that which is permitted or which is indifferent; (4) *makrūh*, that which is reprobate.' (S. G. Vesey-Fitzgerald, 'Nature and Sources of the Shariᶜa,' *Law in the Middle East* [Washington, D.C.: Middle East Institute, 1955], pp. 98ff.)

CHAPTER SIX
An Exposition of the Assumed Need for Patience and that the Servant Cannot Dispense with it under any Condition

KNOW that everything the servant encounters in this life is of two kinds. The first is that which is in harmony with his desire, the other is that which is not and he loathes it. In each case, he is in need of patience. A man is not free from one or the other or both of these things in any state. Therefore, he can never dispense with patience.

The first kind is that which is in harmony with desire: health, safety, wealth, prestige, a large family, prosperity, popularity, supporters, and all the pleasures of this world. How the servant needs patience against these matters! If he does not restrain himself from irresponsible living and a propensity for this, he will lose himself in legitimate pleasures that lead to arrogance and transgression. *Surely man transgresses, for he believes himself to be self-sufficient.*[1]

Some of the gnostics say, 'Tribulation is patiently borne by the believer, while only a righteous man is patient with well-being.'

Sahl [al-Tustarī] said, 'Patience in well-being is more difficult than patience in tribulation.'[A]

When the Companions (may God be pleased with them) were favoured with success, they said, 'We experienced the trial of hardship and were patient, then we experienced the trial of

[A] *Qūt*, I.401. In his study of Sahl al-Tustarī, Gerhard Böwering notes that Ghazālī in his 'monumental work [the] *Iḥyā'* . . . cites about sixty well-chosen sayings of Tustarī.' Three are in this book (*Iḥyā'*, IV.68, 96, 125), (Böwering, *Mystical Vision*, pp. 36–37).

good fortune and were not patient.' For this reason, God warned His servants of the trial of wealth, spouses and children; He said, *O believers, let neither your possessions, nor your children divert you from God's remembrance.*[2] The Mighty and Majestic said, *O believers, in your wives and children there is an enemy to you; so beware of them.*[3]

The Prophet (peace and blessings be upon him) said, 'The son is a cause of greed, a cause of cowardice and a cause of sorrow.'[4] When he looked at his grandson Ḥasan (may God be pleased with him) stumbling on his gown, he came down from the minbar and embraced him. Then he said, 'God spoke the truth—*Your wealth and your children are a trial.*[5] Truly, when I saw my child stumbling, I could not restrain myself from taking hold of him.'[6] This is an admonition for those who discern.

The true man is he who patiently endures well-being. The meaning of patience with respect to well-being is that a man does not rely on it. He knows that well-being is entrusted to him, and it may be that it shall soon be taken back, and so he should not yield himself wholly to its enjoyment. He does not persist obstinately in a life of luxury, physical pleasure, frivolity and amusement. He [must] care about God's claims regarding the expenditure of his wealth, regarding his body, regarding the way he dispenses succour for creation, regarding his tongue in speaking truthfully, and, likewise, regarding all else that God has favoured him with.

This patience is linked to thankfulness. Therefore, it becomes complete only when it is bound up with the duty of thankfulness, as will be explained. Patience in good fortune is more difficult, because it is related to the capacity for endurance. You are not always granted endurance. It is easier for someone to perform bloodletting and leeching on you than that you should perform them on yourself. A hungry man is better able to endure his hunger when food is not available than when delicious, good foods are set before him, and he could [eat]. In this situation the trial of good fortune is great.

The second kind of [situation] is that which is not in harmony with desire and nature. It is either related to the servant's choice, as in acts of obedience and disobedience; or is not related to the servant's choice, as in misfortunes and calamities; or is not related to his choice, yet is an action he can choose to take, such as when he avenges himself against an offender. These alternatives have three divisions.

The first division is what relates to [the servant's] choice. It includes all his deeds that can be described as either obedience or disobedience. There are thus two types [of choice]. The first is obedience, and the servant is in need of patience in this. Patience is difficult, because the self by its nature flees from slavery and covets lordship. About this, one of the [Sufi] gnostics said, 'Every soul has concealed [in its innermost heart] what Pharaoh revealed by saying: *I am your lord, the Most High!*'[7] Pharaoh had the opportunity and the acceptance of his people and he revealed [this aspect of the soul], *for he thought little of his people and [yet] they followed him.*[8] They were a perverse people! And each person does the same [as Pharaoh] with his slave, his servant, his followers and with all those who are under his constraint and command, though he may restrain himself from revealing this. His distancing himself from anger and annoyance when [his servant] falls short in serving him, is a result of hiding pride[A] and struggling with 'lordship' (*rubūbiyya*) in the form of arrogance. Therefore, servanthood (*ʿubūdiyya*) is always an effort for the soul.

Beyond this, among the acts of worship, there are those [the servant] abhors because of laziness, such as prayer (*ṣalāt*), and those he abhors because of stinginess, such as almsgiving (*zakāt*), and those he abhors because of them both, such as the pilgrimage (*ḥajj*) and struggling in the way of God (*jihād*).

Patience in obedience is a hardship. He who is obedient requires patience in his obedience at three stages. The first [stage] precedes obedience and is the correction of the intention (*niyya*), is sincerity and steadfastness against the defects of hypocrisy

[A] To hide here means not to allow it to manifest itself. It is therefore a form of self-control not subterfuge.

(*riyā'*) and the promptings of faults, and is establishing the determination for sincerity and loyalty. Those who know what true intention and sincerity are, [and who know] the defects of hypocrisy and the wiles of the lower self, [also know] that this is a demanding [form of] patience. The Prophet (may God bless him and grant him peace) drew attention to this matter when he said, 'Indeed, actions are judged by intentions, and every man is rewarded according to his intention.'[A] God (Exalted is He!) said, *And they have been commanded no more than this: to worship God, offering Him sincere devotion.*[9] In this matter God gave priority to patience over action, for He (Exalted is He!) said, *save such as are patient and do righteous deeds.*[10]

The second [stage] is the stage of action. [Here the servant] must be mindful of God throughout all his actions, he must not be slothful in what is His due in proper conduct and custom, and he must maintain the conditions of proper conduct to the last and final act. He must persevere in patience against the causes of laxity until the very end. This too is a demanding [form] of patience and perhaps it is the meaning intended in His words, *Excellent is the reward of those who do (good) and persevere in patience*[11] that is, those who are steadfast in the completion of their actions.

The third [stage] follows the completion of the action, since [the servant] needs steadfastness against the temptation to spread news of his good deed, and boast about it so that he may become known for it. The discipline of patience conflicts with acts of self-congratulation and opposes all that voids the action of the servant and dissipates its influence, as God said, *and do not make your works void.*[12] Similarly, the Exalted said, *Void not your charity with reproach and injury . . .*[13] Consequently, he who does not refrain from [lit. is not patient against] reproach and injury makes void his action.

Acts of obedience are divided into obligatory and supererogatory, and [the servant] needs patience for both. God (Exalted is

[A] This is a very important *ḥadīth*, often cited by Muslims. See *K. al-niyya wa'l-ṣidq wa'l-ikhlāṣ, Iḥyā'*, IV.7.

He!) has brought these two together in His words, *Surely God enjoins justice, kindness, and the doing of good to kinsmen . . .* [14] Justice then is obligatory and kindness is supererogatory; while giving to kinsmen and maintaining blood-relations (*ṣilat al-raḥim*)[A] are the ideal of manhood.[B] All these require patience.

The second type [of choice] is disobedience. How necessary for the servant to have patience against it! God (Exalted is He!) has gathered together the different forms of disobedience in His words, *And He forbids indecency, dishonour, and insolence . . .* [15] The Prophet (may God bless him and grant him peace) said, 'The immigrant (*muhājir*) is he who abjures evil, and the one who strives (*mujāhid*) is he who struggles against his passion.'[16] Acts of disobedience are in accordance with the impulse of desire. The strongest kind of patience is steadfastness against acts of disobedience that have become habitual. For habit is a fifth nature. If habit is added to sensual desire, two forces of Satan have aided one another against the forces of God. Then, the religious impulse will not be able to prevail against them.

If a particular act is easy to perform, steadfastness against it is more toilsome to the self. For example, patience is more taxing for the servant when dealing with acts of disobedience of the tongue—such as backbiting, lying, hypocrisy, boasting by insinuation or openly, the varieties of jesting that are harmful to the heart, the kinds of words with contemptuous and disdainful intent, and speaking of the dead and deprecating their knowledge, lives, and positions in society. This deed is slander on the surface, but in reality it is boasting. For in it there are two desires of the self. One is the denial of the other person and the other is the assertion of oneself. Through it [the servant] achieves the lordship that is in his nature and is contrary to the servanthood that is decreed for him. When the [above] two desires, combined with

[A] *Ṣilat al-raḥim* is highly commended in Islam.

[B] Hitti defines *murū'a* as 'manliness,' considered a supreme virtue by the Bedouin Arabs (*History of the Arabs*, p. 25).

the free-flowing nature of the tongue, become habitual in [one's] conversation to the point that they are no longer disapproved and loathed because of the frequency of their use and because they find general acceptance [by people], this becomes difficult to restrain and it is among the gravest of sins. For example, you see a man wearing silk,[A] who puts on airs and slanders people all day long and this conduct is not disapproved [by people, even though] the tradition says, 'Backbiting is worse than adultery.'[17] Solitary life and isolation become incumbent upon him who cannot control his tongue in discussions and who has no capacity for patience in that respect. Nothing else can rescue him. Enduring isolation will be easier [for him] than silence in company.

The degree of patience required [in the face of] different acts of disobedience varies according to how strong or weak the motive for disobedience is. Easier even than the movement of the tongue is that of the inner thoughts that come into play through the stirring of temptations. It is no wonder that internal monologues persist when one is alone; patience against them is impossible, unless [a man's] heart is overtaken by another concern, [such as] religion. Then it is as if a man's [entire] concerns have become one.[B] Otherwise, if reflection is not employed against a particular thing, it is inconceivable to think that the whisperings will die down [on their own].

The second division is that which is not related to [the servant's] choice; however, he does have a choice in its repulsion—for example, in the event that he is wronged in deed or word and a sin is committed against him, directly against his person or his property, then patience in this case is in the abandonment of [earthly]

[A] Wearing silk is prohibited to men in Islam.

[B] Allusion to the *ḥadīth*, 'He who makes all his concerns one concern, the concern of his Hereafter to come, God will protect him from the concerns of this world.' This *ḥadīth* is narrated by Ibn ʿUmar with a slight variant, 'He who makes all his troubles one, God will free him from the trouble of his world.' A. J. Wensinck, *Concordance* (Leiden: E. J. Brill, 1936), VII.107.

recompense, sometimes it is obligatory and sometimes it is a virtue. Some of the Companions (may God be pleased with them) said, 'We do not consider the faith of a man [true] faith if he is not patient with a harm [done to him].'[18] [About these] God says, *we shall certainly bear with patience all the harm you shall cause us. Let those who trust, trust God.*[19] The Messenger of God (may God bless him and grant him peace) once divided a sum of money, and a Bedouin from among the Muslims said, 'This is a division which cannot be pleasing to God.' The Messenger of God (may God bless him and grant him peace) was informed of the incident; his face turned red with anger. Then he said, 'God grant His mercy to my brother Moses, he was wronged in more than this and he was patient!'[20] God (Exalted is He!) said, *Heed not their hurt, but put your trust in God.*[21] And He said, *And bear patiently what they say and forsake them graciously.*[22] And He said, *We know indeed how your heart is distressed by what they say. But celebrate the praises of your Lord, and be of those that bow, and serve their Lord, until there comes to you the Hour that is certain;*[23] and He said, *and you shall hear from those who were given the Book before you, and from those who are idolaters, much harm; but if you are patient and God-fearing, surely that is true constancy.*[24] That is, you should refrain from seeking retribution.

Therefore, God commended those who forego their rights to retaliation and other matters. For God said, *And if you take retribution, then do so in proportion to the wrong done to you. But if you can bear such conduct with patience, indeed that is best for the steadfast.*[25] The Prophet (may God bless him and grant him peace) said, 'Approach him who snubbed you, give him who has deprived you, pardon him who wronged you.'[26] And I have observed in the Gospel that Jesus son of Mary (may the peace of God be upon him) said, 'It has been said to you in the past, "A tooth for a tooth and a nose for a nose,"[A] but I say to you, do not oppose evil with evil. Whosoever

[A] Ghazālī may have wanted to interpolate Matthew's text with Q.v.45. However, neither the Syriac nor the Greek version of Matthew's gospel carry this variation.

strikes your right cheek, turn to him the left cheek. Whosoever takes your coat, give your buttoned garment. Whosoever obliges you to go with him a mile, go with him two miles.'[27A] All these are commendations for forbearance in harm. Thus, patience with the harm [done] by men is among the highest grades of patience, for in it are combined both the religious impulse and the impulses for desire and wrath.

The third division relates to the innumerable [matters] over which [one] has no choice at all. Misfortunes like the death of a loved one, the total loss of wealth, the disappearance of health through illness, the loss of eyesight, the failure of bodily organs and all other kinds of tribulation. Patience in these [misfortunes] is one of the highest stations of patience. Ibn ᶜAbbās (may God be pleased with them both) said, 'Patience in the Qur'ān is of three kinds: patience in fulfilling obligations [prescribed by] God the Exalted and it has three hundred degrees; patience regarding what God the Exalted forbids has six hundred degrees; and patience at the first shock of misfortune has nine hundred degrees.'[28] This [latter] aspect of patience is preferred over the other two even though it is a virtue and the others are obligatory duties (*farā'id*) because every believer should have the ability to be patient against forbidden things. But as for patience with afflictions sent by God the Exalted, no one can bear them except the prophets because it is a trait of the righteous, and it is an extreme [hardship] for the soul. This is why the Prophet prayed, 'I ask You for inner certainty, to ease the misfortunes of life for me.'[29] This is patience supported by the best of certainty.

Abū Sulaymān said, 'By God, we do not endure patiently what

[A] Matthew 5:38-41. Padwick comments on Zwemer's remark that 'nowhere does al-Ghazālī take the familiar position [in Islam] that Christians have tampered with the text of their Gospels. For al-Ghazālī these Gospels are an authority to be wielded in argument, while in the *Iḥyā'* the *logia* attributed to Christ are used for edification.' Constance E. Padwick, 'Al-Ghazālī and the Arabic Versions of the Gospel, An Unresolved Problem,' *Moslem World*, vol. XXIX, no. 2 (April 1939).

we love, then how shall we bear patiently what we loathe?'

The Prophet (may God bless him and grant him peace) said, 'God, Who is Mighty and Glorious, said, "If I afflict one of my servants with a misfortune in his body, wealth, or child, and it is received with graceful patience (*ṣabrun jamīl*), I will be ashamed on the Day of Resurrection to set up for him the scales or open the book."'[30A]

The Prophet (may God bless him and grant him peace) said, 'The period of waiting patiently for release from suffering is an act of worship.'[31] And he said, 'There is no believing servant, stricken by misfortune, but he said as God commanded "*Surely we belong to God, and to Him we return*,[32] Almighty God, reward me in my misfortune and give me good in exchange for it," but that God will do this for him.'[33]

Anas said, 'The Messenger of God (may God bless him and grant him peace) related to me that "God, Almighty and Glorious said, 'O Gabriel, what is the reward for the one whose sight I have taken away?' He replied, 'Praise be to You. We have no knowledge save what You have taught us.' Then God (Exalted is He!) said, 'His reward is immortality in My house and beholding My countenance.'"'[34]

The Prophet (may God bless him and grant him peace) said, 'God, Almighty and Glorious, said, "If I put my servant to the test with a trial [of illness], and he endures it and does not express distrust of Me before those who come to visit him, I shall give him flesh better than his flesh and blood better than his blood. If I grant him health, he [rises] without sin; and if I decree his death, it is to My mercy [he returns]."'[35]

David (peace be upon him) prayed, 'O Lord, what is the reward of the sorrowful person who is patient in misfortune, seeking Your pleasure?' He (Exalted is He!) answered, 'His reward is that I will dress him in the clothing of faith, and I shall never remove it from him.'[36]

[A] To weigh his good and bad deeds and judge his actions.

ʿUmar b. ʿAbd al-ʿAzīz (may God have mercy upon him) said in a sermon, 'God bestows a blessing upon a servant and then snatches it away from him, replacing it with patience in order to compensate the servant with something better than what He has taken away from him.' Then he recited, *Surely the patient will be given their reward in full without reckoning*.[37]

Fuḍayl was asked about patience and replied, 'It is contentment with the decree of God.' It was then asked, 'How can that be?' He replied, 'The contented one does not desire anything beyond the degree he has attained.'

It was said that when Shiblī was confined to the hospital a group of friends came to visit him. He asked, 'Who are you?' They replied, 'Your beloved friends who have come to visit you.' Whereupon he began to throw stones at them, and they started to run. He said, 'If you were my beloved friends, you would have been patient with me in my tribulation.'

One of the [Sufi] gnostics used to take a note out of his pocket every hour and look at it. These words were written on it, *And be patient under the judgement of your Lord: surely you are before Our eyes*.[38]

It is said that the wife of Fatḥ al-Mawṣilī stumbled, and her fingernail became detached. She laughed. It was asked of her, 'Do you feel pain?' She replied, 'The delight of its reward caused the bitterness of its pain to vanish from my heart.'

David said to Solomon (peace be upon them both), 'The piety of the believer is exhibited in three ways: perfect trust in what was not granted him by God's decree; perfect contentment in what was granted; and perfect patience in what he has missed out on in life.'[39]

Our Prophet (may God bless him and grant him peace) said, 'It is out of reverence for God and the knowledge of what is due to Him that you should not complain about your pain, or mention your misfortune.'[40]

It was related that a pious man went out one day with a purse in his sleeve. The purse was stolen. When he noticed this he said, 'God bless it for him who has taken it. Perhaps he needs it more than I do.'

It was related that a Muslim [at the Battle of Yamāma] said, 'I passed by Sālim, a client of Abū Ḥudhayfa, among the slain, and there was still in him a spark of life. I said, "Can I give you water to drink," he replied, "Bring me a little closer to the enemy, and put the water on the shield, for I am fasting. If I live until nightfall, I will drink it."'[41] Thus are those who travel the path to the Hereafter patient with the trials of God, Exalted is He!

If you ask, 'How can one attain to such a degree of patience in misfortunes when the matter does not come about by choice, he is compelled whether he likes it or not.' What is meant by this is that within himself he should not hate the misfortune, which was not his choice. It should be understood that one departs from the station of patience only through anxiety, rending of clothes, striking of cheeks, exaggeration in complaint, making an exhibition of sorrow, changes of habit in dress, possessions, and food. These matters are part of a man's choice. One must avoid them all and show contentment with the decree of God (Exalted is He!), remain continually in his usual way of life, and believe firmly that [what was taken away] was a deposit [that has been] returned.

Just as Ramayṣā' Umm Sulaym (may God have mercy on her) is reported to have said, 'My son passed away while my husband, Abū Ṭalḥa was absent. Then I arose and covered him with a shroud and put him in a corner of the house. Later Abū Ṭalḥa came, and I prepared his breakfast for him and he began to eat. He asked, "How is the boy?" I replied, "In the best of states through God's grace, may He be praised. He has never been as quiet as this night since he [first] complained of the disease." With this, I feigned as best I could, until he had had his fill. Then I asked, "Do you not wonder at our neighbours?" He replied, "What of them?" I said, "They borrowed something and when I asked them for it, and requested its return they were annoyed." He said, "What evil! What an attitude!" Thereupon I said, "This is your son who was a borrowed thing from God, and God has taken him to Himself." He praised God and said, *Surely we belong to God, and to Him we return.*[42] Abū Ṭalḥa went to the Messenger of God (may God bless him and grant him peace) and told him [about this]. The Messenger of God prayed, "Almighty God, bless this night for them."'[43] The narrator said, '[Some time after this] I saw seven [of their offspring], together in the mosque, reciting the Qur'ān.'[44] Jābir related that he (may God bless him and grant him peace) said, 'I dreamed that I entered Paradise and there I was with Ramayṣā', the wife of Abū Ṭalḥa.'

It has been said that patience that is pleasing (*ṣabr jamīl*) is when the one who suffers misfortune [i.e., the one grieving] cannot be identified from those around him. The pain in his heart and the tears that flow from his eyes should not take him beyond the limits of those who are patient, rather he should be the same as anyone else present [at the mourning]. Weeping for the dead causes the heart pain, it is part of human nature that one cannot be rid of until death. For this reason when Ibrāhīm, the Prophet's son, died, he wept and it was said to him, 'Did you not forbid us to do this?' He replied, 'This is a mercy and God is merciful to his merciful servants.'[45]

Moreover, this response also does not contradict the station of contentment. For the one undergoing cupping and bloodletting is content despite the pain involved. He may even weep when the pain becomes intense. This will be discussed in the *Book of Contentment*,[A] God willing.

Ibn Abī Najīḥ wrote the following to one of the caliphs, condoling with him, 'The most deserving of those who know the rights of God (Exalted is He!) regarding what has been taken from him is the one who magnifies the rights of God (Exalted is He!) in what has been left to him by God.'[46]

Know that what has gone ahead of you remains for you and what you leave behind will increase your reward. Know that the reward of those who endure patiently what befalls them is greater than the blessings of being spared [a misfortune]. Therefore, a servant attains the level of those who endure patiently when he

[A] *K. al-maḥabba, Iḥyā'*, IV.333–334.

wards off hatred [of misfortune] by contemplating the blessings of God. Indeed, the perfection of patience is the concealment of illness, poverty and other similar misfortunes. It is said that among the treasures of righteousness is the concealment of misfortunes, ailments and almsgiving.[A]

The [above] divisions will have made it clear to you that the obligations of patience are universal in all states and actions. Even he who has gone beyond all desires and who lives in isolation will still have to be outwardly patient with isolation and solitude, and inwardly patient against the whisperings of Satan, for the stirring of thoughts is never stilled. Most thoughts wander to a past that can no longer be reached or to a future that is invariably decreed, and both are a waste of time.

The tool of the servant is his heart and his merchandise is his life span. If a person's heart neglects a remembrance, through which he gains intimacy with God (Exalted is He!); or [neglects] reflection, by which he gains knowledge of God (Exalted is He!), and, through this knowledge, the love of God; then he has been duped. This is if his reflection and his daydreams are limited to what is lawful. But this is not usually the case. More often, he will contemplate the many ways of circumventing [the law] to satisfy his desires. And throughout his life, he will contend with all those who oppose his desires, or those who he imagines to oppose his desires, or those who appear to prevent him from obtaining his goal. He even believes in the opposition of those who most sincerely love him, like his wife and son. He imagines their opposition to him. He considers intently the means by which he will restrain and dominate them, and the responses that he will make to whatever reasons they give for thwarting him. And [thus] he remains preoccupied with this matter.

Now Satan has two forces, an air force and a ground force.

[A] Ghazālī discusses secrecy in almsgiving in *K. asrār al-zakat* (*Iḥyā'*, 1.5), pp. 233–234. The book has been translated as *The Mysteries of Almsgiving* by Nabih A. Faris (Beirut: Centennial Publications, 1966), our passage being pp. 31–33.

Mental whisperings are the movement of his air force and desires are the movement of his ground force. This is because Satan was created from fire and man from dry clay like pottery.[47] In pottery, the fire and the clay are brought together. Clay, by its nature, is still, while fire, by its nature, is movement. For one cannot imagine a blazing fire without movement; indeed its nature is to always move.

The Accursed One, who was created out of fire, was commanded to cease his motion, and prostrate before what God created from clay [i.e., mankind]. But he refused, displayed arrogance, became recalcitrant, and expressed the cause of his recalcitrance in these words, *You created me of fire, and him You created of clay*.[48] If at that time the Accursed One did not bow down before our father Adam (may God bless him and grant him peace), one should not hope that he will prostrate himself before his [Adam's] children. Whenever the temptations, hostilities, 'flights and wanderings [of Satan]' depart from the heart, it is a sign of his submission and compliance. His submission and compliance are his prostration. They are [in fact] the spirit of prostration, while placing the forehead on the ground is its form and its expression in language. If placing the forehead on the ground were symbolic of contempt, then it would be understood as such. Just as lying on the ground in front of a person of respect is customarily considered disrespectful. The shell of the pearl should not confuse you about the pearl, nor the form of the spirit about the spirit, nor the outer about the inner. [If you allow this,] you will be of those who are totally restricted by the visible world from the invisible world.

You must realise that Satan is among those granted respite.[A] He will not humble himself to you and he will not cease his whisperings until the Day of Judgement, unless you make all

[A] A reference to the Qur'ānic verses VII.13–15 which refer to Satan's expulsion and his request from God that he be reprieved until the Day of Judgement, which he is granted.

your concerns one.[A] So busy your heart with God alone, and the Accursed One will not find a way to reach you. Then you will be among God's sincere servants, those who are beyond the authority of the Accursed One.[B]

You should not think that he [Satan] will leave an empty heart, rather, he is as a liquid that flows through the son of Adam like blood. He is like the air in a cup. If you want the cup to be free of air, and you do not fill it with water or something else, you will be striving in vain. To the extent that the cup is empty of water, it will be filled with air. By the same token, the heart that is not occupied with essential thoughts about religion will not be spared the patrols of Satan. Whoever neglects God, even for an instant, will have Satan as a companion in that instant. Thus, God said, *Whoever turns away from the remembrance of the All-Merciful, to him We assign a devil as companion.*[49] The Prophet (may God bless him and grant him peace) said, 'God hates a youth who is idle.'[50] This, because a youth who is not busy inwardly with what will support him in his religion may appear outwardly idle, but his heart will not remain idle. Rather, Satan builds a nest in him, lays eggs and hatches them. His brood doubles in number and in turn lays eggs and multiplies.

The offspring of Satan reproduce a generation faster than other living beings, because his nature is composed of fire. If he finds dry fodder, his generation is multiplied. For fire will generate more fire and it will not cease. On the contrary, it spreads by contact from one thing to another. For Satan, the desires of the youth's soul are as dry fodder is to fire. Just as fire vanishes when there is no fuel, which is firewood, so Satan enjoys no opportunity when there is no desire. If you reflect on this, you will see that your worst enemy is your desire, and it is an attribute of your self. At the time of his execution, Ḥusayn b. Manṣūr al-Ḥallāj was

[A] See note B p. 38

[B] Allusion to Qur'ānic verses xv.40 and xxxviii.83, in which Satan vows to lead all of humanity astray except for God's sincere servants.

asked what Sufism is and he replied, 'It is your soul. If you do not keep it occupied, it will occupy you.'[51]

Therefore, true and perfect patience is patience [in the face of] every blameworthy action. Inner actions, however, have a greater need for patience as they require continuous patience which ceases only with death. We ask God for the best of success, with His favour and graciousness.

CHAPTER SEVEN
An Exposition of Patience as a Remedy and What is Gained by Resorting to It

KNOW that He Who sends down disease also sends down the remedy and promises healing.[1] Even if patience [seems] arduous or impossible, it is possible to attain it with a combination [lit. a medicinal mixture] of knowledge and action. For knowledge and action are the components from which all medicines for the diseases of the heart are composed. Each sickness, however, needs a different kind of knowledge and a different kind of action. Just as the divisions of patience are varied, so also the divisions of illness that are resistent to patience are varied. If the illnesses differ, their medical treatment differs, since the definition of a cure is the antidote for the illness and its removal.

An exhaustive treatment of this field of knowledge would be lengthy. However, we can show the way by these examples. For example, we say that if a man lacks self-control over the appetite for sexual relations, intense desire overcomes him regardless of whether he controls his sexual urge; or he may control his urge, but he does not control his eyes; or he may control his eyes, but he does not control his heart. If his self continues to speak to him about the demands of desire, this distracts him from the constant remembrance and contemplation [of God], and [the accomplishment of] good deeds. We say: we have already presented patience to you as a struggle between the religious impulse and the impulse of desire. In this struggle, each wants to overcome the other, and there is no alternative for us except to strengthen the one we wish to have the upper hand and weaken the other.

It is our duty at this point to strengthen the religious impulse and to weaken the impulse of desire. As for the impulse of desire, there are three ways to weaken it. The first is for us to consider the source of its strength, [like] delicious foods of various kinds and quantities which arouse desire. It is necessary then to break [the desire] by continual fasting, and [then] break the fast with little food that is not rich, and avoid meat foods that arouse desires.

The second way is breaking the causes of arousal at the time that it occurs. [A servant] will be aroused by a glance at the object of desire, for a glance stirs the heart and the heart stirs the appetite. This [breaking] can be achieved through seclusion and caution at the times when the desired forms are seen, or fleeing from them entirely.

The Messenger of God (may God bless him and grant him peace) said, 'The glance is a poisonous arrow of the arrows of the devil.'[2] It is an arrow that the Accursed One aims accurately. No [human] shield can defend against it, save closing the eyes or fleeing from the direction of his shot. When he shoots this arrow it is with the bow of forms, and if you turn away from the direction of forms, his arrow will not reach you.

The third [way is] to divert the self with permissible sexual relations, and that is [through] marriage. All of what is desired by human nature is available through what is permissible of its kind, to stop [the desire for what] is forbidden. For most people, this is the most effective remedy. Curbing [one's] nourishment weakens all actions, yet restricting the intake of food may not suppress the desire of most men. Therefore, the Prophet (may God bless him and grant him peace) said, 'I advise you to set up a household [i.e., marry]; he who cannot [marry] should fast. Fasting is a deterrent.'[3]

These are the three means [of weakening the impulse of desire]. The first remedy is curbing food. It resembles the curbing of fodder for an unruly beast or a vicious dog in order to weaken him, so his power then collapses. The second resembles hiding meat from a dog or barley from a farm animal so that his innards are not stirred by seeing them. The third resembles diverting them with a little of something that their nature desires, in order that they retain some power to be patient with discipline.

As for strengthening the religious impulse, this is accomplished in two ways. The first is by nourishing it with the benefits of striving (*mujāhada*) and its fruits in this life and in the next. He should then reflect on the traditions that we mentioned on the merits of patience, and the excellence of its outcome in this life and the Hereafter.

In the traditions, it says, 'The reward of patience in the face of misfortune is more than what has been lost.'[4] Due to this, [one] can be envied in misfortune since one has lost only that which lasts for the duration of one's life and one has that which will remain with him after death forever. Whoever relinquishes a base thing for a precious thing should not be sad for the base thing that has passed in this case.

This is the door to knowledge and it is part of faith. Sometimes it is weakened and sometimes it is strengthened. When it is strengthened, then the religious impulse is strengthened and it will stir the person intensely. But if it is weak, it will weaken him. The strength of faith is an expression of inner certainty and it stimulates the resolve for patience. The least of what men have been granted is certainty (*yaqīn*) and the resolve for patience.[5]

The second way [in which to strengthen the religious impulse] is to gradually train it to struggle against the impulse of desire, little by little, until it attains the joy of victory over it. It will thus become bold and its determination will strengthen in its struggle. For habit and the practice of difficult actions bring about the strength from which actions can issue. Thus, the [physical] strength of porters, farmers, soldiers and all those who [regularly] engage in difficult [physical] labour exceeds the strength of tailors, perfumers, jurists and those devoted only to religious practice, because the [physical] strength [of the latter] has not been strengthened by exercise.

Therefore, the first way [of strengthening the religious impulse] is analogous to enticing a wrestler with a robe of honour if he is victorious and with promises of all manner of preferment. Just as Pharaoh had promised his sorcerers, when he incited them against Moses, '*Yes, indeed, and you shall be among those stationed near to me.*'[6]

The second [way] corresponds to the training of a boy who is expected to wrestle and do combat. He becomes accustomed to his conditioning by following training procedures from his early years until it becomes his norm and he gains confidence from them, and his resolve is strengthened by them.

The religious impulse is weakened in the one who completely abandons the struggle of patience and he will not be able to master his desires even if they are weakened. He who accustoms himself to disobeying his desire will overcome them whenever he wishes. This is the method of treatment adopted in all applications of patience. But an exhaustive discussion of this is not possible.

However, the [way that is] most effective is preventing oneself from internal monologues. This is particularly effective for whoever devotes himself to eliminating the outward desires, who prefers solitude, and who sits to monitor [himself], to remember [God] and to reflect [on His creation]. [If] internal whisperings continue to distract him from one side or the other, then there is no remedy for this condition at all, except severing [himself] from [worldly] attachments, outwardly and inwardly, and fleeing from family, children, wealth, prominence, colleagues, and companions;[A] then retiring to a retreat (*zāwiya*) after having provided himself with a small amount of food and being content with it. And yet, none of this would be sufficient if all his concerns have not become one; have not become [centred on] God (Exalted is He!). When [this single concern] overcomes the heart, one must make time for reflection. This inward reflection on the

[A] The remedy that Ghazālī encourages for his readers is the one he employed himself. The very phrase used here is repeated in his autobiography. Cf. Ghazālī, *al-Munqidh*, p. 104 and Watt, *Faith and Practice*, pp. 58, 59.

kingdom of heaven and earth, the marvels of the creation of God (Exalted is He!) and other doors to knowledge of God (Exalted is He!) will overtake his heart. [While] his occupation with them will repel Satan's temptations and whisperings.

If he is [not capable] of inward reflection then he can only be rescued by [the practice of] continuous, ordered litanies at every instant, [such as] recitations [of the Qur'ān], remembrance (*dhikr*) and prayer. He will also require, along with this, that the heart be [fully] attentive. For outward litanies, without inward concentration, cannot engross the heart. Even if he does all this, he will not be successful all the time. For he can never be free of unexpected events that will distract him from contemplation and remembrance. The types of distractions include sickness, fear, harm and oppression from people he interacts with, because he cannot be free from associating with those who help him [obtain] his livelihood.

As for the second type [of distraction], it is far more imperative than the first; it is his preoccupation with [acquiring] food, clothing and earning a living. For acquiring these requires work, whether he does it himself or has someone else do it, [either way] his heart is not free of concern over them. It is only when he severs [himself] from all attachments that he will be free most of the time, unless disaster or accident assail him. At these times, his heart is stilled, contemplation comes easily, and in him, the secrets of God (Exalted is He!) concerning the kingdoms of the heavens and the earth are unveiled to him. It would take him a long time to achieve even one percent [of this] if his heart were still preoccupied with attachments. This is the highest of the stations that are reachable through effort and striving.[A]

As to the scale of what is revealed and the extent of what is to be met with in states and actions from the grace of God (Exalted is He!), this is akin to hunting, in that it is dependent on providence (*rizq*). Sometimes, with little effort, you may gain a great catch,

[A] As opposed to the stations that are attained through divine grace.

and sometimes, with a great effort, your fortune is little. What is imperative in this case is to seek to attain the attractive power of the All-Merciful [lit. an attraction (*jadhba*) from the attractions of][A] for it is equivalent to the actions of both humans and the jinn (*al-thaqabān*). But this is not up to the servant. What the servant can do is expose [himself] to that attraction and sever from his heart the attractions of this world. For he who is attracted (*majdhūb*) by the lowest of the low will not be attracted by the highest of the high. And he who is concerned with this world is attracted (*munjadhib*) to it.[B] Severing [oneself] from these attractive [worldly] attachments is what is meant by the statement of the Prophet (may God bless him and grant him peace), 'Truly, God grants breezes (*nafaḥāt*)[C] in the days of your life. So, place yourself in their way!'[7] These 'breezes' and attractions have heavenly causes. For God (Exalted is He!) said, *And in heaven is your provision, and also what you are promised.*[8] This is among the highest kind of provision (*rizq*).

[But] heavenly matters are concealed from us. We do not know when God (Exalted is He!) will make the means of sustenance easy. We must empty the place (*maḥal*)[D] and wait for the descent of mercy at the appointed time. This is similar to preparing the earth, clearing it of weeds and sowing the seeds. And yet, all this will be to no avail without rain. [The servant] does not know when God will decree the means of rain, but he has confidence in the bounty of God (Exalted is He!) and His mercy, as there has been no year without rain. So, in like manner, rarely will you pass a year, a month, or a day without an attraction from [God] or one of His 'breezes'. The servant must have a heart purified of the weeds of passion and he must sow the seeds of will (*irāda*) and sincerity (*ikhlāṣ*) and expose it to the blowing winds of

[A] *Jadhb* (attraction) is the opposite of *juhd* (striving).

[B] *Majdhūb* and *munjadhib* both derive from the same root *jadhaba*, to attract.

[C] In Sufism, *nafḥa* (pl. *nafaḥāt*) is divine graces or aid.

[D] As we shall see below, Ghazālī here means the heart.

mercy. For just as the expectation of rain increases in the spring and at the appearance of clouds, so the expectation of these breezes increases in the blessed times, when spiritual resolutions and hearts are united, such as on the Day of ʿArafa, on Fridays, and during the days of Ramaḍān. For spiritual resolve and aspirations are means decreed by God (Exalted is He!) to shower His mercy, until, through them, rain is brought forth when the prayer for rain (*istisqāʾ*) is recited. And they are more suited to bring forth the 'rain' of unveilings (*mukāshafāt*) and the subtleties of knowledge (*laṭāʾif al-maʿārif*) from the treasure chests of the divine kingdom than [they are] to bring raindrops by drawing clouds from the mountain-tops and the distant seas.

Moreover, states and unveilings are present in your heart, but you are preoccupied with your worldly attachments and desires, which have become a veil between you and them. All that you need is for desire to abate and the veils will lift, so that the lights of knowledge will shine forth from the inside of the heart. It is easier to draw water to the surface of the earth by digging canals than it is to bring it from a distant, lower place. As it is present in the heart and yet forgotten through [worldly] preoccupations, God (Exalted is He!) has called all the spiritual knowledge of faith 'remembrance' (*tadhakkur*). He said, *It is We Who have sent down the remembrance, and We guard it.*[9] And He said, *Let men of understanding take heed*;[10] and God (Exalted is He!) said, *And We have indeed made the Qurʾān easy to understand and remember. Then is there any that will receive admonition?*[11]

This then is the treatment of patience against inner whisperings and distractions, and it is the last level of patience. Patience regarding [worldly] attachments takes precedence over patience with thoughts.

Junayd (may God have mercy on him) said, 'The journey from this world to the Hereafter is easy for the believer. Forsaking created things (*khalq*) for the love of the Truth is difficult. The journey from one's ego (*nafs*) to God is extremely difficult, while patience in God is even more difficult.'[12] He mentioned the difficulty of [having] patience with the distractions of the heart, then of forsaking created things.

The most entrenched of the soul's attachments is [the attachment] to others and the love of prominence (*jāh*). Indeed the pleasure of leadership, authority, superiority and having a following are the most dominant of worldly pleasures in the souls of those who possess reason (*nufūs al-ʿuqalāʾ*). How can these not be the most dominant and sought after pleasures when one of the attributes of God (Exalted is He!) is lordship. Lordship is coveted and sought by the nature of the heart because of its [the heart's] affinity to matters of lordship. Concerning this, there is a statement from God, *Say: The Spirit is of the command* (amr) *of my lord.*[13]

The heart is not to be blamed for its love of this. It is blamed only for error which befalls it because of the beguiling of the accursed Satan. He was banished from the world of command (*ʿālam al-amr*) because he was envious of it [the heart] being of the world of command, and he tempted and misguided it. How can [the heart] be at fault, when it seeks the happiness of the Hereafter; it seeks permanence without end, honour without disgrace, safety without fear, abundance without want and perfection without defect. These are all attributes of lordship. It [the heart] is not to be blamed for seeking these [attributes]. Indeed every servant has a right to seek a great dominion (*mulk*) without end, and surely seeking this dominion is seeking greatness, honour and perfection.

However, dominion is of two [kinds]. [One kind] is mixed with various pains and is fleeting but is immediate and of this world. And [the second kind] is the everlasting dominion, unmixed with grief and pain, and unending, but it is in the Hereafter. Man is a creature of haste,[14] desirous of [this] world. Satan comes and curries favour with him through haste, which is his nature. He seeks to deceive him with [what can be] gained quickly and make attractive to him the present [world]. Satan lures him through foolishness, makes him illusory promises for the Hereafter and gives him the hope [of gaining] the dominion of the Hereafter in addition to the dominion of this world. It is just as the Prophet (may God bless him and grant him peace) said, 'the stupid man is he who lets his soul follow its own passions and presumes upon God!'[15] This forsaken one is deceived by the delusions [of Satan] and occupies himself with the pursuit of glory and the dominion of this world as much as he can. [While] he who has been rightly guided is not taken in by his [Satan's] delusions, because he knows his [Satan's] entry-ways and plots, and he turns away from this transitory world. God (Exalted is He!) stated clearly about the forsaken, *No indeed, but you love the fleeting life, and leave the Hereafter*;[16] and God (Exalted is He!) says, *Surely, these men love the fleeting life and leave behind them a heavy day*;[17] and God (Exalted is He!) says, *So turn away from those who turn away from Our remembrance and desire nothing but the life of this world. That is as far as knowledge will reach them.*[18]

When Satan's plots agitated the whole of humanity, God sent the angels to the messengers and revealed to them the extent of the destruction and entrapment of creatures by the enemy [Satan]. So [the messengers] went to work calling humanity to the true dominion, away from the dominion of the illusory, which, at best, has no permanence and no foundation. So they summoned people, *O believers, what is amiss with you, that when it is said to you to go forth in the way of God, you sink heavily to the ground? Do you prefer the life of this world to the Hereafter? Yet the enjoyment of this present life, compared to the world to come, is a little thing.*[19]

For the Torah, the Gospels, the Psalms, the Furqān,[A] the books of Moses and Abraham, and every book sent down was sent down only to call humanity to the eternal and ever-lasting dominion (*mulk*). And the intention is for them to be sovereign (*mulūk*) in this world, and sovereign in the Hereafter. [Now] dominion of this world is abstaining (*zuhd*) from it and contentment (*qanāʿa*) with a small portion of it. While dominion of the Hereafter is closeness to God (Exalted is He!), where one attains permanence without

[A] The Criterion, a name for the Qur'ān.

end, glory without dishonour, and the delights of the eye[A] which are concealed in this world and which no soul knows.[20]

Satan calls them to the dominion of this world, because of his knowledge that the dominion of the Hereafter is not his, since this world and the Hereafter are as two wives;[21B] and, again, because of his knowledge that this world is not secure [for man]; were it secure for him, he [Satan] would envy him also for this.

The dominion of this world, however, is not free from contentions, troubles and ongoing anxieties about plans. And, this also applies to the various means of [attaining] prominence. Even when [these] means are available and achieved, life comes to an end, . . . *till, when the earth has taken on its glitter, and has decked itself fair, and its inhabitants think they have power over it, Our command comes upon it by night or day, and we make it as a harvest clean mown as if it had not flourished only the day before. . .* [22] God (Exalted is He!) applies a similitude with His statement, *And strike for them the similitude of the present life: it is as water that we send down out of heaven, and the plants of the earth mingle with it, and in the morning it is straw the winds scatter.*[23]

When renunciation of this world becomes a real possession, Satan envies him [the servant] because of it and [tries to] dissuade him from it. Renunciation means that the servant governs his appetite and wrath, so both are led by the religious impulse and the commands of faith, and this is a true possession, for the owner of this becomes free through it. When the appetite overcomes him, he becomes a slave to his sexual organs, stomach and the rest of his desires. He will be subservient like the beasts, led by the halter of desire, which takes him by the neck wherever it wants and wishes.

How great, therefore, is the deception of the person who presumes he is in possession, and instead is possessed. He presumes that he will obtain lordship, but instead becomes a slave. He is the

[A] *Qurrat al-ʿayn* is an idiomatic phrase meaning 'delight.'

[B] Lit., *ḍurratān*, two women married to the same man and competing with each other.

example of a person who is the opposite of what he should be in this life, and he will have [his fortunes] reversed in the Hereafter. Thus, one of the kings asked an ascetic, 'Have you any need?' He replied, 'How shall I ask anything of you when my kingdom is greater than your kingdom?' He [the king] asked, 'How is that?' He replied, 'The one to whom you are a slave is my slave!' Then [the king] asked, 'How can that be?' [The ascetic] replied, 'You are a slave to your appetite, wrath, sexual urges and stomach, while I rule over all these! For they are my slaves!' This is [true] possession in this world, and this is what leads to dominion in the Hereafter. So [all those] who are deceived by the allurement (*ghurūr*) of Satan, lose both this world and the Hereafter. Those who are successful in holding fast to the straight path triumph in both this world and the Hereafter.

Now that you know the meaning of possession and lordship, the meaning of subservience and slavery, the errors of [understanding] these, and Satan's manner of blinding and deceiving, it will be easy for you to withdraw and turn away from worldly possession and prominence and be patient with their passing. You will become a king [in this world] by abandoning it and expect [to be] a king in the Hereafter.

When these matters are unveiled for the servant who is familiar with prominence, who has found solace in it, and who pursues it as an established habit, mere knowledge and unveiling are not sufficient remedies, it is imperative that he add action to this. His action is of three kinds. The first is that he should flee from the place of prominence in order not to witness its effects. For patience will be difficult for him in the presence of the effects, just as he whose appetite has overcome him should flee from the contemplation of the forms that enthrall him. He who does not do this is ungrateful for the blessings of this spacious earth, as God says, *Was not God's earth broad enough for you to flee away in?* [24]

The second [kind of action] is to force himself to do what is contrary to his habit. Affectation is [then] replaced by modesty and shameful dress by humble apparel. And likewise for every aspect, state and act, in dwelling, clothing, food, standing and sitting which were his habit in order to fulfil his prominent position. He must replace [these] with the opposite, in order to establish a habit that is contrary to what was established in him before and to become accustomed to its opposite. For the treatment is not effective without [replacing it with] its opposite.

The third [kind of action] is to heed this carefully and gradually, for [the servant] does not transform [himself], in one instant, to devotion from the opposite extreme. Nature is averse [to change], and it is not possible to transform one's character except gradually. So as some [of the habits] are abandoned, he occupies himself with others, then, when his self is content with that, he begins to abandon yet another part, until he is content with what is left. And so, little by little he carries on, until he eliminates those characteristics that were established in him. This gradual [process] is indicated in the Prophet's statement, 'This religion is firm, so slowly penetrate into it, and do not make the worship of God hateful to yourself, for he who exhausts his mount does not go far and ruins the back [of his mount].'[25] The Prophet [also] alluded to this in his statement, 'Do not make harsh this religion, for he who makes it harsh will be overwhelmed by it.'[26]

What we have mentioned of the treatment of patience for temptations, desire, [the love of] prominence and the appetite, should be added to what we have said about the rules for striving in *The Book of Disciplining the Soul*, in the quarter of [the *Revival*] on mortal vices.[A] Adopt this as your constitution, so that you will know by it the remedy of patience in all the divisions that we detailed above. For it is lengthy to discuss particular matters.

He who heeds the gradual [method], patience will raise him to a state [such that it will be] hard for him to be without patience, just as patience was hard for him [previously]. So his affairs will be reversed; what he once liked becomes detestable, and what was

[A] This is *K. riyaḍāt al-nafs* (*Iḥyā'*, III.2). See the English translation by T. J. Winter, *On Disciplining the Soul*.

hateful to him becomes palatable and agreeable [to such an extent that] he cannot keep himself from it. This can only be known with practice and experience (*dhawq*). And there is a precedent for this in [how] habits [are established]. For [example], a child, at the beginning, is taught by constriction. He finds it difficult to be patient away from playing and to be patient with studying. When his perception is opened and he begins to enjoy studying, the matter is reversed; it will be difficult for him to have patience away from learning and patience with playing.

This is indicated by what was said by one of the gnostics when he asked Shiblī about patience. [He said,] 'Which [act of patience] is most difficult?' Shiblī replied, 'Patience in the way of God (Exalted is He!) (*al-ṣabr fi'Llāh*)?' The gnostic said, 'No.' Shiblī said, 'Patience for God (*al-ṣabr li-Llāh*).' The gnostic said, 'No.' Shiblī said, 'Patience with God (*al-ṣabr maʿa Allāh*).' The gnostic replied, 'No.' Then Shiblī asked, 'Then what?' The gnostic replied, 'Patience away from God! (*al-ṣabr ʿan Allāh*).' Thereupon Shiblī gave a shout and his spirit nearly departed him.[27]

And it has been said, concerning the meaning of God's statement, *Be patient and vie in patience; be steadfast!*[28] So, *be patient* for God, *vie in patience* to God, and *be steadfast* in God.

It has been said, 'Patience for God (*li-Llāh*) is doing without [what is other than God] (*ghanā'*), patience through God (*bi-Llāh*) is permanence (*baqā'*),[A] patience with God (*maʿa Allāh*) is faithfulness (*wafā'*), and patience away from God (*ʿan Allāh*) is estrangement (*jafā'*).[29]

It has been said that the meaning of patience is,
  Patience away from You,
Blameworthy are its consequences;
  Patience in the rest of things
Is praiseworthy;

[A] Though this is not necessarily the meaning here, *baqā'* in Sufism is the station after *fanā'* (annihilation) and is the highest possible realisation.

Patience is beautiful in all its habitations,
Except away from You;
Then it does not beautify its possessor.[30]

This is the last of what we wish to say about the knowledge of patience and its mysteries.

PART II
ON THANKFULNESS

It is made up of three sections. The first is on the merit of thankfulness: its reality, its divisions, and its rules. The second is on the nature of blessings and their specific and general divisions. The third is an exposition of what is best; patience or thankfulness.

SECTION ONE
ON THE ESSENCE OF THANKFULNESS

CHAPTER EIGHT
An Exposition of the Merit of Thankfulness

KNOW that God the Exalted united thankfulness (*shukr*) with remembrance (*dhikr*) in His Book. Although He said, *God's remembrance is greater,*[1] He said, *So remember Me, and I will remember you; and be thankful to Me and be not ungrateful;*[2] and *Why would God chastise you if you are thankful and believe?*[3] and *We will recompense the thankful.*[4]

God, Almighty and Majestic, says that Iblīs the accursed one says, *'I shall surely sit in ambush for them on the straight path.'*[5] It has been said that this path is the way of thankfulness. Due to the elevated nature of thankfulness, the Accursed One accused humanity and said, *You will not find most of them thankful.*[6] God (Exalted is He!) said, *For few indeed are those that are thankful among My servants.*[7]

God (Exalted is He!) declared that increase is joined to thankfulness without condition, *If you are thankful, surely I will increase you.*[8] He made five [other] things conditional: wealth (*ighnā'*), response [to personal prayer] (*ijāba*), provision (*rizq*), forgiveness (*maghfira*) and repentance (*tawba*). He (Exalted is He!) said, *God shall enrich you with His bounty, if He wills;*[9] and He said, *He will remove that [distress] for which you call upon Him, if He wills;*[10] and

He said, *And God bestows His abundance without measure on whom He wills*;[11] and He said, *He forgives other than [associating partners with God] to whomsoever He wills*;[12] and He said, *God accepts the repentance of whom He wills.*[13]

[Thankfulness] is one of the qualities of lordship. God (Exalted is He!) said, *God is All-Thankful, All-Clement.*[14]

God [also] made thankfulness the first utterance of the people of Paradise, for He said, *And they shall say, 'Praise belongs to God, Who has been true in His promise to us*;'[15] and He said, *And their supplication ends, 'Praise belongs to God, the Lord of all the worlds.'*[16]

As for the traditions, the Messenger of God (may God bless him and grant him peace) said, 'He who eats and gives thanks is equal to he who fasts and is patient.'[17]

It has been narrated that ʿAṭāʾ visited ʿĀʾisha (may God be pleased with her) and said, 'Tell us the most wonderful thing that you saw of the Messenger of God.' She wept and replied, 'And which matter was not a wonder? He once came to me at night and entered into bed with me, (or 'under my blanket so that my skin touched his skin') and said, "O daughter of Abū Bakr, give me leave that I may pray to my Lord." I said, "I love to be near you, but I prefer that you have what you wish." So I gave him leave, and he arose to get a vessel of water. Then he performed his ablutions, not pouring out much water. Thereupon he stood in prayer and wept until his tears flowed down his chest. Then he knelt in prayer and wept, then he prostrated in prayer and wept, and then he raised his head, still weeping. He continued to weep in this manner until Bilāl came and made the call to prayer. I said, "O Messenger of God, what makes you weep when God has forgiven you what has passed of your sin and what will come to pass?" He replied, "Should I not be a thankful servant? And how can I not be when God has revealed to me, *In the creation of the heavens and the earth. . .* "[18A]

[A] The verse continues: *and the alternation of night and day; in the sailing of the ships through the ocean for the profit of mankind; in the rain that God sends down from*

This incident points to the fact that weeping should never cease. This mystery is alluded to in what was narrated about one the prophets who passed by a small stone from which much water was gushing and he marvelled at it. Then God (Exalted is He!) made it speak. [The stone] said, 'Since the time I heard His words "*whose fuel is men and stones*"[19] I have been moved to tears out of fear of Him.' And the stone asked the prophet if he would rescue it from the Fire, and he agreed to protect it. Some time later, the prophet saw the stone in the same state and said, 'Why do you weep now?' [The stone] replied, 'The former was the weeping of fear, while this is the weeping of thankfulness and joy.'[20] The heart of the servant is like the stone, or even harder.[A] Its hardness is removed only by weeping from a state of either fear or thankfulness.

It is narrated that the Prophet (may God bless him and grant him peace) said, 'On the Day of Resurrection a summons will be made to 'those who praise' (*ḥammādūn*). A group will rise and a standard will be raised up for them and they will enter Paradise.' It was asked, 'Who are those who praise?' He replied, 'Those who thank God (Exalted is He!) under all circumstances.'[21] Another version of the tradition is, 'Those who thank God both in prosperity (*sarrā'*) and hardship (*ḍarrā'*).'[22]

The Prophet (may God bless him and grant him peace) said, 'Praise is the robe of the Merciful.'[23]

In a long discourse, God (Exalted is He!) revealed to Job (peace be upon him), 'I am content with thankfulness as a reward from my saints.'[24] God also revealed to him the description of those

the skies, and the life that He gives therewith to an earth that is dead; in the beasts of all kinds that He scatters through the earth; in the change of the winds, and the clouds that they trail like their slaves between the sky and the earth; (Here) indeed, are signs for a people that are wise.

[A] Allusion to Qur'ānic verse II.74: *Then after that, your hearts were hardened and became as rocks, or even harder. For there are rocks from which rivers gush forth, and there are rocks that shatter and water flows from them, and there are rocks that fall down in awe of God; and God is not unaware of what you do.*

who are patient, 'Their dwelling is the house of peace in Paradise. When they enter it, I inspire them to thankfulness and it is the best of speech. And when [they express] thankfulness, I increase them, and it is with vision of Me that I increase them.'[25]

When there were sufficient funds in the Treasury, ᶜUmar (may God be pleased with him) asked, 'What wealth shall we take?' The Prophet replied, 'Let each of you take a tongue in [continual] remembrance and a thankful heart.'[26] Therefore, he commanded the acquisition of a thankful heart in place of wealth.

Ibn Masᶜūd said, 'Thankfulness is half of faith.'[27]

CHAPTER NINE
An Exposition of the Definition and Nature of Thankfulness

KNOW that thankfulness is one of the stations of those who follow the spiritual path. [Like patience] it is made up of knowledge, state, and action.[A] Knowledge is the foundation, it generates the state, and the state generates the action. As for knowledge, it is to perceive that the blessing (*niʿma*)[B] is from the Bestower of blessings.[C] The state is the joy that results from the blessing. The action is the performance of what is intended and loved by the Bestower, and relates to the heart, limbs, and tongue. All three must be engaged so that the servant can attain a complete understanding of the reality of thankfulness. Yet, all that can be said about thankfulness falls short of encompassing its full meaning.

The first principle is knowledge, and it is knowledge of three matters: the blessing itself; the way in which it is a blessing with respect to the servant; the nature of the bestower and his different attributes which are active in bestowing and through which the [act of] bestowing proceeds from him to the other. For it is necessary that there should be a blessing, a bestower, and the one

[A] Here Ghazālī uses the singular *ʿilm* instead of the plural *maʿārif* and *ḥāl* and *ʿamal* instead of *aḥwāl* and *aʿmāl*.

[B] *Niʿma*, and its plural *niʿam*, is an essential term in the second section of the book. It includes all the different levels of divine provision. In his discussion of *shukr*, Othman renders the plural *niʿam* as 'bounties' (*Concept of Man*, p. 93).

[C] *Al-Munʿim*. Ghazālī does not discuss this in his commentary on the beautiful names, *al-Maqṣad*. Nor does this form occur in the Qur'ān. However, Ghazālī employs it as though it were an epithet of that rank.

upon whom the blessing is bestowed according to the intention and will of the bestower. Knowledge of these matters is absolutely necessary, [especially] with respect to the rights of other than God (Exalted is He!). As to the rights of God (Exalted is He!), this knowledge is complete only when [the servant] knows that all blessings come from God and He is the Bestower and the means are subservient to Him [alone].

This knowledge lies behind the knowledge of God's unity (*tawḥīd*) and transcendence (*taqdīs*),[A] because transcendence and unity are part of it. For the first degree of realisation of faith (*maʿārif al-īmān*) is to acknowledge a transcendent Essence. When [the servant] comes to know that there is only One in transcendence and that all else is not transcendent, [he has affirmed] divine unity. The servant, then, comes to know that everything in the world exists from that One only and everything is a blessing from Him. This is the third degree of knowledge as it includes, in addition to transcendence and unity, [knowledge of] the omnipotence [of God] and His being the unique active Agent.

About this, the Messenger of God (may God bless him and grant him peace) said, 'The person who says, "Glory be to God (*subḥān Allāh*)," receives ten good merits (*ḥasanāt*); he who says, "There is no god but God (*lā ilāha illa Allāh*)" receives twenty good merits; and he who says, "Praise be to God (*al-ḥamdu li-Llāh*)," receives thirty good merits.'[1] He (may God bless him and grant him peace) also said, 'The best remembrance is "there is no god but God," the best invocation is, "thanks be to God."'[2] And he said, 'There is nothing among the remembrances of God that multiplies merits as "thanks be to God" multiplies [them].'[3]

But do not think that these good merits are achieved [simply] by the tongue repeating these phrases without the heart having

[A] Ordinarily the verbal root *qaddasa* means to sanctify, hallow, declare holy; it occurs only in Q.II.30 in connection with the perpetual praise of God by the angels. Here, we have followed Jabre's translation of *taqdīs* as 'transcendence' (*Lexique de Ghazali*, p. 228).

attained to their meanings. Thus 'glory be to God' is an utterance that points to transcendence; 'there is no god but God' is an utterance that points to divine unity; and 'praise be to God' is an utterance that points to the knowledge that blessings are from the One, the Truth. [Each] good merit, then, is derived from [a particular] knowledge and is among the categories of faith and [inner] certainty.

Know that perfection of this knowledge precludes the association of others with God (*shirk*) in action. For when a king favours [someone] with something, and [the person] believes that the king's minister or steward had a share in facilitating it when handing it to him, [this belief] is an association of the blessing with [someone] other than the king. He does not see that the blessing is solely from the king; rather as partly from him and partly from others. His joy [at the receipt of the gift] is divided between them and will not be solely (*muwaḥḥad*)[A] for the king. However, to recognise that the blessing has reached him by means of the pen that [the king] used to sign with and the paper on which the signature appears, do not negate his exclusive acknowledgement (*tawḥīdih*) of the right of the king and the fullness of his [the person's] thankfulness. For he does not rejoice in the pen and the paper, nor does he thank them as they themselves were not [independently] involved; rather, they were employed at the command of the king. Likewise, the steward and the treasurer are both compelled to convey [things] for the sake of the king. If it were up to them and was not a definite command of the king for which they fear being punished if they neglect it, they would not give [the person] anything. When [the person] understands this, his regard for the treasurer will be like his regard for the pen and the paper; that is, it will not result in him associating anyone with the unity of relating the gift to the king.

[A] *Muwaḥḥad* and *tawḥīd* derive from the same root *waḥada*: to make into one, to unify. The choice of *muwaḥḥad* links the example Ghazālī is giving back to *tawḥīd*, which is the main focus of his argument here.

Similarly, whoever knows God and His acts knows that the sun, moon, and stars are subservient to His command[4] like the pen in the hand of a writer. The animals that are capable of choosing are subservient in their very choices. For God (Exalted is He!) controls their impulses, determining what they desire or reject, just like the treasurer, who is compelled by the king's command and cannot disobey him. Left to himself, he [the treasurer] would not give you a tiny particle of what he has. Everyone who conveys a blessing of God to you through his hand is compelled, since God empowers him with a will and stimulates him to do His bidding and puts in his soul [the conviction] that what is good for him in this world and the Hereafter is giving you what [God] wishes, and that he will not attain his goal in this life and in the Hereafter unless he does so. When God creates this belief in him, the servant cannot go against it, as he [will be under the conviction] that he is serving his own purpose not your purpose. If he did not have any personal motive for giving, he would never give [anything to] you; and, if he did not know that his benefit lies in your benefit, he surely would not benefit you. So he seeks to benefit himself by benefiting you and he is thus not your benefactor as he only adopts you as a means of attaining a blessing he seeks. Your true benefactor is He who made [this person] subservient to you and who placed in his heart convictions and desires which compelled him to convey [something] to you.

When you know that matters are like this, you know God (Exalted is He!) and you know His acts. You [truly] affirm God's unity and you are capable of thanking Him. In fact, you are thankful simply through this knowledge. For this reason, Moses (peace be upon him) in his personal devotions said, 'My God, you created Adam with Your hand. And You did this and this.[A] How can You be thanked?' God, Almighty and Majestic, answered, 'By knowing that all this is from Me.' [Moses'] knowledge was thankfulness.[5] Therefore, you are not thankful until you know

[A] Meaning that it is not possible to number God's gifts.

that everything is from Him. If doubt preoccupies your mind in this, you lack knowledge of the blessing or of the Bestower; and your delight will not be solely in the Bestower, but in other than Him. Because of your lack of knowledge, your state is diminished in joy; and because of the lack of joy, your action decreases. This is the exposition of the [first] principle [of thankfulness].

The second principle [of thankfulness] is the state that is derived from the principle of knowledge. It is joy in the Bestower while maintaining an attitude of submission and humility. In itself [this joy] is thankfulness, just as knowledge is thankfulness. However, it is thankfulness only if it contains the condition of thankfulness, and its condition is that your joy be in the Bestower, not in the blessing [itself] nor in the act of kindness [towards you].

Perhaps this statement is difficult for you to understand. Let us give an example. We say that a king who desires to make a journey grants a man[A] a favour [in the form] of a horse. He imagines that the man to whom it is granted will be delighted with the horse for three reasons. Firstly, he will be delighted because it is a horse and because it has [monetary] value which can be of benefit to him; because he can use it for riding, and that suits his purpose; and because it is a valuable racer as well. This [kind] of joy is for one who has no interest in the king, rather, his interest is only in the horse. Had he found it [the horse] in a desert, he would have taken it, and his joy would have been similar to this joy.

The second kind [of joy] is when he delights in it, not because it is a horse, but because he infers the care of the king expressed in it, and his [the king's] compassion for him. Had he found the horse in the desert, or someone other than the king had given it to him, he would not really be happy with it because, in principle, he has no need of the horse and it is of no significance to him compared to his desire to have a place in the heart of the king.

The third kind [of joy] is when [the servant] delights in the horse in order to ride it, to go out in the service of the king and

[A] The meaning here is 'a man in his entourage'.

bear the toil of the journey in his service, and to obtain the rank of nearness to the king. Perhaps he will be promoted to the position of a minister, because he is not content that his position in the heart of the king should be limited to his [the king's] giving him a horse and caring for him only to this degree. Rather, he does not want the king to convey [favours] from his wealth on anyone, except through him. Yet, he does not want the ministry for the sake of the ministry, rather he wants to see the king and be near him. If he had to choose between this proximity to him without the ministry, and the ministry without proximity, he would choose proximity.

These are the three levels [of joy]. In the first, there is no thankfulness at all because the vision of the one possessing it [this level of joy] is confined to the horse and his joy lies in the horse, not in the one who gave it. This is the state of all those who are made happy by a blessing because of the pleasure of it and because it is agreeable to their purpose. This is far from the meaning of thankfulness.

The second [kind] enters under the definition of thankfulness, in that the person delights in the giver, but not exactly because of him [the giver], rather, because of the knowledge of his care; this incites [the person] to seek favour in the future. This is the state of the righteous, who worship God and are thankful to Him for fear of His punishment and hope for His reward.

Perfect thankfulness is found only in the third kind of joy. It is when the joy of the servant in the blessing of God (Exalted is He!) is because it enables him to reach a place of proximity to Him (Exalted is He!), to reside in His companionship, and enjoy the vision of His countenance continually! This is the highest level [of attainment]. Its characteristic is joy in this world only for what it is, a field under cultivation for the Hereafter and the means to assist him to it. He grieves at every blessing that diverts him from the remembrance of God (Exalted is He!) and turns him away from His path. He does not desire the blessing because it is pleasurable, just as the possessor of the horse does not desire the horse because it is a racer or an ambler, but because it carries him in company with the king, that he may continue to see the king and be near him.

Thus Shiblī (may God grant him His mercy) said, 'Thankfulness is the vision of the Bestower, not the vision of the blessing.'[6]

Khawwāṣ (may God grant him His mercy) said, 'The thankfulness of the common people is for food, clothing, and drink; the thankfulness of the elect is for sudden inspirations in the heart.'[7]

This degree cannot be known by those whose experience is confined to the pleasures of the stomach, sexuality, and sensory perceptions of colour and sound, and is devoid of the pleasures of the heart. For the heart, when it is in a state of health, takes pleasure only in the remembrance of God (Exalted is He!), in knowledge of Him, and encountering Him. It takes pleasure in something else only when it has become ill with bad habits, just as some people [when ill] take pleasure in eating mud, or when sick people regard sweet things as distasteful and bitter things as delightful. It was said,

> And he who possesses a bitter mouth is sick
> And the sweet water he finds bitter.[8]

Therefore, this is the condition for [true] joy in the blessing of God (Exalted is He!). If the servant [has not attained] this, then he is at the second level. As for the first, it is not worthy of consideration. How great is the difference between one who desires the king for the horse, and one who desires the horse for the king! And how great is the difference between he who desires God that He may grant him favour and one who desires the blessings of God in order to draw closer to Him!

The third principle [of thankfulness] is action which is in accord with the joy that comes from the knowledge of the Bestower. This action is connected with the heart, the tongue, and the limbs. The aim of the heart is goodness towards all of creation; the tongue must express thankfulness to God (Exalted is He!) by praising Him without restraint; while the limbs should use the blessings of God (Exalted is He!) in obedience to Him and guard themselves from disobedience to Him. There is even [a form of] thankfulness for the eyes: it is to veil every shameful thing they see in a Muslim. The thankfulness of the ears is that they veil every shameful thing they hear about him [a Muslim]. All these are included under thankfulness for the blessings of God (Exalted is He!) by the parts of the body. Thankfulness of the tongue is to express contentment with God (Exalted is He!), as He commanded. Thus, the Prophet (may God bless him and grant him peace) said to a man, 'How are you this morning?' He replied, 'Fine.' He (may God bless him and grant him peace) repeated the question until [the man] responded after the third inquiry, 'Fine. I praise God and thank Him.' Thereupon the Prophet said, 'This is what I desired of you.'[9]

Our predecessors used to question each other with the intention of eliciting thankfulness to God (Exalted is He!) and providing the means for he who thanks to be obedient and for the one questioning him also to be obedient. Their purpose was not ostentation through the appearance of longing. For every servant who is asked about his state is found to be either thankful, complaining, or silent. Thankfulness is obedience and complaining is shameful disobedience for the people of religion. How can complaining of the King of kings, of He who holds in His hand everything [needed] by the servant, to another [servant] who is unable to do anything for himself, be anything but shameful? The best conduct for the servant who is not able to be patient in affliction and with what is decreed, and whose weakness leads him to complaint, is for his complaint to be to God (Exalted is He!). For He is the Afflicter (*al-Mublī*)[A] and He is the Capable (*al-Qādir*)[B] of removing

[A] *Al-Mublī*. Ghazālī does not discuss an epithet of this form in *al-Maqṣad*, nor does this epithet for God occur in the Qur'ān.

[B] *Al-Qādir*. Ghazālī discusses the epithet *al-Qādir* among the beautiful names for God along with *al-Muqtadir*. Both of these mean, 'One who the affliction. The humility of a servant towards his Lord is [an] honour; [while] complaint to other than Him is humiliation. The exposure of weakness to another man, who is only a servant like the complainer himself, is a shameful weakness. God (Exalted is He!) said, *Those you serve, apart from God, have no power to provide for you. So seek your provision with God, serve Him, be thankful to Him.*[10] And God (Exalted is He!) said, *Those on whom you call, apart from God, are servants like you.*[11]

Thus, thankfulness with the tongue is one of the expressions of thankfulness. It is said that a delegation approached ʿUmar b. ʿAbd al-ʿAzīz (may God show him His mercy) and a youth among them rose to speak. ʿUmar said, 'The aged, the aged [should speak]!' The youth replied, 'O commander of the believers! Were it a matter of age, there would be among the Muslims someone who is older than you!' Then ʿUmar said, 'Speak!' [The youth] said, 'We are not a delegation desiring anything, nor a delegation fearing anything. As to desire, your bounty has delivered it to us; as to fear, your justice has made us secure from it. We are only a delegation of the thankful, we came to thank you with the tongue, and [when we have done so] we will depart.'[12]

These, then, are the principles of the definitions of thankfulness, which comprise the whole of its reality. As to he who has said, 'Thankfulness is the acknowledgment of the blessings of the Bestower on the basis of submission.' This is a view of how the tongue acts [in harmony] with some of the states of the heart. The statement 'Thankfulness is praise for the One Who does good (*al-Muḥsin*)[A] by remembering His goodness,'[13] is to consider the act of the tongue only. The statement, 'Thankfulness is to remain uninterruptedly on the carpet of the vision [of God] while

possesses power and the second is the most expressive of it' (*al-Maqṣad*, p. 145; Burrell and Daher, pp. 131–132). Both occur in the Qur'ān as epithets for God.

[A] *Al-Muḥsin*. Ghazālī does not discuss this epithet in *al-Maqṣad*. In the Qur'ān all three references to *muḥsin* refer to the believer who surrenders his life to God, but not to God. See Q.ɪɪ.112, ɪᴠ.125, and xxxɪ.22.

permanently maintaining reverence,'[14] brings together most of the meanings of thankfulness except for the work of the tongue.

The saying of Ḥamdūn al-Qaṣṣār, 'Thankfulness for blessing is that you see yourself as an intruder in thankfulness,' indicates that thankfulness is part of knowledge.

The saying of Junayd, 'Thankfulness is that you should not consider yourself worthy of blessing'[15] alludes to a particular state of the heart.

These sayings [of notable Sufis] express their states. Therefore, their rejoinders differ and do not agree. Furthermore, the reply of each may differ in two different states, because they speak only through the state that prevails with them and they are occupied with what concerns them and not with what does not concern them. Or, perhaps they speak of what they see as the immediate concern of the questioner, discussing a matter only to the extent that it concerns him and remaining silent about what does not. You should not think that what we mentioned above is a criticism of them, or, if they had been presented with all the definitions that we have explained, that they would have denied them. No reasonable person would think that, unless something disputable became apparent from the standpoint of language. That is to say, linguistically, does the word 'thankfulness' include all meanings, or are some of them intended and the rest are only implied in the meaning of thankfulness? We do not intend to offer linguistic explanations in this book, because it is not a science of the way of the Hereafter in any respect! And God grants success through His mercy!

CHAPTER TEN
An Exposition of How to Raise the Veil on the Thankfulness Due to God

IT MAY have occurred to you that thankfulness [is conceivable only] with respect to the right of the benefactor to receive thanks. When we thank kings by praising [them], we increase their esteem in the hearts [of their subjects] and make manifest their magnanimity to people, thereby increasing their renown and influence; or [we thank them] through service to them, which helps them [accomplish] some of their purposes; or by appearing before them as their servants, which in turn increases their influence. For [one] cannot be thankful to [kings] except through acts such as these.

This notion is inconceivable with regard to the rights of God for two reasons. The first is that God (Exalted is He!) is far from needing benefit or having an interest. He is exalted above the need for service and help, [above the desire to] spread [His] glory and reverence through praise and extolment or the amassing of standing, kneeling, and prostrating servants. Our thankfulness to Him does not benefit Him. [This] thankfulness may be likened to [the benefit] that a beneficent king derives from us sleeping in our homes, and from us prostrating ourselves or kneeling [in prayer]; the king derives no benefit from this, for he is absent and knows nothing of what we do. God (Exalted is He!) does not benefit from any of our acts!

The second reason is that every action we choose to undertake is an additional blessing of God upon us, since our limbs, our ability, our will, our motives, and all our means of movement are the creation and blessing of God (Exalted is He!). Then how can we be thankful for a blessing through [another] blessing? If the king gives us a riding horse and we take another of his horses, and ride it; or the king gives us a second horse, [thankfulness for] the second horse would not express thankfulness for the first. Thankfulness for the second is required just as it is required for the first. Furthermore, we cannot give thanks for thankfulness save through another blessing, thus leading to [the notion that] thankfulness is impossible with respect to God (Exalted is He!) in both cases. Yet, there can be no doubt about [the necessity for thankfulness in] both of them. The law addresses this. So how do we resolve the matter?

Know that this observation occurred to both David and Moses (peace be upon them). For Moses said, 'O Lord, how do I thank You when I [can] only thank through a second blessing from Your blessings?'[1] In another version, 'and my thankfulness to You is another blessing from You, which necessitates thankfulness from me.'[2] God (Exalted is He!) revealed to him [Moses], 'If you know this, you are thankful to Me.'[3] In another report, 'When you know the blessing is from Me, I accept this as a form of thanks from you.'[4]

If you say, 'I have understood the question, but I fail to understand what God revealed to them [David and Moses]. I know for myself that thankfulness to God (Exalted is He!) is impossible. If knowledge of the impossibility of thankfulness *is* thankfulness, then I do not understand it. For this knowledge is also a blessing from Him. So how does it become thankfulness?' The conclusion to this may lead [one to think] that by not expressing thankfulness, one has been thankful; that the acceptance of a second robe of honour from the king constitutes thankfulness for a first robe of honour. This understanding falls short of grasping the mystery in [the matter]. It is possible to clarify this with a simile, as this is an important matter in itself.

Know that [we are here] knocking at the door of knowledge (*maʿārif*) which is higher than the sciences of practical transactions

(*ʿulūm al-muʿāmala*). We will point to some of its allusions. We say that there are two ways of seeing (*naẓarān*). [The first] is vision of divine unity (*bi-ʿayn al-tawḥīd*). This vision gives absolute knowledge that He is the One Who gives thanks and the One Who is thanked; He is the One Who loves and the beloved.[A] This is the perspective of [a servant] who knows that there is none other than He in existence, that everything perishes save His countenance, and that this is true in every state, always and forever.[B] For a being other than God to exist, it would have to subsist through itself. Such a being does not exist; in fact, it is impossible for it to exist. Real Being (*al-wujūd al-muḥaqqaq*) is That which is self-subsistent (*al-qā'im bi-nafsih*).[C] That which cannot subsist through itself, cannot exist through itself. If it is sustained by an other, then it exists through an other. In itself, it has no existence at all.

That which exists (*al-mawjūd*) is that which is self-subsistent, and the self-subsistent is that which remains in existence when others cease to be. If in addition to its self-subsistence, it is the cause of its own existence and the existence of others, then it is the self-subsisting (*qayyūm*); there is only One Who is the Self-Subsisting (*al-Qayyūm*)[D] and it cannot be otherwise conceived. Thus in existence, there is only the Ever-Living One (*al-Ḥayy*),[E]

[A] *Al-Muḥibb* and *al-Maḥbūb*. Neither of these forms occur in the Qur'ān and Ghazālī does not list them in *al-Maqṣad*. However, the cognate roots *aḥabba* and *ḥabbaba* occur as follows: *God loves those who do good* (Q.II.195); *Truly, God loves those who repent, and He loves those who keep themselves pure* (Q.II.222); '*Say: if you love God, follow me, and God will love you, and forgive all your sins; God is All-Forgiving, All-Compassionate*' (Q.III.31).

[B] The first is *azal*, eternity in the past, and the second is *abad*, eternity in the future.

[C] This epithet is referred to under *al-Qayyūm* in *al-Maqṣad* (p. 143; Burrell and Daher, pp. 129–130).

[D] *Al-Qayyūm* is one of the beautiful names of God mentioned in the Qur'ān (Q.II.255; III.2; XX.111).

[E] *Al-Ḥayy* is one of the beautiful names of God mentioned in the Qur'ān (Q.II.255; III.2; XX.111; and XL.65). Ghazālī summarises his discussion of this epithet, 'The absolute living is He Who incorporates all the cognitions within the Self-Subsisting (*al-Qayyūm*), He is the One (*al-Aḥad*),[A] the Eternal (*al-Ṣamad*).[B] From the viewpoint of this station, you will know that all things emanate from Him as their source, and to Him they return.[5] He is the Thankful and the One thanked;[C] He is the Lover and the Beloved.

This was the vision of Ḥabīb b. Abī Ḥabīb when he said after reciting, *Truly We found him full of patience. An excellent servant! Ever did he turn* [*to Us*],[6] 'How marvellous! He gives and He praises!'[7] pointing to the fact that when He praises His own giving, He praises Himself. God is the One Who praises and is the one praised.[D] This also was the vision of Shaykh Abū Saʿīd al-Mayhanī when [the verse] *God loves them and they love Him*[8] was recited in his presence. He said, 'Upon my life! God loves them, so let Him love them! For in truth, when [God] loves, He only loves Himself!'

His discernment, and all existing things within His activity: God Almighty and Majestic. For He is the Living, the Absolute' (*al-Maqṣad*, p. 142; Burrell and Daher, p. 129).

[A] Ghazālī discusses this under *al-Wāḥid al-Aḥad* (*al-Maqṣad*, p. 144; Burrell and Daher, pp. 130–131).

[B] *Al-Ṣamad* is one of the beautiful names of God and occurs only once in the Qur'ān (Q.cxii.2). Following Arberry, Watt comments on the English translation that God is 'the Everlasting Refuge: the usual interpretation of *ṣamad*. However, it is also rendered 'eternal,' 'the only one' (Watt, *Companion to the Qur'ān* [London: George Allen and Unwin, 1967], p. 332). Pickthall renders *al-Ṣamad* as 'the most eternally besought of all' (*Koran*); Muhammad Ali translates it as 'He on whom all depend' (*Holy Qur'ān* [Lahore: Ahmadiyya Anjuman Isha'at Islam, 1963], p. 1219).

[C] *Al-Shākir* and *al-Mashkūr*. Ghazālī, in his discussion of the divine name *al-Shakūr*, does not discuss these active and passive participle forms as epithets for God (*al-Maqṣad*, pp. 114–115; Burrell and Daher, pp. 101–102), although the first occurs twice in the Qur'ān (Q.ii.157; iv.147). Arberry translates it as 'All-Grateful' and 'All-Thankful,' respectively. The second form also occurs in the Qur'ān, but not in reference to God (Q.xvii.19 and lxxvi.22). Louis Gardet, does not include these two as alternate forms in the list of the beautiful names ('al-Asmā' al-ḥusnā',' *EI*², pp. 714–717).

[D] *Al-Muthnī* and *al-Muthnā ʿalayhī*. Ghazālī does not list either of these epithets in *al-Maqṣad*.

[The Shaykh] was indicating that God is both the Lover and the Beloved.

This is a high degree [of knowledge] that you can understand only through a simile, and according to the level of your intelligence. You know well that if an author loves his literary work, he loves himself! When an artisan loves his craft, he loves himself! When a parent loves his child, he does so because the child is *his* child and he loves himself. All that exists aside from God (Exalted is He!) is created and made by God. If God loves it, then He only loves Himself; and if He only loves Himself, He does so through what He has loved. All this can [only] be perceived through divine unity (*bi-ʿayn al-tawḥīd*). Sufism expresses this state of experience as the annihilation of the self (*fanā' al-nafs*); that is, his self and all that is other than God ceases to be for him, and he sees only God (Exalted is He!).

Whoever does not understand this will find fault with them [the Sufis] and say, 'How can a person be annihilated when his shadow remains four forearms [long] and he eats several weights of bread every day?' Ignorant people laugh at them [the Sufis], because they do not understand the meaning of their words and because gnostics will [always] be the laughing stock of the ignorant. And this is indicated in the statement of God (Exalted is He!), *Those in sin used to laugh at those who believed, and whenever they passed by them, used to wink at each other (in mockery); and when they returned to their own people, they would return jesting; and whenever they saw them, they would say 'Behold, These are people truly astray!' But they had not been sent as keepers over them.*[9] God has also made it plain that the gnostics will have the last laugh, since God (Exalted is He!) has said, *But on this Day the believers will laugh at the non-believers, on thrones (of dignity) they will command (a sight of all things).*[10] This is similar to when the people of Noah (peace be upon him) laughed at him for being busy with building the Ark. He said, *If you scoff at us, we shall surely scoff at you, as you scoff.*[11] [The above] then is one of the two [possible] visions.

The second vision is that of those who have not attained to the station of extinction of themselves. They are [divided into] two groups. [First], there is a group that confirms only their own existence and denies having a lord to worship. These people are blind and astray; their blindness afflicts both eyes, because they deny what is truly constant, that is, the Self-Subsisting One, Who is self-subsistent in Himself, and Who gives subsistence to every soul and every subsistent [thing] subsists through Him. These people are not content with this [denial]; they wish to prove their own self-subsistence. If only they knew, they would surely understand that, being who they are, they have no subsistence or existence through themselves. They exist because they have been brought into existence, and not because they have existentiated themselves. There is a difference between that which exists (*mawjūd*) and that which is brought into existence (*mūjad*). In existence, there is only One Being (*Mawjūd*) and One Originator (*Mūjid*). Thus, Being is the Real (*al-Ḥaqq*) and that which is brought into being (*mūjad*) is in its very self illusory. Being is Self-Subsistent and Self-Subsisting (*Qā'im wa-Qayyūm*); while that which is brought into existence passes away and perishes. Indeed, *All that is on the earth will perish: But will abide (forever) the countenance of your Lord, Majestic and Splendid.*[12]

The second group are not blind, but are one-eyed. With one eye they see the One Real Being, and they do not deny Him. Should the other eye be completely blind, they will not be able to use it to see that all which is other than the Real Being will perish. Thus, they affirm another with God (Exalted is He!). And they are thus confirmed polytheists (*mushrik*); just as those mentioned above are confirmed apostates (*jāḥid*).

If [a person] goes from being blind to having blurred vision, he will discern that there are degrees of existent beings and, consequently, that there is a servant and a Lord. Thus the ability to discern degrees and imperfections in existent beings is part of the affirmation of divine unity (*tawḥīd*).

If the servant's sight is anointed with something that increases its light, its blurriness will decrease. And to the extent that his sight is increased, he perceives the deficiency of that which he had affirmed aside from God (Exalted is He!). If he continues in this way, the increased [perception of] deficiency will lead him to extinction and the extinction of all that he perceived aside from God; he will [then] only see God. He will have reached the perfection of affirming divine unity. When he had [first] perceived the imperfection of that which is other than God, he had [just] entered the beginning of divine unity. And between the two[A] are innumerable degrees. Herein lie the degrees of those who profess the unity of God (*muwaḥḥidūn*).

God ordained that the station [of divine unity] be revealed through the teachings of His messengers. [The teachings] are the ointment that grants the lights of vision, and the prophets are those who apply the ointment. They come calling to divine unity, and to elucidate the statement, '*There is no god but God*.'[13] It means that the servant sees only the One, the Real. Those who reach the perfection of divine unity are very few. The apostates and polytheists are also few in number. They are on the far side, opposite the side of divine unity. The worshippers of idols said, *We only serve them that they may bring us nearer to God*.[14] These people have barely entered the first levels of divine unity. Most people are in the middle. Among them is he who, in some states, acquires vision of divine unity but only like a flash of lightening; it is not permanent. And among them is he who acquires this [vision of divine unity] and it remains [with him] for a while. Yet [again], it is not permanent; for permanence in it is rare.

> For all men there are movements toward the highest ambition,
> But rare among men are those who persist.[15]

[A] That is, between the first perception of divine unity and its perfection.

When God (Exalted is He!) commanded His Prophet to seek nearness [to Him], He told him, *Prostrate yourself, and draw near.*[16] [The Prophet] said, in his prostration, 'I take refuge in Your pardon from Your punishment, I take refuge in Your contentment from Your anger, and I take refuge in You from You. I cannot enumerate Your praise. You are just as You have praised Yourself.'[17] The statement of the Prophet (may God bless him and grant him peace), 'I take refuge in Your pardon from Your punishment,' is based on the vision of the act of God. It is as if he saw God and His acts only, so he sought refuge in His act from His act. Then he drew nearer and he ceased to see the acts, and he advanced to the sources of the acts, which are the attributes of God, and he said, 'I take refuge in Your contentment from Your anger,' and these are two attributes. Then he perceived that this was an imperfection [in the affirmation of] divine unity. So he drew nearer and progressed from the station of seeing God's attributes (*ṣifāt*) to the vision of the Essence (*Dhāt*) and he said, 'I take refuge in You from You.' This is a flight from Him to Him without perceiving act or attribute. He saw himself fleeing from Him to Him, [both] when he sought refuge and when he praised. So he ceased seeing his own self when he perceived that it is a limitation. He drew nearer and said, 'I cannot enumerate Your praise. You are just as You have praised Yourself.' So [the Prophet's] statement, 'I cannot enumerate' refers to the extinction of his self and passing beyond seeing it. His statement, 'You are just as You have praised Yourself' is a declaration that God is the One Who praises and the One praised; that all things originate from Him and return to Him, and that *all things perish, save His countenance.*[18] The first of his [the Prophet's] stations (*maqāmāt*)—that he only saw God and His acts, and he sought refuge in one [divine] act from another [divine] act—is the final station of those who profess divine unity (*muwaḥḥidūn*). Observe, then, what ended the matter; it ended with the One, the Real, [everything] was lifted from his vision and perception save the True Essence.

Whenever he (may God bless him and grant him peace) advanced from one station to another, he would observe that the first [station] was at a greater distance [from God] than the second. So the Prophet (may God bless him and grant him peace) sought God's pardon from the first station, seeing in it a limitation on his path and a shortcoming in his station. This is indicated in his words (may God bless him and grant him peace), 'I find a veil on my heart until I have begged for God's pardon each day and night, seventy times.'[19] This [statement] indicates his attainment of seventy stations, one above the other. The first [station], despite exceeding the highest aspirations of human beings, was yet less complete than the final [station]. His appeal for God's pardon was made for that reason.

When ʿĀ'isha (may God be pleased with her) said, 'Has God not forgiven you both your previous and later sins? So why this weeping in prostration and this strenuous effort?' He replied, 'Should I not be a thankful servant?'[20] Its meaning is, 'Should I not seek more of the higher stations?'[A] Thankfulness, therefore, is the means of increase, whence God (Exalted is He!) said, *If you give thanks, I will give you more*.[21]

Now that we have penetrated the oceans of unveilings, let us draw in the reins and return to the sciences of practical transactions (*ʿulūm al-muʿāmalāt*). So we say, the prophets (may God grant them peace) were sent to call humanity to the perfect [understanding] of divine unity as we have described it. But between [humanity] and the attainment of [this goal] is a great distance and serious obstacles. The Law (*sharʿ*) in its entirety is instruction in the way of traversing that distance and passing through these obstacles. When this is [achieved], [one] sees with a different vision and [one attains] a different station. This station grants, in addition to this [new] vision, [an understanding of] thankfulness, the thankful One and the One being thanked. But this is comprehended only by simile.

[A] Ghazālī here gives this tradition a specifically Sufi interpretation.

Therefore, I say: It is possible for you to understand that a king despatches to a servant a riding beast, clothing, and money for provisions on the way, that he may traverse a great distance and return to the presence of the king. In doing so the king can have one of two purposes. The first is that he intends for the servant to enter into his presence in order to undertake a matter of state and to engage in his service. [While] in the second, the servant brings no benefit to the king, who has no need of him, rather [the servant's] presence does not increase his [the king's] kingdom because he [the servant] is not able to undertake a service that increases the wealth of the king, nor does [the servant's] absence diminish his kingdom. The purpose of the gift of the riding animal and the provisions is for the servant to draw near him, enjoy the pleasure of being in his presence, to benefit the servant himself, not to benefit the king through the servant and his employment. The position of servants to God (Exalted is He!) is that of the second purpose, not that of the first state. The first is impossible with respect to God (Exalted is He!), while the second is possible.

Moreover, know that in the first case the servant is not thankful just by riding and coming into [the king's] presence, until he completes the service that the king desired of him. As for the second case, [the king] has no need of service at all, even though he [the servant] may be either thankful or ungrateful. His thankfulness is when he uses what has been granted to him for the sake of his master, not for his own sake. His ingratitude is when he does not use it for the purpose it was intended for, or when he uses it to increase his distance from him [the king]. For whenever the servant dresses in the clothing, rides the horse, and spends the provision only in journeying [to the king], he thanks him, since he [the servant] used his blessings out of love for him; that is, in what he loves for his servant, not for himself. If he rides away and turns his back on his [the king's] presence and distances himself from the king, then [the servant] is ungrateful for his blessing; that is, he uses it for something that his master hates for his servant, not for himself. If the servant desists and does not ride, neither seeking proximity nor distance, again he is ungrateful for his [the king's] blessing, as he is careless with it and does not make use of it, even if this error is somewhat less than distancing himself from him [the king].

Thus God, glory to Him, created humans, who, in infancy, need to use the appetites in order to reach maturity. They are distanced [subsequently] from His presence [because of the appetites], while their happiness lies only in nearness to Him. God prepares blessings for them, which they can use to reach a degree of nearness. God (Exalted is He!) expressed His purpose with respect to their distance and their nearness, saying, *We indeed created man in the fairest stature then We abased him to the lowest of the low—save those who believe and do righteous deeds: they shall have a reward unfailing.*[22] Thus God (Exalted is He!) provides instruments by which the servant advances from being the lowest of the low. God created these for the sake of the servant, that he may obtain the happiness of nearness. God (Exalted is He!) is free from any need for proximity or distance. The servant either uses them [the instruments given by God] in obedience, and in accordance with what his Lord loves; or he uses them in disobedience to Him, and he is then ungrateful, [doing what] his Lord hates and what He does not wish. Indeed, God does not wish thanklessness and disobedience for His servants. [Finally,] if a servant is careless and does not use [the instruments], in obedience or disobedience, then he is also ungrateful for the blessing, which is squandered.

All that was created in this world was created only as an instrument for the servant to use to reach the happiness of the Hereafter and to attain nearness to God (Exalted is He!). Consequently, every obedient person, to the extent of his obedience, is thankful for the means he uses in that obedience, as these are a blessing from God. Whereas every slothful person who abandons the use [of the means of obedience], or the disobedient person who uses them on a path that distances him from God, is ungrateful, deviating towards something other than the love of God (Exalted is He!). Disobedience and obedience fall under [individual] choice, but likes and dislikes do not. For a desired thing may be either loved or hated. Hidden in this allusion is the secret of divine predestination (*qadar*), but it is prohibited to reveal it.

The first problem has [now] been solved by this, that is: if there is no benefit for the one thanked how then is there thankfulness? With this, also, the second problem is solved. Indeed, by thankfulness we mean only the total use of the blessing of God to proceed in the direction of God's love. If the blessing proceeds in the direction of love through an act of God, the intention is fulfilled. Your [own] act is a gift from God (Exalted is He!). [Yet] when you accomplish it, God praises you and His praise is another blessing from Him to you. He is the One Who gives, and He is the One Who praises. One of His acts has thus become the means by which His second act moves in the direction of His love. Thankfulness, then, belongs to Him in every state. [If] you are described as being thankful, it is in the sense that you become 'the vessel' for the expression of thankfulness, not that you are its originator. This is the same as when you are described as a gnostic (*ʿārif*) or as a scholar (*ʿālim*); this does not mean that you are the creator or originator of knowledge, but that you are a 'vessel' for it and it has been placed in you by the power of the Eternal. To describe you as thankful is to grant 'thingness' (*shay'iyya*) to you; for you are a thing when the Creator of things makes you so. You are not a 'thing' if you think that you are so through yourself. Therefore, you are considered something because God made you a thing. But if He ceases His [creative] act, you are in reality nothing. There is an allusion to this in the response that the Prophet (may God bless him and grant him peace) gave when he was asked, 'O Messenger of God, what is the use of action if things have been predestined?' He said, 'Act! For each thing will be guided[A] to that for which it was created.'[23]

[A] We have chosen to translate the word *muyassar* here as guided. However, the literal meaning is: things are made easy, or things will come easily, or you will be led.

Know [then] that created things are the channels for the power of God (Exalted is He!) and the 'vessels' of His acts even when they themselves are of His acts; for some acts are the causes of others. Though 'Act!' was pronounced by the Prophet (may God bless him and grant him peace), it is [in fact] one of His acts. Its purpose is [on the one hand] to inform humanity that to act is beneficial, and [on the other hand] for them to come to know one of God's acts. For knowledge is a cause that generates a distinct motive for [both] action and obedience. The generation of a motive is also one of God's acts. It causes the movement of the limbs, which is another of God's acts. Some of His acts are secondary causes (*asbāb*) of others, that is, the first is a precondition (*sharṭ*) of the second. Thus the creation of material form (*jism*) is a precondition for the creation of accidents,[A] as accidents cannot exist without them. The creation of life is a precondition for the existence of knowledge. The existence of knowledge is a precondition for the existence of the will. The whole [process] is of the acts of God (Exalted is He!); some [acts] being causes and preconditions of others. The meaning of them being preconditions is that only what possesses substance can possess life, only a living being can possess knowledge, and only that which possesses knowledge can possess a will. In this sense, therefore, some of His acts are causes for others. This does not mean that some acts bring others into existence; only that they facilitate conditions for the existence of others. The realisation of this [knowledge] advances [the servant] to the level of divine unity that we have mentioned.

If you say 'Why did God (Exalted is He!) say—"Act or you will be punished and condemned for disobedience." Why are we held accountable when the whole [process belongs] to God (Exalted is He!) alone?' Know that this statement from God (Exalted is He!) is a cause for us: the existence of a conviction in us; that conviction causes fear; fear causes the abandonment of the desires and

[A] Accidents (*aʿrād*, sing. *ʿarad*) is a philosophical term for possible beings and is the opposite of substance (*jawhar*).

withdrawal from the abode of delusion. And this is a cause that leads to nearness to God, and God (Exalted is He!) is the Causer of the causes[A] and their Arranger.[B] For the one who is predestined to salvation, the chain of causes that will lead him to Paradise will come easily to him. He is an example of the statement, 'Everything is guided to that for which it was created.' As to he who is not predestined to salvation, he is distanced from hearing the words of God (Exalted is He!), the statements of the Messenger of God (may God bless him and grant him peace), and the words of learned men. Since he does not hear, he does not know; and since he does not know, he does not fear; and since he does not fear, he does not abandon preference for this world; and since he does not abandon preference for this world, he remains in the party of Satan, and surely, *Hell is the promised abode for them all.*[24]

If you know this, you will marvel at a people who are led to Paradise in chains. There is none who is not conducted to Paradise by the chain of causes, through the prevailing of knowledge and fear over them. There is none forsaken but that he is conducted to the Fire in chains,[25] through the prevailing of heedlessness, false security and delusion over him. Thus the pious are driven to Paradise by force and the sinners are driven to the Fire by force. There is no compeller save God the One (*al-Wāḥid*),[C] the Omnipotent (*al-Qahhār*),[D] and no one has power save the King

[A] *Musabbib al-asbāb*. Ghazālī does not treat this term separately among the beautiful names in *al-Maqṣad*. He does include it in his exposition of the epithet *al-Ḥakam*, 'the Judge,' or 'the Arbiter' (*al-Maqṣad*, pp. 98–105; Burrell and Daher, pp. 85–92).

[B] *Al-Murattib*. Ghazālī does not include this epithet among the beautiful names in his exposition, nor does it occur in the Qur'ān.

[C] This epithet appears in *al-Maqṣad*, p. 144 (Burrell and Daher, pp. 130–131).

[D] *Al-Qahhār*. This epithet is one of the beautiful names that Ghazālī discusses; 'the Omnipotent' (*al-Qahhār*) is He Who shatters the pomp of His enemies and subdues them with mortification and humiliation' (*al-Maqṣad*, p. 86). This is linked to *al-Wāḥid* ('the One') in all five Qur'ānic passages where it (*al-Malik*),[A] the All-compeller (*al-Jabbār*).[B] If the veil is removed from the eyes of the heedless, they will witness the matter likewise. And they will hear the summons of the summoner, *Whose is the kingdom today? That of God, the One, the Omnipotent.*[26] Certainly, the kingdom belongs to God, the One, the Omnipotent, every day, not just that day[C] in particular. Yet, the heedless do not hear this summons, except on that day. For this is a prophecy of how things will be revealed to the heedless at the time when this knowledge will avail them not. We, therefore, seek refuge in God, the All-Clement, the All-Gracious, from ignorance and blindness, for they are the preconditions of the causes of destruction.

occurs (Q.xii.39; xiii.16; xiv.48; xxxviii.65; xxxix.4; and xl.16). Arberry consistently translates it as 'the Omnipotent.' It is the intensive adjectival form of the root *qahara* ('to subject, subjugate, or conquer'). A second epithet from this root, *al-Qāhir*, occurs once (Q.vi.18). Arberry also translates it as 'the Omnipotent' (Arberry, *Koran*, i.150).

[A] *Al-Malik* appears in *al-Maqṣad*, pp. 70–71 (Burrell and Daher, pp. 57–59); *Mālik al-Mulk* at p. 152 (Burrell and Daher, pp. 139–140).

[B] *Al-Jabbār*. 'The All-Compeller.' In the Qur'ān this form in the singular occurs eight times. However, it is used only once as an epithet for God (Q.lix.23), and appears in a passage containing sixteen of the beautiful names together in one place. Ghazālī comments that 'the All-Compeller, absolutely, is God. . . He compels everyone, but no one compels Him' (*al-Maqṣad*, pp. 78–79; Burrell and Daher, pp. 66–67).

[C] The Day of Judgement.

CHAPTER ELEVEN
An Exposition of the Distinction Between What God Loves and What He Hates

KNOW that the act of thankfulness and the abandonment of ingratitude (*kufr*)[A] are complete only with knowledge of what God (Exalted is He!) loves as opposed to what He hates. The meaning of thankfulness is using His (Exalted is He!) blessings for that which He loves. The meaning of ingratitude is the opposite of this, either abandoning [the blessing] or using it for that which He hates.

There are two faculties by which to distinguish between what God (Exalted is He!) loves and what He hates. One is [the faculty of] hearing and it relies on the verses [of the Qur'ān] and on the Traditions. The second [faculty] is the vision of the heart (*baṣīrat al-qalb*), and it is to see with the eye of contemplation (*bi-ʿayn al-iʿtibār*). This is difficult and for that reason it is rare. Thus, God (Exalted is He!) sent the messengers and through them made the way easier for mankind. This knowledge [they taught] is knowledge of all the rules of law governing the acts of the servants. For whoever does not follow the rules of law in all of his actions can never be truly thankful.

With respect to the second [faculty], it is to see with the eye of contemplation, and it consists in understanding the wisdom

[A] The verb *kafara* is usually taken to mean 'to disbelieve in God'. However, the meaning of the root form is 'to cover over'. Here *kufr* and *kufrān* are used as synonyms for ingratitude; literally 'to cover the blessings of God' or 'to turn a blind eye to the blessings of God.'

(*ḥikma*) of God (Exalted is He!) in every thing He has created. For there is a wisdom in each thing. Underlying the wisdom is a purpose (*maqṣūd*), and the purpose is what is loved (*maḥbūb*) [by God]. The wisdom is divided into what is evident and what is hidden. Evident matters are those like knowledge of the wisdom of creating the sun to demarcate night from day. For the day is for [earning one's] livelihood, while the night is the means for rest.[1] One can see easily [during the day], and one can rest during the cover [of darkness]. This is only part of the wisdom [behind the creation of the] sun, not its entire wisdom, as there is, in it, many other subtle [forms of] wisdom.

Likewise, is the knowledge of the wisdom relating to clouds and the descent of rain, which exist so that varieties of plants can come forth as food for mankind and grazing pasture for livestock. In some [verses], the Qur'ān includes the evident wisdom that people can understand without [including] the subtleties that [people] cannot understand. God (Exalted is He!) said, *We poured out abundant rain, then We split the earth in fissures and there caused the grains to grow and vines [and reeds]*.[2]

As to the wisdom in the various celestial bodies, both moving and fixed, it is obscure and most people do not comprehend it. The part that humans can comprehend, is that they adorn the heavens, so that the eye may take pleasure in gazing at them. The words of God (Exalted is He!) indicate this, *We have adorned the lower heaven with beauty in the stars.*[3]

In all the particulars of the world—its heavens and stars; its winds, seas, mountains, and minerals; its plants, animals, and the limbs of the animals—there is not a single atom that is devoid of wisdom; [in] it may be one, ten, a thousand, or ten thousand wisdoms. The same [is true] for the limbs of the animals, which are divided into those whose underlying wisdom is known, for example, the knowledge that the eye is for sight, not for grasping; the hand is for grasping, not for walking; the leg is for walking, not for smell. As to the internal bodily organs, like the intestines, the gall bladder, the liver, the kidneys, the individual veins, the nerves and muscles, and their cavities, layers, interconnections and separation, their thinness, thickness and the rest of their properties, the majority of people do not understand their wisdom. Those who do understand it, possess only a limited knowledge of the knowledge of God (Exalted is He!), *You have been given but little knowledge.*[4]

Therefore, everyone who uses something for a purpose other than that for which it was created, that is, not properly in the manner intended for it, denies the blessing of God (Exalted is He!). Whoever strikes another with his hand denies the blessing of the hand, since the hand was created for his defence from what would harm him and for the acquisition of what would benefit him, and not for harming another with it. He who looks at the face [of a woman who is] not a member of his household denies the blessing of the eye and the blessing of [the light of] the sun, since sight is made complete through both. These two were created only for [the servant] to see through them what is useful for his religion in his world and for protection from what harms him. The one [who looks at what is not lawful to him] has used [his eyes] for other than what they were meant for. This is because the purpose behind bringing creation into existence and the creation of this world, and its means of subsistence, is to assist mankind to reach God (Exalted is He!) through them.

There is no reaching God except by what He loves, and intimacy with Him in this world [comes from] shunning the delusions of this world. There is no intimacy except through continual remembrance (*dhikr*); and no love except through knowledge gained through continual reflection (*fikr*). And continual remembrance and contemplation are not possible except through the continuity of the body. The body can only be maintained by food, and food can only exist through the earth, and the water, and the air; and those can only exist through the creation of the heavens and the earth, and the creation of all the organs, visible and hidden.

All of this is for the sake of the body, and the body is the repository of the soul. What returns to God (Exalted is He!) is the soul that is serene through worship and knowledge. This is why God (Exalted is He!) said, *I have created jinn and mankind only that they should worship Me. No sustenance do I require of them [nor do I require that they should feed Me]*.[5] So whoever uses a thing other than in obedience to God, has denied the blessings of God in all the means which he necessarily had to use to commit the particular sin.

Let us give an example of a hidden wisdom that is not totally obscure, so that you may discern and recognise the ways of thankfulness and ingratitude for blessings. We say: silver and gold coins are a blessing created by God (Exalted is He!), through which this world is sustained. They are two minerals with no benefit in themselves, but mankind is obliged [to use] them insofar as every person needs food, clothing, and other things. A man may lack what he needs, but possess what he can dispense with, as for instance, someone may possess saffron but need a camel to ride. Someone who possesses a camel, perhaps, can do without it, but may need saffron. For an exchange to take place between the two, an evaluation must be made of the amounts [to be exchanged], since the owner of the camel will not exchange his camel for just any amount of saffron. As there is no comparison between saffron and a camel, it cannot be said that he should be given what is similar in weight or appearance. The same is true for whoever [wants to] buy a house with clothing, a slave with shoes, or flour with a donkey. These items do not resemble each other and it is not possible, therefore, to evaluate the worth of a camel compared to saffron. Thus, transactions will be very difficult.

These distinct, incongruous goods require a mediator to judge them fairly, and to reckon the degree and level of each. If the levels are determined and the degrees set in order, after that [we will] know the unequal from the equal. God (Exalted is He!) created gold and silver coins as two judges and mediators among the various kinds of wealth, so that wealth may be evaluated by them. So one may say: this camel is worth one hundred dinars and this amount of saffron is worth one hundred [dinars]. So these two things, since they are equal in one thing, are made equal. The settlement becomes possible by the two currencies, as there is no similarity in the substances of the two. If there is a similarity in their substances, it may be that an object has a special [value] for its owner but not necessarily for another, and the transaction will not be settled. Thus, God (Exalted is He!) created them [the coins] to be circulated and as fair judges between goods.

Another wisdom, is that through them, one has access to other things. This is because they are rare in themselves and there is nothing comparable to them. Their relation to various kinds of goods is one. He who possesses them is like he who possessed everything. He is not like he who owns a garment and does not own [anything] except the garment. [The owner of the garment] may need food, while he who has food may not need a garment as his need is for an animal to ride. The necessity then arises for something that has no form in itself and yet has the value of everything. Now a thing is on equal standing to different objects when it has no particularly beneficial characteristic; like a mirror that has no colour and yet reflects every colour. Similarly, coins are of no use in themselves, but they are a means to everything needed. It is like a letter [of the alphabet]; it has no meaning in itself, but makes apparent the meanings of other [words]. This then is the second wisdom. And in them [coins] is other wisdom which would be lengthy to narrate.

Anyone who uses them in a way that is incompatible with the wisdom [in them] contradicts the intended purpose of the wisdom and is ungrateful for the blessing that God (Exalted is He!) has placed in them. Therefore whoever hoards them, wrongs them and nullifies the wisdom in them. He is like one who places the ruler of Muslims in jail, thereby preventing him from making rulings. Indeed, when coins are hoarded, the wisdom [in them] is lost, as is their intended purpose. Gold and silver dirhams and dinars were not created, for example, for Zayd or for ʿAmr specifically, since individuals have no need for them in themselves. They are two minerals, created to be circulated. They are standards among people and identify the value and measure of things.

God (Exalted is He!) reveals to those who are incapable of reading the divinely written lines written on the tablets of creation with a divine script, without any letters or sounds and which cannot be perceived with the eye of sight, but only through inner vision—He reveals to them through what they hear from His Messenger (may God bless him and grant him peace), in the form of letters and sounds, the meaning of that which they were unable to understand. For the Exalted said, *Those who hoard up gold and silver and do not expend them in the way of God—give them the tidings of a painful chastisement.*[6] Anyone who makes out of dinars and dirhams vessels of gold or silver is ungrateful for the blessing and is worse than he who hoards. His example is that of one who seeks to subject the ruler of a country [to the labours of] weaving, tax collecting and manual work; imprisonment is easier than this! This is because pottery, lead and brass are suitable substitutes for gold and silver in storing liquids; and vessels are [only] for storing liquids. But pottery and iron are not suitable for the purpose for which coins are used. For he who is incapable of discerning this for himself, God has interpreted it and said [through the Prophet] that, 'He who drinks from a vessel of gold or silver, it is as if he were pouring into his stomach the fire of Hell.'[7]

All those who charge interest on silver and gold coins are ungrateful for the blessing and commit a transgression. For they were created for something other than themselves; as there is no purpose in their substances. If [a servant] trades in their substances, he uses them for a purpose contrary to the wisdom that was intended, since seeking money for other than what money was intended for is wrong. If one possesses a garment but no money, he may not be able to buy food or a riding animal, since food and a riding animal are not sold for a garment. Then the man is excused for selling it [the garment] in order to obtain money. For with this he reaches his goal. Therefore, [gold and silver coins] are two means to something else and are not ends in themselves. Their position among [the various kinds of] wealth is like the function of a letter (*ḥarf*) among words. As the grammarians say, 'The particle is that which brings meaning in conjunction to other [elements of the sentence].'[8] [It is] like the role of a mirror [in relation] to colours. If he who has money is permitted to sell it for money, he takes the exchange as the end purpose of his action, so the money is tied to him, and becomes equivalent to a hoarded treasure. To shackle a ruler is wrong, as it is wrong to despatch mail incorrectly or to withhold it [completely]. Thus the only purpose in selling money for money is hoarding, and it is an injustice.

You may ask, 'Why is the purchase of one sort of coins by another permissible and not the purchase of the same [sort of] coins?' Know that coins differ from each other in the attainment of their purpose. If the attainment is facilitated by one of them, because it is available, like silver coins, it can be used. The prevention [of the circulation] of money is what confounds its specific purpose: facilitating the acquisition of something else with it. The sale of a silver coin for a silver coin is lawful because they are equal, though an intelligent person would not desire it, and no merchant works in this manner, for it is nonsense. It is like putting a dirham on the ground and picking the same [dirham] up again. We do not fear that intelligent people will spend their time putting a dirham on the ground and picking it up again, so we do not prohibit it.

[There is no reason] to prohibit what people do not covet, except [in the case] when one thing is better than the other. And that also is not likely to happen because the owner of something of quality will not accept [to exchange it] for its inferior.[9] Consequently, no contract is entered into. It is possible that [someone] demands a greater quantity of what is inferior [in exchange for the same superior item]. Certainly, we could prevent him from doing it as we consider 'superiority' or 'inferiority' to be meaningless [in themselves]; superiority and inferiority must only be taken into account in terms of their applications. There is no need to go into detailed descriptions of the attributes of something that is not an end in itself. The one who transgresses is the one who mints the coins unequal in their good and bad [qualities], causing them to be desired in themselves when they should not be so desired.

But if he sells a dirham with a dirham as a loan, no one would undertake this except a forgiving person who intends to do good. For in the loan is a kindness [which is] honourable and voluntary, so he [the one making the loan] is praised and rewarded. Whereas a loan for profit is neither praiseworthy nor rewarding. Even more, it is an injustice because it does away with a form of kindness and replaces it with profit.

Just as [money was created for a purpose], foods were created to nourish and heal, so they should not be diverted from their purpose. If it [food] is allowed to become a commodity, it will become restricted in the hands [of those who trade in it] and its consumption will be held back. God created food only to be consumed and the need for foodstuffs is great. It is necessary for foodstuffs to be released by whoever can dispense with them to those in need. Only he who is not in need of foodstuffs trades in them. If he possesses food and is in need of it, why does he not consume it? Why does he turn it into a saleable commodity? If he turns it into a saleable commodity, then he should sell it to someone who needs it for something, other than food, which he [himself] needs and not for another transaction of food which he does not need. This is why the law curses the hoarder.[10] We have discussed the penalties for this in the *Book of Earning a Livelihood*.[A]

Certainly, one who sells wheat for dates is excused, since one item does not fill the place or purpose of the other. Whereas one who sells a quantity of wheat for [the same] quantity of wheat is without excuse. [What he does] is a mockery. Yet, there should be no need to prohibit this because people would not consider it except in the case of a difference in quality. To exchange that which is superior with its poorer equivalent would not be

[A] *K. ādab al-kasb wa'l-maʿāsh* (*Iḥyā'*, II.3, pp. 62–88).

acceptable to he who owns the superior one. However, the superior can be exchanged with two inferiors.

But as foodstuffs are among the necessities of life, when that which is superior [among them] is equal in usefulness to that which is inferior, differing only in it being a luxury, the law no longer considers it a luxury when it [fulfils] a necessity. Therein lies the wisdom of the law in prohibiting usury. This was made clear to us after we left the realm of *fiqh*.[A] So let us return to the realm of *fiqh* in this, as it is here superior to other sciences. We give preference to the legal school of Shāfiʿī (may God grant him His mercy) as, among those [things] that can be weighed, it gives priority to foodstuffs. For if gypsum can be included [as it is among those things that can be weighed], then it would be even more appropriate to include clothing and animals.[B] Were it not for his inclusion of salt as a foodstuff (*qūt*), the legal school of Mālik would be the most correct of all the schools of law in this matter.[C] Now, everything the law concerns itself with must be given a definition. This [salt] can be defined as a '*qūt*,' a foodstuff, or as a '*maṭʿūm*,' an edible thing. The law considered it best to include all that which is necessary for survival under '*maṭʿūm*.'[D]

The definitions the law gives may encompass rulings, the reasons for which are not at first obvious. The definitions must be made, because if they are not clear people may become confused in following the purpose of the law as it applies to different cases and peoples. The particular legal ruling (*ḥadd*) is then imperative while the fullness of its applicability differs according to different situations and peoples. This is why God (Exalted is He!) said, *Whosoever trespasses the bounds of God has wronged himself.* [11]

[A] Ghazālī means when he stopped teaching *fiqh*.

[B] Because the latter are of more immediate use for humanity than gypsum.

[C] *Qūt* is here understood as a foodstuff that is sufficient for survival and not just something that can be eaten.

[D] Meaning that the other schools of law, and Ghazālī himself, disagree with Mālik's definition.

The laws of the different religions agree on the principles, where they differ is in the restrictions they apply. For example, the law of Jesus son of Mary (peace be upon him) sets the ruling on wine at not becoming drunk. Our law sets the ruling at it [wine] being an intoxicant and [on the concern] that a small amount [of consumption] may lead to a greater amount. Just as the definition of something is part of its totality, all that falls under a ruling because of its type falls under the prohibition.

This is one of the hidden wisdoms of the rule of the two currencies [gold and silver]. It is necessary to consider thankfulness for, and denial of, a blessing in this way. The particular wisdom for which a thing was created should not be deviated from. No one understands this except he who knows the wisdom—*and the one who is given wisdom, has been given abundant good.*[12] The essence of wisdom, however, cannot be encountered by hearts that are the dung-heaps of desires and the playgrounds of the devils. *Only those who possess insight* (ulu'l-albāb) *heed* [*this*].[13] Therefore, he (may God bless him and grant him peace) said, 'Were it not that the devils hover over the hearts of the children of Adam, they would surely see the kingdom of heaven.'[14]

If you understand this statement, then measure your movement, stillness, speech, silence and every one of your deeds by it. For every act that proceeds from you is either thankfulness or ingratitude; as it is impossible to be free of both. We sometimes describe these [acts] through the language of jurisprudence which is common to most people with [terms like] 'disliked' (*karāha*) and 'prohibited' (*ḥaẓar*). And all [such acts] are considered prohibited for the people of insight (*arbāb al-qulūb*).

I shall give an example. Were I to purify myself [after a call of nature] with the right hand, I will have denied the blessing of both hands.[A] God created both hands for you and made one stronger than the other; because of its superiority, the stronger deserves the maximum honour and preference. Preferring the

[A] In Islam, the right is always given preference over the left.

weaker hand is straying from justice and God commands only justice. He Who has given you two hands made actions necessary for you, some of which are honourable, such as taking up the Qur'ān; some of which are lowly, such as the removal of impurity. If you pick up a Qur'ān with the left hand and cleanse impurity with the right, you have used what is honourable for what is base, depriving it of its right and wronging it.

Likewise, if I spit in the direction of the *qibla*,[A] for example, or I relieve myself in its direction, I deny the blessing of God (Exalted is He!) in the creation of the directions of space and the spaciousness of the world. For He created [four] directions to be your range of movement, and He divided the directions into those He does not honour and those He honours, by placing in one of the directions a house which He ascribed to Himself.[B] He did this in order to bind your heart to it, and bind your body in that direction through the binding of the heart, thus giving it constancy and dignity whenever you worship your Lord.

Your deeds, then, are divided into those which are honourable (*sharīf*), such as acts of obedience, and those which are base (*ḥasīs*), such as relieving oneself and spitting. If you spit in the direction of the *qibla*, you wrong the *qibla* and deny the blessing God (Exalted is He!) gave you in the position of the *qibla*, which He positioned for the perfection of your worship.

Similarly, if you put your shoe on and begin with the left foot, you have done wrong, because the shoe is a protection for the foot and the foot benefits by it. In everything from which benefit is derived precedence must be given to what is most honoured. This is justice and the fulfilment of wisdom. Its opposite is a sin and a denial of the blessing of the shoe and the foot. [To do] thus is a great [sin] among the gnostics, even though the jurists call it 'disliked' acts (*makrūh*). [It is so] to the extent that one of them gathered measures of wheat to give in charity, and when he

[A] The direction taken in prayer towards Mecca.

[B] The Kaʿba in Mecca.

was asked why, he replied, 'I once put my shoes on and inadvertently began with the left foot. Now, I desire to atone for it with charity.' Excellent is the jurist who does not enlarge upon these matters because they are simple. Rather, [what is required] is to reform the common people, whose level is close to the level of cattle. They are immersed in wrongs, more overwhelming and far beyond any examples [that can be given] of these wrongs.

It is shameful to say that whoever drinks wine and takes the goblet with his left hand has transgressed [the law] in two respects: one is the drink, the other by using the left hand. It is [also] shameful to say that he who sells wine on Friday at the time of the call to prayer is unfaithful [to his religious obligations] in two respects: one is in selling wine, the other is in selling it at the time of the call to prayer. [Likewise] it is shameful to say that he who relieves himself in the prayer niche of a mosque with his back to the *qibla* [has transgressed in two ways]. It is a disgrace to combine his abandonment of manners when fulfilling a call of nature, by saying that he did not keep the *qibla* to his right. The [acts of] disobedience are all wrongs! Some are greater than others and some of them surpass others!

The master, therefore, may punish his servant for using his knife without his permission. Yet if the dearest of his sons were killed by that knife, [disobedience of his] command and vexation would not remain within him about the use of the knife without his permission.[A]

The conduct of the prophets and saints, and what we [each] forbear of the law with regards to the general public, is necessary for this reason. [In reality] every disobedience deflects from justice, denies the blessing and distances one from the degrees that lead the servant to the levels of nearness [to God]. Yes, some of these vile things render the servant unable [to attain] nearness and reduce his rank! Others take him entirely beyond the limits of nearness to the distant world which is the abode of the devils!

[A] That is, because of the far greater gravity of the murder of his son.

Similarly, he who breaks the branch of a tree needlessly, for no immediate and essential purpose, nor a true need, denies the blessing of God (Exalted is He!) in the creation of trees and the creation of the hand. As for the hand, it was not created for foolishness, but for obedience and the acts that aid in obedience. As for the tree, God (Exalted is He!) created it and created roots for it and watered it. He created the power of nourishment and growth in it to enable it to attain the utmost limit of its growth so that His servants benefit from it. Cutting it before it reaches its full potential, without [a good cause that] benefits His servants, contradicts the aims of His wisdom and strays from justice. But, if one has a rightful objective for that, then cutting [it] is permitted for him, since trees and animals can be sacrificed for the purposes of humanity. They are both transitory things, fading away, and the dissolution of the base thing [in order] that the more honoured thing may survive for a time is closer to justice than wasting them both. This is indicated in His words, *And He has subjected to you, as from Him, all that is in the heavens and on earth.*[15]

If [a branch] is broken off from a tree belonging to someone else, [the person] has committed a wrong, even if he is in need! This is because each tree cannot supply the needs of all the servants of God; it is sufficient for the needs of one. It would be unjust to give preference and a special claim to one servant over others, [unless] the possessor of the special claim is he who obtained the seed, put it into the ground, watered it with care and kept up its maintenance; he would thus have priority over all others and his case would be stronger because of that fact. If that seed grows in uncultivated ground,[16] not by the effort of any man who has a special claim in its place of planting, or its planting, then a different claim becomes necessary. He who claims it first has a right to it. For to him belongs precedence. It is fair that he should merit it more [than others]. The jurists have expressed this preference by the term 'property'. However, it is a completely figurative [term], since there is no property save that which belongs to the King of kings, to Whom belong the heavens and the earth. How shall the servant be a property owner when he does not own himself, but is owned by Another? Indeed, created beings are the servants of God and the earth is the table of God![17] He has permitted them food from His table to the extent of their need, just as the king prepares a table for his servants. Thus when someone takes a morsel with the right hand and his finger joints encompass it, and another servant comes along wanting to snatch it from his hand, [the second servant] would have no right to it, not because the morsel became the possession of [the first servant] when he took it in his hand, for the hand and the owner of the hand are also owned [by God]. [He has no right to it] because each morsel in itself does not satisfy the need of all the servants. Thus the personal claim is fair in its preference [of one person] and in its particularity. Picking something up is a special act that makes the servant its sole owner. It prohibits the second, who has no special claim rivalling [that of the first].

It is in this manner that we should understand the command of God in His servants. We say: whoever takes more than he needs of the riches of this world, hoarding it and holding fast to it, while among the servants of God someone needs it, is unjust. He is of those who hoard gold and silver, expending none of it in the way of God. And the way of God is obedience to Him. Through obedience to God, the riches of this world become a provision for people, and their necessities and needs are satisfied and fulfilled through them.

The above does not enter within the bounds of legal juristic opinions,[A] because it is not possible to judge [individual] needs and because individuals differ in their perception of future poverty and because the length of a life span cannot be known. So when dealing with uneducated people (*al-ʿāma*), one should use the same means as one uses to teach children sobriety, humbleness

[A] *Fatāwā* (pl of *fatwa*). The practice of issuing a legal opinion on a matter began in the period of the rightly-guided caliphs (*al-rāshidūn*, 11–40/632–661). See Ṣubḥī Maḥmaṣānī, *Falsafat al-tashrīʿ fī'l-Islām: The Philosophy of Jurisprudence*, trans. Farhat Ziadeh (Leiden: E. J. Brill, 1961), pp. 17, 18.

and silence with regard to all speech that is unimportant. This is because of their [the children's] immaturity; they are not able to bear more. That we desist from objecting to their play and frivolity does not mean that play and frivolity are right. Therefore, we permit the common people to keep [their] possessions and confine charitable handouts (*infāq*) to *zakat*[A] because of their tendency towards avarice and not because this is the extent of its reality. The Qur'ān indicates it in His saying (Exalted is He!), *If He should ask you for all of them, and press you, you would hoard it.*[18]

Indeed, the truth that is not obscure and the justice that has no injustice in it is that the servants of God should not take from the wealth of God save what is needed for a travellers provision. For all the servants of God are riders on their bodies [that are like mounts moving] towards the presence of the King, the Judge. The one who takes more [than he needs] for himself, thus denying another rider who is in need, is unfair; he abandons justice; he goes beyond the aim of the [intended] wisdom; he is ungrateful for the blessings of God (Exalted is He!) in the Qur'ān, the Messenger of God, the intellect, and all the reasons by which he knows that anything greater than the rider's provision is harmful to him in this world and the Hereafter.

Whoever understands the wisdom of God (Exalted is He!) in all the varieties of existents is able to undertake the duty of thankfulness. An exhaustive [listing] of this requires volumes, and even then, we will have done only little justice to it. We have elucidated this much to show the truth in His (Exalted is He!) statement, *For few indeed are those that are thankful among My servants.*[19] Iblīs, the Accursed One, delights in the saying, '*You will not find most of them thankful.*'[20] He who has not understood the meaning (*ma*ʿ*nā*) of all the above will not be able to understand the meaning of this verse and [the meaning of other] matters beyond this

[A] Ghazālī discusses this subject earlier in *K. asrār al-zakāt* (*Iḥyā'*, I.5, pp. 215–237). It was translated by Faris, *Almsgiving*, pp. 27, 28; in it, Ghazālī discusses niggardliness.

in which lives have been spent without even attaining their first principles. The interpretation of the verse and of its words is clear to all those who know the language. [Yet,] you will find there is a difference between the [literal] interpretation of the verse and its [true] meaning.

You may say: The conclusion of this discussion is that God (Exalted is He!) has a wisdom [for every thing] and He has made some of the deeds of the servants a way to fulfil this wisdom and to attain its intended goal, and He has made some of their deeds obstacles to the fulfilment of the wisdom. Every act that conforms to the requirement of the wisdom, such that the wisdom may reach its goal, is thankfulness. Every [act] that opposes and obstructs the causes [of things] from reaching the intended goal is ingratitude. All this is understood. Nevertheless, there is still a problem: the acts of a servant which are divided into what fulfils wisdom and what impedes it are also an act of God (Exalted is He!). So, where is the servant in all of this that he may be sometimes thankful and sometimes ungrateful?

Know that a full realisation of this is based in the flow of a great ocean from the knowledge by unveilings (*ʿulūm al-mukāshafāt*). We have, earlier, given intimations of allusions to them [unveilings]. Now we will embark on a concise interpretation of their end and goal and whoever knows the speech of birds will understand.[A] He who denies it is not able to walk along the path, let alone roam in the heavens like a bird in flight.

We say: God, Almighty and Majestic in His Might and Pride, has an attribute from whence creation (*khalq*) and origination (*ikhtirāʿ*) proceed. This attribute is higher and more majestic than the sight of those who formulate languages [lit., ones who put

[A] *Manṭiq al-ṭayr* ('the speech of the birds,' Q.xxvii.16) refers to Solomon's wisdom and the prosperity of the children of Israel at the time of his reign. The verse reads, *Solomon was David's heir and he said, 'Men, we have been taught the speech of the birds, and we have been given of everything; surely this is indeed the manifest bounty.'*

language on paper].[A] They are unable to express the very essence of the majesty and the particularity of its reality. There is not, in the world, a verbal expression for its height, and the language used by writers falls short of expressing the beginnings of its emanation.[B] Their vision falls short of its summits, just as the vision of bats decreases in the light of the sun; not because of the obscurity of the sunlight, but because of the weakness of the vision of the bats. Those who have acquired vision, so that they see its majesty, are compelled to borrow from the base world of language-users an expression to convey the outlines of its reality in a very feeble way. So they borrow the term 'power' (*qudra*) for it.

This 'borrowing' has emboldened us to give expression and say: God (Exalted is He!) has an attribute that is [called] power and it is the source of creation and creative ability. In existence (*wujūd*), creation is divided into parts and particular attributes. The source of the division of these parts and their particularities is another attribute, for which we are compelled as above to borrow a term: 'will' (*mashī'a*). For language-users, [this term] evokes a matter with a general application. The inadequacy of the term 'will' to describe that attribute and its reality is similar to the inadequacy of the term 'power.'

Now, the acts that proceed from power are divided into those that progress towards the purpose of their wisdom, and those that fall short of the goal. Each [act] is connected to the attribute of the will because of its dependence on the particularities through

[A] That is, an attribute that cannot be seen by people or described through language.

[B] *Ishrāq* ('emanation' or 'radiance') became a technical term in later Sufism; it refers to the combination of philosophical reflection and mystical experience. See L. Massignon, 'Taṣawwuf,' *SEI*, p. 581. Attempts were made to trace it back to earlier mystics, both Muslim and non-Muslim. Ghazālī may not have intended all the meanings that later Sufis gave the term, rather he points to the failure of language to convey the depth of religious experience. Cf. Henry Corbin's *Creative Imagination in the Sufism of Ibn ʿArabī*, trans. Ralph Manheim (Princeton, NJ: Princeton University Press, 1969), pp. 20, 36, 299, 300.

which parts and differences come about. So we have borrowed the expression 'love' (*maḥabba*) to denote that which achieves its goal, while the expression 'hatred' (*karāha*) is utilised for that which falls short of the goal. It is said that they are both included in the attribute of will, but for each there is a particular application. [Yet,] those who seek to understand [solely] through words and languages imagine that the terms love and hatred are general [terms].

His servants, who are part of His creation and creative ability, are divided into those for whom the everlasting will has decreed that [God] will use them to hamper His wisdom from attaining its goal—this is predestined in them by the exigencies and incentives that dominate them—and those for whom it was predestined in eternity that He will use them, in some circumstances, in the pursuit of His wisdom towards its goal.

Each group has a specific relationship to the will. I borrow the expression 'approval' (*riḍā*) for those who are utilised for the fulfilment of the [divine] wisdom, and I borrow the expression 'wrath' (*ghaḍab*) for those who are utilised to hamper wisdom from reaching its goal. An act which hampers wisdom from reaching its goal will issue from he who is the subject of eternal wrath, and for it I will borrow the term 'ingratitude' (*kufrān*), and will add to it 'the affliction of being cursed' (*naqmat al-laʿn*) and 'censure' (*madhamma*) as additional punishments.

From he who is the subject of eternal approval issues an act that drives wisdom to its goal. [For this], I will borrow the term 'thankfulness' (*shukr*) and will add to it the mantle of 'praise' (*thanā'*) and 'reward' (*iʿṭā'*) as an increase in contentment, acceptance and drawing near. This is followed by a robe of praise and profuse commendation, an overflow of contentment, acceptance and a [welcome] reception.

The conclusion is that it is God (Exalted is He!) Who grants beauty and it is He Who then praises it. It is He Who warns, then He Who rebukes and destroys. An example of this is the king who cleans his filthy servant, then clothes him with the best of his clothes. When his attire is complete, the king says, 'O handsome one! How beautiful you are, how beautiful your clothes, how clean is your face.' In reality, He is the beautifier and He is the praiser of beauty. It is He Who is praised in every case. Thus, the 'meaning' (*maʿnā*) is that He only praises Himself; while the servant is the goal of praise in that which is outward (*ẓāhir*) and that which has form (*ṣūra*).

This is how matters are in eternity. Thus, causes and effects are linked together by the Lord of lords, the Causer of causes. This does not occur through agreement and discussion, but by will, wisdom, rule of truth and decisive command, for which I borrow the term 'divine decree' (*qaḍā'*). It [all happens] in the blink of an eye or quicker. Thus, the ocean of what is preordained overflows by order of that absolute decree, with that which has been predestined. The term 'divine predestination' (*qadar*) is used for the succession of individual things which are predestined, one after another. Therefore, the term 'divine decree' (*qaḍā'*) is applied to the one, whole, command; while the term 'divine predestination' is applied to details continuing endlessly. It has been said that nothing escapes the decree and predestination.

For some servants, the question arises as to why the division [into parts] requires this amount of detail. And, how can there be justice given the [degrees] of difference and preference? Some of them, because of their shortcomings, cannot grasp the essence of this matter and cannot encompass its totality. They are restrained by a bridle that prohibits them from rushing headlong into a profusion they cannot bear. It was said to them, 'Be silent, for you were not created for this!' *He shall not be questioned about what He does, but they shall be questioned.*[21]

For some, their niche[A] is filled with light borrowed from the light of God (Exalted is He!) in the heavens and the earth. Their oil was from the start pure, almost luminous, *though no fire had*

[A] Allusion to the heart and its light and vision. Ghazālī's discussion here is based on the Verse of Light (Q.xxiv.35).

touched it. Then it was touched by fire and it lit up, *light upon light*. The world of sovereignty, then, shone before them by the light of their Lord, and they came to know things as they are in themselves. It was said to them, 'Conduct yourselves according to the conduct [worthy] of God (Exalted is He!) and keep quiet. If what is predestined is discussed, then be silent,[22] for the walls have ears and around you are those whose vision is weak. So, follow the course of your weaker ones, and do not lift the veil of the sun to the sight of bats, for that would be the cause of their destruction. Take on yourselves the character traits of God (Exalted is He!) and descend to the heaven of this world from your distant loftiness, that the weak may befriend you and borrow something of the permanence of your radiant lights from behind your veils, just as the bats borrow [their sight] from the remaining light of the sun and of the stars at night. They [the weak] will live by it a life that is suited to their character and state, though not the life of those who reside in the fullness of the light of the sun. They will be like those about whom it was said,

> We drank a good drink in the presence of the Good,
> Likewise, the drink of the good is [always] good.
> We drank and we poured its excess on the ground,
> The ground also receives a portion from the cup of the generous one.[23]

Such is the first of this matter and its last. You will only understand it if you are worthy of it. If you are worthy of it, the eye [of the heart] (*baṣīra*) will open and you will see. You will have no need of a guide to lead you. The blind can be led, but only to a certain extent. For if the way becomes narrow and sharper than a sword and finer than [a strand of] hair,[A] the bird is able to fly over it, but cannot pull along a blind person. If the passage is narrow and fluid, like the fluidity of water, and the crossing is possible

[A] This is an allusion to the *sirāt*, the path or bridge, on which all will pass on the Day of Judgement.

only by swimming, and he possesses the skill of swimming, [he can] cross over by himself, although he may not be able to pull another along behind him.

Treading along the path of these matters, in comparison to the path that the majority of people follow, is equivalent to walking on water in relation to walking on earth. Swimming can be learned, but walking on water is not acquired by learning, rather it is acquired by the power of certainty. For this reason, when it was said to the Prophet (may God bless him and grant him peace) that, 'Jesus (peace be upon him) is said to have walked on water,'[A] he (may God bless him and grant him peace) replied, 'Had he increased in certainty, he would surely have walked on air.'[24]

These, therefore, are allusions to the meanings of hatred and love, contentment and wrath, and thankfulness and ingratitude, [all of which] do not come under the sciences of practical transactions. With respect to this, God (Exalted is He!) gave an example on the level of human understanding, [when He said] that jinns and mankind were created only to worship Him.[25] Consequently, the wisdom in their creation is their worship.

God then says that He has two servants, one of whom He loves. His name is Gabriel, the Holy Spirit, the Faithful. He is beloved [of God], obedient, honest and unshakable. God hates the other and his name is Iblīs [Satan]. He is the accursed who was given respite until the Day of Judgement. [God] assigned guidance to Gabriel, for He (Exalted is He!) said, *Say: 'The Holy Spirit sent it down from your Lord in truth;'*[26] and He (Exalted is He!) said, *By His command He sends the Spirit to any of His servants He pleases;*[27] and [God] assigned temptation to Iblīs, for He said, *he will lead [others] astray from His way.*[28] To lead astray is to impede the servants from reaching the goal of wisdom. Observe, then, how He has attributed it to the servant with whom He is wrathful. Guidance is conducting them to the goal. And observe how He attributes it to the servant whom He loves. This pattern is before you in

[A] Matthew 14:25–33; Mark 6:48–52; and John 6:16–21.

ordinary life. A king, if he needs someone to give him [something] to drink and someone to cup him and clean his house of all that is dirty, appoints two servants. He will appoint the worst and the basest to cupping and cleaning only; and he will entrust the carrying of good drink to the best, the most perfect and the most loved by him.

You must not say, 'This is my deed, and His deed is not possible without mine.' You are mistaken if you attribute it to yourself! Rather, it is He Who turns your motive to the hateful deed specifically by means of the hateful one, and the loved deed by [means of] the beloved one, for the fulfilment of justice. His justice is fulfilled sometimes by matters [of which] you have no part, and sometimes it is fulfilled in you, as you are also among His acts. Your motivation, your ability, your knowledge, your actions, and all that causes your movements are all His act, which conform to justice and from which harmonious acts issue.

However, you only see yourself. You think that what appears before you in the visible world has no [underlying] cause in the invisible world and the world of sovereignty. Therefore, you attribute it to yourself. You are like the boy, who, at night watches a display of puppets, whose images appear from behind a curtain. They dance, shout, stand and sit. They are made of rags, which do not move by themselves. They are made to move by fine, thin threads (like hairs) that cannot be seen in the darkness of night. The ends [of the threads] are in the hands of the puppeteer, who is hidden from the sight of the boys. They [the boys] have fun and marvel because they think that these rags dance, play, stand and sit. But the adults[A] know that these [puppets] are moved and do not move [themselves], even if they do not know exactly how it happens. The spectator who knows some of the details [of how it happens], does not know it as the puppeteer knows it; for the command is his and the [strings] are pulled by his hands.

The same can be said for the people of this world who are like

[A] Literally, 'the intelligent.'

children. [In fact,] all of mankind are like children in comparison to scholars (*ʿulamāʾ*). [The former] look and think that they are the movers; they credit themselves with this, while the majority of scholars know that they are 'moved,' even if they do not know how the movement occurs. As to the gnostics and those who are firmly established in knowledge (*al-rāsikhūn fī ʾl-ʿilm*), they perceive with the acuteness of their vision fine spidery threads, and even finer [ones], hanging from the heavens and attached to the limbs of the people of the earth. These threads cannot be perceived by physical sight because of their fineness, [but those firmly established in knowledge] can see the places from which the ends of the threads are suspended. They see that the places of suspension are handles in the hands of the angels, the movers of the heavens. They also witness the angels of the heavens awaiting the command that has descended to the angels of the Throne from the lordly presence, for *they do not disobey God in what He commands and they perform what they are commanded.*[29] These spectacles are mentioned in the Qur'ān, *And in heaven is your provision, which you are promised.*[30] He has described the angels of the heavens as waiting for what He sends down to them of predestination and command in His saying, *He created seven heavens and of the earth a similar number. Through the midst of them (all) descends His Command: that you may know that God has power over all things, and that God comprehends all things in (His) Knowledge.*[31]

These are matters whose interpretation no one knows except God and those firmly established in knowledge.[32] Ibn ʿAbbās (may God be pleased with both of them) spoke about the special [claim] of those firmly established in knowledge to possess knowledge that others cannot comprehend, reciting the words of God (Exalted is He!), *Through the midst of them (all) descends His Command.*[33] He then said, 'Were I to tell [you] what I know of the meaning of these verses, you would surely stone me.' And in another version, 'You would surely say, "He is a non-believer."' But, let what we have said suffice. For the reins of speech have fallen away from the grip of the will and what is not from the sciences of practical transactions has become mingled with it, so we must [now] return to the objectives of thankfulness.

We say: If the reality of thankfulness is the use of the servant in the fulfilment of the wisdom of God (Exalted is He!), the most thankful servant is the most beloved of God and the closest of them to Him. The closest of them to God are the angels, and they also have a hierarchy, and a known station. The highest of them in degree of closeness is an angel whose name is Isrāfīl (peace be upon him).[A] Their level is high because they are themselves noble and devoted.[34] God (Exalted is He!) blessed the prophets (peace be upon them) through them, and they [the angels] are the most honoured of what is created on the face of the earth. The level of the prophets follows their level. They are a select [number] and God has guided the rest of humanity and perfected His wisdom through them.

The highest of them is our Prophet (may God bless him and grant him peace), since God perfected religion and sealed the prophets through him. Following them [the prophets] are those scholars who are heirs to the prophets.[35] They are, in themselves, righteous (*ṣāliḥūn*). God has made the rest of humanity better through them. The level of each of them is in relation to how much he has improved himself and others. Then just rulers follow them, because they have improved the world for people, just as the scholars have improved [the practice of] their religion. Because he combined religion, kingship and authority, our Prophet Muḥammad (may God bless him and grant him peace) was better than the rest of the prophets. God perfected the goodness of their religions and their world through him. The sword and rule were not given to any other prophet. After the scholars and just rulers come the

[A] Wensinck comments, 'He is considered the angel who reads out the divine decisions from the well-kept Tablet and transmits them to the Archangel to whose department they belong' (A. J. Wensinck, 'Isrāfīl,' *SEI*, p. 184). Chittick mentions the anticipated blowing of the Trumpet on two occasions by Isrāfīl, preparing for the accounting of Judgement Day (*Sufi Path of Knowledge*, p. 122).

righteous, who have only perfected their religion [for themselves] and improved themselves. The wisdom of God, therefore, was not completed through them, but rather in them. Beyond these are the rabble, the basest of the people.

Know that religion is established through the ruler. He should not be belittled, even if he is unjust and corrupt. ʿAmr b. al-ʿĀṣ (may God be pleased with him) said, 'An unjust *imām*[A] is better than persistent civil strife.'[36] The Prophet (may God bless him and grant him peace) said, 'There will be rulers over you whom you know and those whom you do not know. They will be corrupt but God may put much right through them. For if they do well, they are rewarded and thankfulness is incumbent upon you; while if they do evil, the fault is with them and patience is incumbent upon you.'[37]

Sahl said, 'He who denies the authority of the ruler is a heretic; and he whom the sultan summons, and he does not go, is an innovator.[B] He who goes to him [the sultan] without being summoned is ignorant.'

He was asked, 'Who is the best of men?' He replied, 'The ruler.' So it was said, 'We thought that the worst of men was the ruler.' He [Sahl] replied, 'Do not be hasty! God (Exalted is He) has two glances every day: one is for the safety of the possessions of Muslims; another is for the safety of their bodies. Then, God looks in [the ruler's] book and forgives him all his sins [for his protection of both].'[38]

He [Sahl] used to say, 'The black boards suspended on the doors are better than seventy storytellers reciting tales.'[39C]

[A] *Imām* here means leader.

[B] *Mubtadiʿ*: a person who brings something new into religion without knowledge of the law. *Bidʿa* is an important legal term.

[C] Böwering explains, 'the black pieces of wood suspended [*muʿallaqat*] at the doors of the [rulers of the] Muslims are of more use [*anfaʿ*] than seventy Qāḍīs passing judgement in the mosque [*qāḍiyan yaqḍūna fī'l-masjad*]' (*Mystical Vision*, pp. 58–75, and p. 67).

SECTION TWO

THE APPLICATIONS OF THANKFULNESS

[Thankfulness] is for blessings. Here we will discuss the meaning of a blessing, its divisions, levels, kinds and what is common to a particular and a general [blessing]. Indeed, enumerating the blessings of God (Exalted is He!) to His servants is beyond the capacities of mankind, as God said, *If you count the blessings of God, you will never number them.*[1] We will [first] present general matters which will be like laws for the understanding of the blessings. Then, we will concern ourselves with discussing particulars. And God guides to what is right.

CHAPTER TWELVE
An Exposition of the Nature of the Blessings and Their Divisions

KNOW that every good thing, [every] pleasure, [or] happiness—everything sought after and preferred—is called a blessing. But the true blessing is the happiness of the Hereafter (*al-saʿāda al-ākhiriyya*). To call something else a blessing or happiness is either erroneous or figurative. This is the case when worldly happiness (*al-saʿāda al-dunyawiyya*), which does not lead to the Hereafter, is called a blessing; this is a clear mistake. It may be correct to call something a blessing, but it is more correct to use [blessing] for the happiness of the Hereafter. Thus, every means that leads to the happiness of the Hereafter and facilitates it, either by one or more expedients, is designated as a sound and true blessing, because it leads to the real blessing. We shall [now] explain the divisions of the means that facilitate [happiness in the Hereafter] and the pleasures that are called blessings.

The first division: All that concerns us can be divided into what is beneficial in both this world and in the Hereafter, such as knowledge and good character (*ḥusn al-khuluq*); what is harmful in both, such as ignorance and bad character; what benefits in the present and harms in the Hereafter, such as delight in sensual pleasures; and into what harms and is painful in the present but benefits in the Hereafter, such as the suppression of desires and restraining the soul.

What is beneficial in the present and in the Hereafter together, such as knowledge and good character, is the real blessing. What is harmful to them and [what] contradicts them both is the real affliction. What is beneficial in the present and harmful for the Hereafter is an absolute calamity (*balā' maḥd*) [according to] those endowed with insight, while the ignorant consider it a blessing. An example of this is a hungry man who finds honey with poison in it. He counts it a blessing, being ignorant [of the poison]; if he learns of it, he knows that it leads to a calamity for him. That which is considered by those who have insight to be harmful in the present but of benefit in the Hereafter is considered by the ignorant as a calamity. An example of this is foul-tasting medicine, which is distasteful at the time it is taken, but cures diseases and illnesses and brings about health and safety. The ignorant child, when he is obliged to drink it, thinks it a trial, while the sensible person counts it as a blessing and assumes it is an act of kindness from the one who guides him to it, brings it closer, and prepares it as a means [to restore his health].

Likewise, a mother may prohibit cupping for her son, while the father may guide him to it. For the father sees the end result, because he focuses on his reason, while the mother is concerned about the present, because of her excessive love and ignorance [of the outcome]. The boy, because of his ignorance, assumes that his mother, unlike his father, acts out of kindness. He seeks her company and compassion and deems his father an enemy. Had he the intelligence, he would surely know that his mother is a hidden enemy in the form of a true friend, because preventing him from the cupping leads to diseases and suffering worse than the cupping. An ignorant friend is worse than a reasonable enemy. Now, every person is his own friend,[A] but an ignorant friend. This is why he may deal with it [his soul] as an enemy may not.

The second division: Know that the things of this world are intermingled—good mixed with evil. What is good in them—such as wealth, family, progeny, relatives, prominence and other matters—is never unequivocally so. However, they are divided into what is more beneficial than harmful, such as sufficient wealth,

[A] Literally, a friend to his own soul (*nafsihi*).

prominence and other matters; what is more harmful than beneficial to most people, such as much wealth and widespread prominence; and that in which harm and benefit are equal, but these matters differ according to [each] individual. A pious man may benefit from lawfully gained wealth, even if it is substantial. He will expend it for the sake of God in good deeds, and this wealth is a blessing for him. A man may also be harmed by possessing little if he persists in deeming it little, complains of his Lord and seeks increase for himself, then this will be a trial for him and a humiliation.

The third division: Know that from a different angle, good things are divided into what is desired for itself, not for an other; what is desired for an other; and what is desired both for itself and for an other. Now, the first is what is desired for itself, not for something else, such as the delight of beholding the countenance of God (Exalted is He!) and the happiness of encountering Him. In short, it is the happiness of the Hereafter, which has no end. [This kind] is not sought to gain access to another desired objective beyond it, rather it is sought for its own sake.

The second is what is intended for something else and is not desired originally for itself—like dirhams and dinars. For if needs were not fulfilled [by these monies], surely they would be equivalent to pebbles. But when they are a means to quick pleasures, they become loved in themselves among the ignorant, such that they gather them, hoard them, and transact with them usuriously. They consider them an end [in themselves]. A simile for these [people] is that of one who loves a person, and because of his love for this person, he also loves the messenger who brings them together. Then, in the love of the messenger, he forgets the original love and turns away from him for the remainder of his life. He continues in his preoccupation with, and care and regard for the messenger. This is the epitome of ignorance and error.

The third is what is sought [both] for itself and for something else—such as health and safety. These are sought after so that [the servant] may through them [engage in] remembrance and reflection which will lead to the encounter with God (Exalted is He!). Or they [are sought after] to gain the pleasures of this world. They are also sought after for themselves. [For example] a man may be able to dispense with something because he desires to save his leg [which was at risk], and yet he can, at the same time, desire the safety of his leg simply for its own sake.

Therefore, the thing that is only desired for itself is truly a good and a blessing. What is desired for itself and for something else, too, is a blessing, but less than the first. As for what is desired only for something else, such as the two currencies, they cannot be considered in themselves—in terms of their substances—as a blessing, but only in terms of their being a means. They are a blessing for the one who, aiming to obtain something, can do so only through them. If knowledge and worship are his purpose, and he has sufficient for the necessities of life, then to him gold and clay are equal and their existence and non-existence are the same. Perhaps their existence would divert him from reflection and worship. [In that case], they would be a trial and not a blessing.

The fourth division: Know that from another point of view good things are divided into the beneficial (*nāfiʿ*), the pleasurable (*ladhīdh*) and the beautiful (*jamīl*). The pleasurable is that which is enjoyed in the present; the beneficial is that which is of good in the long term; and the beautiful is what is preferred in all the states. Evils are also divided into [three]: the harmful (*ḍār*), the ugly (*qabīḥ*) and the painful (*mu'lim*).

Each of these two categories has two applications: total and limited. The total is that in which the three qualities are included. In the case of what is good, there is knowledge and wisdom, for they are beneficial, beautiful and pleasurable to the people of knowledge and wisdom. While in the case of the evil, there is ignorance, which is harmful, ugly and painful. The ignorant man feels the pain of his ignorance when he comes to know that he is ignorant. That is, when he sees another who is informed and sees himself ignorant. He experiences the suffering of inadequacy and the pleasurable desire for knowledge is stimulated in him. Thereupon, envy, pride and the bodily desires may attempt to prevent him from learning. Two opposing inclinations pull him back and forth, increasing his suffering. If he abandons learning, he suffers from ignorance and the onslaught of inadequacy; if he is occupied with learning, he suffers from abandoning the desires, putting aside pride and from the servitude imposed by studying. To be sure, such a person is in continual torment.

The second application is the limited. It brings together some, but not all, the attributes. There is that which is beneficial but painful, such as the cutting of a gangrenous finger or a foreign cyst from the body; and that which may be beneficial but is ugly, such as stupidity, which is beneficial in some cases. It has been said: he who has no intelligence is at ease. He does not concern himself with the consequences [of his actions]; so he relaxes in the present, until the time of his death. [Then] there is that which is beneficial from one aspect and harmful from another, such as when one casts wealth into the sea when one fears drowning. There is harm in [lost] wealth, but a benefit in the safety of the person.

The beneficial is divided into two: that which is necessary—like faith and good character—in the attainment of happiness in the Hereafter. Also, knowledge and action, since nothing can ever take their place. And, that which is not necessary. For example, [in medicine] oxymel will treat the yellow bile, but it [yellow bile] can also be treated by other means.

The fifth division: Know that 'blessing' describes every pleasurable thing. Pleasurable things, whether man partakes of them exclusively, or shares them with others, are of three types: intellectual (*ʿaqliyya*), bodily (*badaniyya*) shared with some animals, and bodily shared with all animals. As for the intellectual, like the pleasure of knowledge and wisdom, the hearing, sight, smell, taste, stomach and sexual organs do not derive pleasure from them. It is the heart that takes pleasure in them because of its exclusive possession of the faculty known as the intellect (*ʿaql*). This [intellectual] pleasure is the rarest and the most noble. It is rare because knowledge is only pleasing to a scholar, and wisdom is only pleasing to a sage. How few indeed are the people of knowledge and wisdom and how many are called by their name and designated by their appearances!

The nobility [of intellectual pleasure] derives from it being permanent; it does not perish, not in this world and not in the Hereafter, and you can never weary of it. One can have enough of food and grow tired of it, and when the sexual act is over one can be wearied by it. But it cannot be imagined that knowledge and wisdom can satiate or be wearisome. When he who is capable [of attaining to what is] noble and everlasting finds pleasure in the transitory and contemptible, then he is afflicted in his intelligence and will [consequently] be denied [what is noble] due to his fallen nature and his rejection.

The least that [can be said] about knowledge and intelligence is that, unlike wealth, they need no help or protection, since knowledge protects you while you protect wealth. Knowledge increases with expenditure, while wealth decreases with expenditure. Wealth can be stolen and public office taken away, but the hands of the thief cannot reach to snatch away knowledge, nor can it be exiled at the hands of the rulers. For its possessor is always in a spirit of tranquillity, while the owner of wealth and prominence is always gripped by apprehension.

Thus knowledge is always beneficial, pleasurable and beautiful in every state. Wealth sometimes leads to perdition, and sometimes leads to salvation. This is why God (Exalted is He!) criticised wealth in some verses of the Qur'ān and called it a good thing in others.[A] But most people are unable to grasp the pleasure

[A] The Qur'ān uses the singular and plural forms of *māl/amwāl* eighty-six times to refer to wealth and possessions. Positive and negative references are about evenly divided. Some address the 'believers', and others address the 'non-believers'. The first passage of the Qur'ān that brings *fitna* (test, trial, temptation) together with *amwāl* (wealth, property, possessions) is Q.VIII:28. It reads, *Know that your wealth and children are a test.* See also: Q.LXIV.7, 8, 10, 14; VI.53; XX.85.

of knowledge. This may be due to a lack of experience (*dhawq*),[A] for he who has no experience has no knowledge and no yearning; as yearning follows experience. Or, it may be due to a corruption of natures and a sickness of hearts, from indulging the desires—as when the sick person, who cannot sense the sweetness of honey, finds it bitter. Or, due to the inadequacy of the intelligence when [the person] has not yet attained to the quality by which he takes pleasure in knowledge—as when the nursing infant, who does not know the deliciousness of honey and fowl, takes pleasure only in milk. This does not mean that [honey and fowl] are not delicious, nor does the infant's love of milk indicate that it is the most delicious of things.

Those who fail to know the pleasure of knowledge are of three [kinds]: he whose intellect has not matured [lit. come to life], like a child; he who died after living [because of his] pursuit of desires; and he who falls ill from following his desires. His (Exalted is He!) statement, *in their hearts is a sickness*[2] refers to the sickness of the intellects. His (Almighty and Majestic) words *that he may warn whosoever is living*[3] refer to [the person] whose inner life is not active. For every person who is alive through his body but whose heart is dead [is considered by] God among the dead, even if the ignorant consider him alive. Likewise, martyrs are alive with their Lord, provided for and joyful, even if their bodies are dead.

The second type [of pleasure] is the pleasure that man shares with some animals, like the pleasure of leadership (*riyāsa*), conquest (*ghalaba*), and mastery (*istīlā'*). This is to be found among lions, tigers, and other animals.

The third type is the pleasure that man shares with all animals, like the pleasure of the stomach and of sexuality. These are the most widespread and the basest [of the pleasures]. All that crawls

[A] Literally, 'tasting,' Watt renders *dhawq* in Ghazālī's *al-Munqidh* as 'immediate experience' (*Faith and Practice*, p. 55) as does Othman (*Concept of Man*, p. 29).

and walks shares in them, even the worms and insects. He who overcomes this degree will [then] be confronted by the pleasure of conquest; and it is the most tenacious [of the pleasures] for the negligent. When this [too] is overcome, he ascends to the final [level], and the pleasure of knowledge and wisdom becomes the most dominant in him; especially the pleasure of the knowledge of God (Exalted is He!), and the knowledge of His attributes and His acts. This is the degree of the truthful (*ṣiddīqūn*). The perfection of this [level] is attained only when the grip of the love of leadership disappears from the heart. For the last fixation of the righteous is the love of leadership. Curbing the evil of the stomach and of sexuality is within the ability of the pious (*ṣaliḥūn*), [while] curbing the desire for leadership is only possible for the righteous. Repressing it completely so that it is no longer sensed at any time nor in any state is almost beyond the capacity of mankind. In some states the pleasure of knowing God (Exalted is He!) overwhelms the pleasure of leadership and conquest, but that does not continue throughout life. Rather, these [states] are followed by periods when the servant returns to [purely] human qualities. They exist [for him] but they are subjugated, and are not strong enough to prevent the soul from straying away from what is right.

For hearts may be divided fourfold: a heart that loves only God (Exalted is He!) and that only rests in an increase of knowledge of Him and contemplation of Him; a heart that does not know the pleasure of knowledge and the meaning of intimacy with God [because] its pleasure is prominence, leadership, wealth and all the bodily desires; a heart, the majority of whose states are intimacy with God (glory be to Him!) and delight in knowledge of Him and contemplation of Him, although [the servant] may descend in some states to human qualities; and a heart, most of whose states delight in human qualities, that occasionally takes pleasure in knowledge and gnosis.

As to the first [type of heart], if it is to be found at all, it borders on the impossible. As for the second, this world overflows with it. The third and fourth exist, but they are rare. It should not be imagined that they can be other than rare and exceptional. But, despite them being rare, their numbers vary, increasing and decreasing. The numbers [of the former] are greater in the eras that are close to, or at the time of the prophets (peace be upon them). With the passing of time, such hearts become increasingly scarce until the Hour draws near *when God's decree comes to pass.*[4]

This [third state] is rare because it is the beginning of the kingdom of the Hereafter. [Now] kingdom is precious and kings are few in number. So, just as [the person with both] great possessions and beauty is rare and most people are without either, so it is in the kingdom of the Hereafter. Indeed, this world is the mirror of the Hereafter; it is defined as the visible world, while the Hereafter is defined as the invisible world. The visible world belongs to the invisible world, just as the image in the mirror belongs to he who is looking in the mirror. The image in the mirror, even if it is second in degree of existence, is first with respect to your vision. For you cannot see yourself; you only do so through your image in the mirror. As a result, you come to know your image as a whole and, then, what it is made up of [lit. woven of]. This is a kind of reversal. In knowledge, that which in existence 'follows' becomes that which is 'followed'; what is behind comes to the fore. Reversal and inversion are necessary for this world.

Thus, this visible world of dominion is 'woven' of the invisible world of sovereignty. Among people, there are those for whom it has been made easy to see through contemplation (*naẓar al-iʿtibār*). No sooner do they look at anything in the world of dominion than they see it as an expression of the world of sovereignty. This expression is called a symbol. God has set forth the truth about it, for He said, *therefore, take heed* (iʿtabirū),[A] *O you who have eyes.*[5] Then, there are those whose vision is blinded and they do not take heed. Consequently, they are imprisoned in the world of dominion and the visible world. From this prison, the gates of Hell will

[A] *Iʿtabirū* comes from the same root (*ʿabara*) as *iʿtibār*.

be opened to them. This prison is filled with a fire whose purpose is to observe the hearts.[6] There is a veil between them [those whose sight is blinded] and the contemplation of essentials. When the veil is raised at death, they will come to know. God (Exalted is He!) has revealed the truth about this through the speech of those whom He made to utter the truth. They said, 'Paradise and the Fire are two created things. However, Hell can be perceived either by what is called the "knowledge of certainty" (*ʿilm al-yaqīn*) or by what is called the "vision of certainty" (*ʿayn al-yaqīn*).[A] The vision of certainty is only in the Hereafter, while the knowledge of certainty may be in this world, but only for those who have fully realised the "light of certainty" (*nūr al-yaqīn*).' For this reason God (Exalted is He!) said, *No, indeed, should you know through the knowledge of certainty you would surely see Hell,*[7] that is, in this world; and, *You shall surely see it with the eye of certainty,*[8] that is, in the Hereafter.

It is [now] clear why the heart which is worthy (*ṣāliḥ*) of the kingdom of the Hereafter cannot be other than rare; just as [is rare] the righteous (*ṣāliḥ*) in the kingdom of this world.

The sixth division: a summary of all the [above] blessings. Know that blessings are divided into what is sought as an end in itself and what is sought for a purpose. This purpose is the happiness of the Hereafter and it is summed up in four matters: permanence in being with no annihilation (*baqāʾ lā fanāʾ lah*); joy with no grief; knowledge with no ignorance; and riches with no subsequent poverty. These are the real blessings.

The Messenger of God (may God bless him and grant him peace) said, 'There is no life, save the life of the Hereafter.'[9] He said this once as a consolation for the soul during the heat of noon while digging the trench.[10B] He said this on another occasion in joy, to dissuade the soul from relying on the joy of this world; this

[A] Literally, the 'eye of certainty.'

[B] This is an allusion to the Battle of the Trench, fought for two weeks from 5 Dhū 'l-Qaʿda 5/31 March 627.

was when people encircled him before his farewell pilgrimage.[11]

A man prayed, 'Almighty God, I ask you for the most complete blessing (*tamām al-niʿma*).' The Prophet (may God bless him and grant him peace) then asked, 'And do you know what perfect blessing is?' He replied, 'No.' He [the Prophet] said, 'Perfect blessing is entrance into Paradise.'[12]

As for the means [to blessings], they are divided into [first]: the foremost and most essential, such as the virtues of the soul; these are followed in descending [order] of importance by the good qualities of the body which come in second [place]; then the degree of that which is outside the body, such as the things that surround the body, including wealth, kinsmen, and clan; and [finally] there are the means that combine what is external to the soul and what is internal to the soul, such as success and guidance.

Therefore the means to blessings are of four kinds. The first and most essential are the virtues of the soul (*al-faḍā'il al-nafsiyya*). Despite their variety, their source is in faith (*īmān*) and good character traits (*ḥusn al-khuluq*). Faith [itself] is divided into the knowledge by unveiling, that is, the knowledge of God (Exalted is He!), His attributes, His angels and His messengers; and the sciences of practical transactions. Good character is divided into two parts: abandonment of the demands of the desires and of wrath; this is called 'abstinence' (*ʿiffa*); and compliance with justice, both in renouncing the requirements of the desires, and in satisfying them so that one does not abstain completely nor does one proceed as one wishes [unrestrained]. Partaking and abstaining will then be in accordance with the scales of justice which God (Exalted is He!) revealed by the tongue of His Messenger (may God bless him and grant him peace) when He (Exalted is He!) said, '*In order that you not transgress the balance, establish weight with justice and fall not short in the balance.*'[13] Therefore, he who castrates himself to curtail the desire for sex; or he who desists from marriage while able [to marry], being safe from all defects; or he who abandons eating until he is too weak for worship, for the remembrance [of God] and for contemplation, [all these] 'fall short' in the balance of the scale. He who becomes completely engrossed in the appetite of the stomach and in sexuality has 'transgressed' the scale. Justice lies in the weight and valuation [of the scales] being free of 'transgression' or 'falling short'; [only] then are the two sides [of the scales] balanced.

Therefore, the specific virtues of the soul which bring one near God (Exalted is He!) are four: knowledge by unveiling, the sciences of practical transactions, abstinence and justice. These are not complete in most cases, except through the second kind, and these are bodily qualities. They are four in number: health, strength, beauty and longevity. These four conditions are not attained except by a third means, namely, the external blessings that surround the body and they are: wealth, kinsmen, prominence and nobility of the clan. Yet, [the servant] does not benefit from any one of these external and bodily means except by the fourth means, and they are what unite [the external means] with the inner virtues of the soul. These are four: the guidance of God (*hidāya*), His good counsel (*rushd*), His direction (*tasdīd*) and His support (*ta'yīd*).

The total sum of these blessings is sixteen. If we divide them into four, and we divide each [group] of four into four then [we will find] that they are all in need of each other, either 'by necessity' (*ḥāja ḍarūriyya*) or 'through benefit' (*ḥāja nāfiʿa*).

As to necessity, it is like the dependence of the happiness in the Hereafter on faith and good character; there is no possibility at all of achieving the happiness of the Hereafter except through them. *Man has only what he strives for,*[14] and all that one has in the Hereafter is what one has prepared [for oneself] in this world. The same [necessity] applies to the virtues of the soul through which this [above] knowledge is gained. Likewise, the disciplining of conduct is necessary for the health of the body.

As for benefit, in general it is like the need of the soul and bodily blessings for external blessings, such as wealth, renown, and kinsmen. For, perhaps, if [they were] lacking, then obstacles would affect some of the inner blessings. You may ask: how can the path to the Hereafter be in need of external blessings like wealth, family, prominence and kinsmen? Know that these secondary causes are similar to the wing that allows [a bird] to reach [its destination] and the tool that facilitates the goal.

As for wealth, the poor [person] with insufficient means who seeks knowledge and perfection is like a soldier going into battle without a weapon, or a falconer poised for the hunt without a bird. This is why the Prophet (may God bless him and grant him peace) said, 'Blessed is rightly [gained] wealth for the righteous man.'[15] And he (may God bless him and grant him peace) said, 'The best support in piety (*taqwā*) is wealth.'[16] And how can it not be so! A person without wealth loses his time seeking provision, finding clothing, a residence and the necessities of life. He is also exposed to all kinds of harm that keep him from the remembrance [of God] and contemplation. These [harms] are driven back only by the weapon of wealth. In addition, he [who has no money] is deprived of the excellence of the pilgrimage, *zakat*, voluntary charity (*ṣadaqāt*) and numerous [other] good deeds.

A wise man was once asked, 'What is true happiness?' He replied, 'Riches, for I observed that there is no life for the poor [person].' Then, it was asked, 'Tell us more!' He replied, 'Security, for I observed that there is no life for the fearful [person].' It was asked, 'Tell us more!' He replied, 'Good health, for I observed that there is no life for the sick [person].' It was asked, 'Tell us more!' He replied, 'Youth, for I observed that there is no life for old age.'[17] It may seen that [all] he mentioned are the good things of this world, but they are a blessing only to the extent that they are an aid to the Hereafter.

So the Prophet (may God bless him and grant him peace) said, 'He who awakens healthy in his body, secure in his home, with enough provision for his day, it is as if he were given the world in its entirety.'[18]

As for family and righteous children, one cannot deny the need for both. The Prophet (may God bless him and grant him peace) said, 'The best help in religion is a righteous wife.'[19] And regarding children, he (may God bless him and grant him peace) said, 'When the servant dies, his work comes to an end except from three [things]: a righteous child who will pray for him ...'[20] We have mentioned the benefits of a family and children in the *Book of Marriage*.[A]

As for near relations, when a man has many children and relatives, they are like eyes and hands to him. Through them the important worldly matters of his religion are made easier, [matters] which, were he alone, would occupy him at length. All of what frees your heart from the necessities of this world is a help to you in religion and is, therefore, a blessing.

As for renown and prominence, a man uses them to defend himself against humiliation and injustice. A Muslim cannot dispense with them. He will not be rid of an enemy who harms him or an oppressor who disturbs his knowledge, his work, his leisure time and his heart, which is his capital, except through renown and prominence. This is why it has been said, 'Religion and authority are twins.' And God (Exalted is He!) said, *Had God not driven back the people, some by means of others, the earth would surely have been corrupted.*[21] So, there is no purpose for prominence other than the possession of hearts, just as the only purpose of wealth is possession of dirhams. He who possesses wealth can have those who possess hearts[B] subservient to him and ward off harm from him. For, just as man needs a roof to protect him from the rain, a cloak to ward off the cold, a dog to drive back the wolf from his sheep, so he needs others to repel evil from him.

This is why prophets who did not possess kingship and power themselves appealed to rulers and sought prominence through them. Likewise, the scholars of religion [do not frequent rulers] with the intention to take from their coffers or achieve prominence and plenty in this world by following them. Surely you do not think that the blessing of God (Exalted is He!) upon His

[A] *Iḥyā'*, II.28.

[B] That is, those who have influence over others.

Messenger (may God bless him and grant him peace) in His helping him, perfecting his religion, granting him victory over his enemies, securing love in the hearts of his followers, until his renown and prominence were extended by God was less than His blessing upon him was when he was molested and struck, to the point that he was forced to flee and emigrate![22]

You may ask, 'Are the nobility of the clan and the honour of near relations blessings or not?' I will say: Yes. This is why the Messenger of God (may God bless him and grant him peace) said, 'The religious leaders are from the Quraysh.'[23] For this reason, he (may God bless him and grant him peace), who was among the most noble of men, was desirous of [affirming] his descent from Adam (peace be upon him).[24] He (may God bless him and grant him peace) said, 'Choose for your seed those who are most suitable.'[25] And he (may God bless him and grant him peace) said, 'Beware the "young woman from the dunghill."' So it was asked, 'Who is "the young woman from dunghill?"' 'The beautiful woman raised in a bad environment.'[26]

This [nobility of birth] is therefore among the blessings. I do not mean by it to marry into [the families] of iniquitous and worldly men, but to marry into the lineage of the Messenger of God (may God bless him and grant him peace), and that of the leading scholars, the righteous and the pious who are burnished with knowledge and [good] actions.

You may then ask, 'What is the meaning of the bodily qualities?' I reply that there is no hiding the great need for health, strength and longevity, since knowledge and action are only complete through them. For this reason, the Prophet (may God bless him and grant him peace) said, 'The greatest happiness is a long life in obedience to God (Exalted is He!).'[27]

Beauty receives slight consideration among matters pertaining to them [bodily qualities]. For it is said that it is sufficient for the body to be free from diseases that detract from the pursuit of good deeds. By my life, I must say that beauty is the least of the riches. Nevertheless, it, too, is a good thing both in this world, where its benefits are obvious, and in two ways with regard to the Hereafter. The first is that that which is ugly is disliked and is naturally repellent. The needs of a beautiful person more readily receive response, for beauty's effect within the breasts of people is greater. In this respect, it is like a useful tool, and like wealth and prominence, since it is a kind of power; the beautiful face can achieve what the ugly cannot. Everything that is helpful in fulfilling needs in this world can be helpful as a means to the Hereafter.

The second way is that beauty, on the whole, indicates the excellence of the soul, because the light of the soul, when its illumination is complete, enhances the body. The outer appearance and the inner reality are often inseparable from each other. Therefore, people who are discerning in the knowledge of the noble traits of the soul depend upon the physiognomy of the body. They say, 'The face and the eye are the mirror of the inner.' Therefore, the effect of anger, joy and grief appear on it [the face]. For this reason it was said, 'The brightness of the face is a sign of what is in the soul.' And it is said, 'All that is on the earth is ugly, yet the face [of each thing in it] is the best of what it contains.'

[The caliph] al-Ma'mūn[A] once inspected an army and in it was an ugly man. He questioned him, and when the man stammered, [al-Ma'mūn][28] struck his name from the registry and said, 'The spirit (*rūḥ*) when it illuminates the outward grants beauty and in the inward grants eloquence. This man has neither outward nor inward.'

The Prophet (may God bless him and grant him peace) said, 'Seek the good from the beautiful of face.'[29]

ʿUmar (may God be pleased with him) said, 'When you send out a messenger, see that he be handsome and of good name.'

The jurists said, 'If those who are to lead the prayer are equal [in merit], then he who has the most beautiful face is more worthy of leading the prayer.'

In emphasising this, the Exalted said, *God has chosen him over you,*

[A] The seventh ʿAbbāsid caliph, al-Ma'mūn (d. 218/833).

and has increased him broadly in knowledge and body.[30]

We do not mean by beauty what stimulates desire, for that pertains to women. We mean a straight and upright build, evenly filled out, with proportionate limbs and a regular countenance, whereby men's natures are not repelled at the sight of him.

You may say, 'You have incorporated wealth, prominence, lineage, family and children within the scope of blessings; yet God (Exalted is He!) has found wealth and prominence blameworthy, and so has the Messenger of God (may God bless him and grant him peace)[31] and also the scholars.'

The Exalted said, *In your wives and children then is an enemy for you; beware of them.*[32] God, Almighty and Majestic, said, *Your wealth and children are mere trial.*[33]

ʿAlī (may God ennoble his countenance) said, in derogation of kinship, 'People are the offspring of their accomplishments. The worth of every person is in what he does well.'

And it is said, 'A person is [valued] for himself, not for his father.'

So, what does it mean to be a blessing but to be blameworthy according to the law? Know that whoever acquires knowledge from words transmitted in writing and from commonly held beliefs is likely to be in error unless he is guided by the light of God (Exalted is He!) to grasp knowledge as it is. Only then will written knowledge coincide sometimes with its metaphorical (*ta'wīl*) and sometimes with its particular (*takhṣīṣ*) interpretation.[A]

[In answer,] these blessings are an aid to the Hereafter and cannot be rejected, yet they [also] contain temptations and dangers. For example, wealth is like the blessing of a snake that has a useful antidote and a deadly poison. When the snake handler

[A] Arberry notes that 'in the early days of Islam *tafsīr* and *ta'wīl* were regarded as more or less synonymous terms; later, *ta'wīl* was used to distinguish "esoteric" as opposed to "exoteric" interpretation' (Arberry, *Revelation and Reason in Islam* [London: Allen and Unwin, 1957], p. 16). Ghazālī's use of *ta'wīl* here suggests that the transition was well on its way to being used as the primary term to express 'esoteric' interpretation, particularly in Sufi circles.

knows how to be careful of its venom and how to extract its useful antidote, then it is a blessing. However, if a foolish, careless person approaches it, it will be a calamity for him and he will perish. It is like the seas within which are varieties of jewels and pearls. Whoever is skilful at sea and knows how to swim, to dive and guard against the perils of the sea, will gain its blessings. But if he dives into it ignorant of these, he will perish.

So, God (Exalted is He!) praised wealth, and called it a good thing. The Messenger of God (may God bless him and grant him peace) praised it and said, 'The best support in piety is wealth.' He also praised prominence and renown, because God (Exalted is He!) favoured His Messenger (may God bless him and grant him peace) by revealing the whole religion to him and making him dear to the hearts of creatures; this is the meaning of prominence.

And yet, that which is transmitted in praise of both is little and that which is transmitted condemning wealth and prominence is plentiful. Whenever ostentation (*riyā'*) is condemned, prominence is also condemned, since the purpose of ostentation is to attract the hearts [of people] and prominence is possessing their hearts. This [evil of ostentation] increases and that [goodness of prominence] decreases, because most men are ignorant of the antidote of the 'snake' of wealth and how to dive into the 'sea' of prominence. And so, they must be warned of them. For they will surely perish by the 'poison' of wealth before extracting its antidote, and the 'crocodile' of the sea of prominence will surely devour them before they discover its jewels! Had [these blessings] been blameworthy in their substances and with respect to everyone, then it would not have been possible to add sovereignty to prophethood as is the case with our Prophet (may God bless him and grant him peace), and it would not have been possible to add to it wealth as in the case of Solomon (peace be upon him).

For all people are children and possessions are snakes. The prophets and the gnostics are like the snake-handlers. The child may be harmed by what cannot harm the snake-handler. Indeed, [suppose] a snake handler had a son whose survival and welfare he desires. He finds a snake, but knows that if he captured it for its antidote, his son would surely imitate him and grab the snake when he saw it to play with it. The boy may perish. [The snake-handler] has two objectives: the antidote and the protection of the child. It is his duty to weigh his objective of obtaining an antidote against ensuring the survival of his son. If he does without the antidote, he is not harmed greatly. But were he to capture it [the snake], the boy would surely grab hold of it [too], and he would lose his son. It is his duty, therefore, to flee from the snake, if he sees it, and direct the boy to flee and to make its image hateful to him. He should tell him that it has a fatal poison from which no one can save him. He should never discuss with him the benefit of the antidote it contains, for this might mislead the boy and he may approach it without full knowledge.

Likewise, if the diver dives into the sea in full view of his son, he will surely follow him and perish. It is his duty to warn the boy about the coast and the river bank. If the boy will not be restrained by mere reprimand whenever he sees his father near the shore, it is then his [the father's] duty to stay away from the shore with his son and not to go near it in his son's presence.

Similarly, the community of believers are, to the prophets (peace be upon them), like foolish children. This is why he (may God bless him and grant him peace) said, 'I am to you like the parent is to his child.'[34] And he (may God bless him and grant him peace) said, 'You tumble over one another into the Fire as the moths tumble [into the flame], and I restrain you.'[35] They [the prophets] have the greatest share in protecting their 'children' from peril. For they surely were only sent for this. They had no use for wealth, except what provides sufficient food. They were content with sufficient food and what was left over they did not retain but distributed. In the distribution is the antidote and in the retention, the poison.

If the door of acquisition of wealth were opened for men and they were to covet it, they would surely incline towards the poison of avarice and would tend away from the antidote of charitable giving. This is why wealth has been condemned and the meaning [of this condemnation] is to make abhorrent its retention, attachment to it, desire for its increase and the propagation of its luxuries, which lead to dependence on the world and its pleasures. But acquiring wealth in sufficient measure and spending the surplus on good deeds is not blameworthy. Every traveller should carry only the provisions he needs on the journey if he is resolved to provide for himself alone. But if he wishes to feed others and to add to the provision of his companions, then there is no harm in carrying more.

He (may God bless him and grant him peace) said, 'Let each of you acquire of this world the provision of the traveller;'[36] this means [take] only what you need. There was one who used to relate this tradition and abided by it. He received one hundred thousand dirhams in one place, and distributed it in the very same place and did not hold on to a grain of it.

When the Messenger of God (may God bless him and grant him peace) mentioned that the rich enter Paradise with difficulty, ʿAbd al-Raḥmān b. ʿAwf (may God be pleased with him) asked him permission to give away all that he possessed. The Messenger of God granted him permission. Then Gabriel (peace be upon him) descended and said, 'Command him to feed the poor, clothe the naked and serve the guest …'[37]

Therefore, worldly blessings are intermingled. The remedies in them are mixed with their diseases, what is desired from them with what is feared, and what is beneficial with what is harmful. So whoever has confidence in his insight and the perfection of his knowledge should draw near to them, fearing their disease but extracting their medicine. He who does not have confidence in them should run far, far away; he should flee quickly from the inherent dangers! Nothing will be safe for the likes of him and such are all creation except for those whom God (Exalted is He!) protects and guides to His way.

If you ask, 'What is the meaning of the blessings that grant success (*tawfīq*), such as [divine] guidance (*hidāya*), counsel (*rushd*), support (*ta'yīd*) and direction (*tasdīd*)?' Know that none can do without the success granted [by God]. It is an expression of the uniting and bringing together of the will of the servant with the decree and the divine predestination. This includes good and evil, happiness and misfortune. However, the common usage for success granted by God is what leads to happiness in the decree of God (Exalted is He!) and what He predestines. This is the same [as the common usage] or [the word] *ilḥād*,[A] which means 'to incline'; it has become restricted to what inclines towards the false. Certainly, there is no disagreement as to the need for success [granted by God]. Therefore, it was said,

> If there is no help from God for the young man,
> It is mostly his striving that brings him injury.

As for guidance (*hidāya*), it is not possible to attain to salvation except by it. For the motive of a man may incline to what will benefit him in the Hereafter. But if he does not know what will bring him salvation in the Hereafter, supposing even that corruption is righteousness, how will [his] will alone benefit him? There is no advantage in the will, ability and the means except after following guidance. Hence, God (Exalted is He!) said, *Our Lord gave everything its creation, then guided it.*[38] And He said, *But for God's bounty to you and His mercy, no one would have ever been pure. God purifies whomever he wills . . .* [39] He (may God bless him and grant him peace) said, 'No one enters Paradise save by the mercy of God (Exalted is He!),' that is, by His guidance. It was said, 'Not even you, O Messenger of God?' And he replied, 'Not even I.'[40]

Guidance is on three levels. The first is knowledge of the way of good and evil, as mentioned in God's words, *And have we not guided him on the two highways?*[41B] God (Exalted is He!) has blessed all His servants by it [this knowledge], some through the intellect and others through the words of the messengers. This is why

[A] *Ilḥād* can also be translated as apostasy.

[B] That is, the difference between good and evil.

He (Exalted is He!) said, *As for Thamūd, We guided them, but they preferred blindness above guidance.*[42] The means to guidance are the books and the messengers and the insight of the intellect (*baṣā'ir al-ʿuqūl*). All these are granted [by God]. Nothing obstructs them except envy, pride, love of this world and those causes that blind the hearts even though the eyes are not blinded. He (Exalted is He!) said, *It is not eyes that are blind, but blind are the hearts inside the breast.*[43] Among the causes that blind are convention, daily habit and the love of maintaining them both. An expression of this can be found in the words of God (Exalted is He!), *We found our fathers following a religion ...*[44] [While] an expression of pride and envy can be found in His statement, *They say, 'Why was this Qur'ān not sent down upon some leading man of the two cities?'*;[45] and His statement, '*What, shall we follow a mortal, one from among us?*'[46] These [causes of] blindness are that which prevent right guidance.

The second is beyond this general guidance. It is [the guidance] that God (Exalted is He!) extends to the servant in one state after another. It is the fruit of spiritual striving (*mujāhada*), as God (Exalted is He!) said, As to *those who struggle in Our cause, surely We shall guide them in Our ways.*[47] It is intended in His words, *But those who accept guidance, He increases in guidance.*[48]

The third guidance goes beyond the second. It is the light that shines in the world of prophethood (*nubuwwa*) and sainthood (*walāya*) at the end of spiritual striving. By it, the servant is guided to that which cannot be acquired through rational thought and through knowledge that can be learnt. It is pure guidance, anything else only veils it and serves as an introduction [to it]. It is [the guidance] that God (Exalted is He!) has exalted by attributing it to Himself even when all [of guidance] is from Him. God (Exalted is He!) said, *Say: God's guidance is the true guidance.*[49] It is called life in the words of the Exalted, *Can he who was dead, to whom We gave life, and a light whereby he can walk amongst men, [be like him who is in the depths of darkness]*;[50] and it is the intention in His statement (Exalted is He!), *Is he whose breast God has opened to Islam so that he follows a light from his Lord [no better than one hard-hearted?]*.'[51]

By counsel (*rushd*), we mean the divine care that helps people in their way towards [God's] intended purposes. It strengthens them in what is good for them and reduces their desire for what corrupts them. This takes place inwardly. Just as God (Exalted is He!) said, *We gave Abraham aforetime his counsel, for We knew him.*[52] Counsel, therefore, is an expression of guidance that propels and compels towards salvation. So, when a boy gains experience in accumulating wealth, in the ways of commerce and investment, but despite this knowledge he squanders his possessions and does not invest them [properly], he is said not to be well-counselled (*rashīd*). This is not from his lack of guidance but because of the insufficiency of his guidance in motivating him. For how many people proceed knowingly towards what they know will harm them! They have been granted guidance, and by it they are distinguished from the ignorant [person] who does not know that a thing will harm; however, they have not been granted counsel. For counsel in this respect is more complete than mere guidance in particular aspects of conduct. It is a great blessing.

As for direction (*tasdīd*), it directs [the servant's] movements toward what is correctly sought. It facilitates [things] for him so that he is strengthened and achieves the goal more quickly. Indeed, guidance by itself is insufficient, it requires [another form of] guidance to stimulate the motive and it is [called] counsel. And counsel is not sufficient. Rather, it is necessary to habituate the movements with the help of the organs and the limbs, until what gave rise to the motive is accomplished. Guidance is the primary introduction; counsel draws in the motive to awaken and stir movement; direction assists by moving the limbs and granting them assistance towards that which is right. As for support, it unites all of these. It strengthens [the servant's] aim by insight from within, and by supporting action and assisting the means [of achievement] from without. It is what God intended by, ...*when I confirm you with the Holy Spirit.*[53] It draws him near sinlessness

(*ʿiṣma*).[A] It is an expression for a divine presence which spreads inwardly, strengthening the person in the pursuit of good and the avoidance of evil. It resembles an imperceptible preventative in his inner self. Related to this support are the words of God (Exalted is He!), *For she desired him and he would have taken her, had he not seen the proof of his Lord.*[54B]

These, therefore, are the sum total of blessings. They cannot be realised except when God (Exalted is He!) grants [the servant] pure penetrating understanding; conscious hearing; a humble, perceptive heart that is aware; a guiding teacher; and wealth sufficient to provide for essentials, [but] which is not so abundant that it distracts him from religion; and renown that protects him from the foolishness of stupid people and the injustice of enemies.

Each of the above sixteen [means to blessings] are dependent on other means. And these other means require others until they finally arrive at He Who guides the perplexed, Who is the refuge of the oppressed, He is the Lord of lords and the Causer of causes. As these causes are numerous, a book such as this is not sufficient to investigate them [all]. Let us now give some examples to make known the meaning of His statement, *If you count God's blessings, you will never be able to number them.*[55] And success is granted by God.

[A] Jabre suggests 'infallibility' for *ʿiṣma*, 'with also a nuance of impeccability,' and cites this very passage (*Lexique de Ghazali*, p. 178).

[B] The verse focuses on part of the story of Joseph and his resistance to temptation.

CHAPTER THIRTEEN
An Exposition of Examples of God's Abundant Blessings, their Inter-connectedness and that they Can Neither be Limited nor Counted

KNOW that we summed up the blessings into sixteen kinds. We have explained that the health of the body is one of the blessings that occurs at the lowest level. Yet, were we to examine the causes by which this one blessing is arrived at, we would not be able to do so. Eating is one of the means to health. Let us, therefore, mention a few examples by which the blessing of health is achieved. For it is well understood that eating is an action. Every action of this kind is a movement, and every movement needs a body that can move: its instrument. [This instrument] must possess the power of movement and possess a will for movement. [In addition,] there has to be a knowledge of what is desired and an understanding of it. There has to be an act of eating and the thing eaten. What is eaten must have a source from which it is acquired, and there must be a producer to make it ready [for eating]. Let us thus mention, by way of allusion and not in detail, the means of knowing; next, the means of willing; the means of ability [to perform what the will wants]; and finally, the means by which the food is acquired.

First Example: On the Blessings of God in the Creation of the Means of Perception

KNOW that God (Exalted is He!) created plants and they are more perfect than stones, clay, iron, brass or other substances, which do not grow and do not require nourishment. Indeed, plants were created with an innate ability to draw nourishment through their stems and their roots, which are in the ground. These are their instruments, through which nourishment is drawn up. They are the fine veins that you see in every leaf. Their stems grow thick; then, they spread out and become fine and sub-divide into a network of veins, spreading through the parts of the leaf until they can no longer be seen.

But despite their perfection, if they are deprived of the nourishment that reaches them and that strengthens their roots, they become parched and dry up. They cannot seek nourishment from another place because seeking [depends on] knowledge of what is sought and [the ability] to reach it, and plants are incapable of both. One of the blessings of God (Exalted is He!) upon you, therefore, is His creation for you of instruments of sensation and movement [to aid] in the acquisition of nourishment.

Observe the wisdom of God's order in creating the five senses that are the instruments of perception! The first [instrument] of perception is the sense of touch. It was created for you to feel the burning fire or sharp sword when it touches you, so you will avoid them. This is the first sense He created for the animals. It is inconceivable that an animal can exist without this sense because if it could not feel at all it would not be an animal. The lowest level of sensation is to feel that with which you are in [direct] contact and which touches you. There is no doubt that the sensing of what is at a distance from you is more complete. The [former] is present in every animal, even the worm in the soil. For when one pricks the worm with a needle, it contracts [itself] for flight, unlike the plant. When a plant is cut, it does not contract, as it does not feel the cut. If you had been created with only this sense, you would surely be lacking, like the worm, and you would not be able to acquire food that is distant from you. You would only be able to [acquire food] from what touches your body and what you feel. You are thus in need of a sense to perceive what is at a distance from you.

Therefore, smell was created for you to sense odour, though you may not know from which direction the odour comes. So you wander about in many directions. Then, perhaps, you will discover the food whose odour you smelled. However, had this been the only [sense] created for you, then you may not have found [food] and you would be in dire need. Thus sight was created for you that you may perceive what is far from you, know its direction and can proceed towards it.

Were only this sense created for you, you would surely be lacking, since you would not know what is beyond the walls and the barriers. You would be able to see food when there is no barrier between you and it, and you would be able to see an enemy when there is no barrier between you and him. But as to where a barrier exists between you and something, you would not be able to see the thing. This barrier might not be lifted until the enemy approaches and you are incapable of flight. Therefore, hearing was created for you to perceive sounds of movement behind walls and barriers. For with sight you can only perceive what is immediately before you. As for that which is out of sight, you cannot have knowledge of it except through speech made up of letters and sounds that you perceive by means of the sense of hearing. Your need for [hearing] was so important that your ears were created for you, and you are distinguished from the other animals by [your] understanding of speech.

None of this would be of any use to you, if you had no sense of taste. For you would not be able to perceive if the food you ate was wholesome for you or disagreeable, and you would eat it and it would kill you. A tree, which has no taste, draws in any liquid poured on its roots, even if it causes it to wither.

All of these [sensory faculties] would not be sufficient for you, if another sense of perception had not been created in the forepart of your brain. This is a 'shared sense' (*ḥiss mushtarak*), in which these five senses come together. If it had not been so, the matter would be unmanageable for you. For example, if you eat something yellow and find it bitter and disagreeable, you leave it. The next time you see it, you would not know that it is bitter and harmful, something not to be tasted a second time, had it not been for this shared sense. The eye sees the yellow, but does not know its bitterness. How, therefore, are you kept from it? The taste recognises the bitterness, but does not know the yellow; thus there must be a judge before whom the yellow and the bitterness are brought together, so that, when you see the yellow, you judge it bitter and refrain from eating it a second time.

All this the animals share with you, for sheep have all of these senses. Yet, if you had these faculties only, you would surely be lacking. An animal is beguiled into a trap set for it, since it does not know how to avoid the trap, or how to escape if it is fettered. It may cast itself down into a well, not knowing that this would kill it. An animal may eat what it takes pleasure in at the time and be harmed by it later, so it sickens and dies because it has only the sense of the present. As for perception of the consequences, it has none. God (Exalted is He!) distinguished you and honoured you with another attribute which is the most honourable of all—the intelligence (*ʿaql*). Through it you recognise harmful and beneficial foods in the present and the future, and by it you know how to cook foods, combine them and prepare their ingredients. Therefore, through your intelligence you benefit from the food which is the source of your health. This is the most immediate benefit of the intelligence and the least of the wisdom in it.

For the greatest wisdom in it is the knowledge of God (Exalted is He!), knowledge of His acts and knowledge of the wisdom of His created world. At this [level], the advantages of the five senses are transformed for you. The five senses then become like spies and informers about the regions of the kingdom [of God]. Each of them has been charged with a special task. One is [charged with] information on colours; another with information on sounds; another with information on odours; another with information on tastes; and another with information on heat, cold, roughness, smoothness, softness, hardness and others. These messengers and spies gather information from the regions of the kingdom and deliver it to the shared sense. The shared sense is seated in the forepart of the brain, like the minister of information who sits at the king's door and gathers verbal and written reports received from the various regions of the world. He takes them and delivers them [to the king]—still sealed—he has only to receive, gather and preserve them. As for knowledge of what they really are, he has none. Likewise, when it [the shared sense] meets the discerning heart (*al-qalb al-ʿāqil*)—which [takes the place of] the prince or the king— it delivers the gathered information, which is sealed. The king, then, peruses it [the information], observes the secrets of the kingdom through it and passes wonderful judgements due to it. But, we will not [undertake] a detailed investigation [of these matters]. In accordance with the decisions and beneficial deeds that seem necessary, he [the king] moves the troops, which are the bodily members: one time searching, another time retreating, still another in completing the stratagems that are appointed to them.

This is the succession of the blessings of God (Exalted is He!) upon you in the [sensory] perceptions. But do not think that we have exhausted them here! For the external senses are only some of the perceptions. Sight is one of the senses and the eye is one of the organs. The eyes are constructed of ten different levels. Some are layers and some are coverings, and some of the coverings are like the weaving of a spider. Some are like placenta; some like the white of eggs; and others are solid. Each of these ten levels has a quality, form, class, appearance, width, sphere and arrangement. If one of the ten layers were faulty or one of the qualities of each layer [were faulty], sight surely would be faulty and no physician or oculist would be able to correct [the condition].

This is but one sense! And the sense of hearing and the rest of the senses should be similarly viewed. It would not be possible, even in many volumes, to do justice to the wisdom of God (Exalted is He!) and the blessings in respect to the organ of sight and its construction, although in itself it does not exceed [the size] of a small walnut. So what then do you think of the whole body, its remaining organs and wonders? [All of] these are pointers to the blessings of God (Exalted is He!) in the creation of the means of perceptions.

The Second Example: On the Blessings of God in the Creation of the Means to Will

KNOW that if sight were created only so that you can recognise food from a distance, and [if] a natural inclination, craving and appetite were not created to incite you to movement, sight would surely be useless. For how many a sick man sees food, the most beneficial of things for him, but does not take it because his appetite is gone; his sight and perception are [thus] ineffective for him. Therefore, it is imperative that you be inclined towards that which agrees with you—this is called 'appetite' (*shahwa*)—and [it is imperative that you] be averse to that which disagrees with you—this is called 'repulsion' (*karāha*). You seek through the appetite and flee through repulsion. God (Exalted is He!) created in you the appetite for food. He gave it authority over you and placed it in your charge. You become like someone subject to legal prosecution; you are compelled to eat and to take food and nourishment, and thus you are sustained by it. This [process] is what you share with the animals, but not with plants.

Should this appetite fail to subside after you satisfy your need, it would exceed all bounds and destroy you. God created repulsion when satiated, so that by it, you cease to eat. You are not like plants that continue to draw up water so long as water flows down to their roots until they rot. They are in need of a human being who can adjust their nourishment according to their needs; at times giving them water and at times cutting it off.

Just like the appetite to eat was created for you in order that your body may survive, [God] created the desire for sexual relations so that you may have descendants. Were we to relate to you the wonders of God in the creation of the womb—the blood of menstruation and the composition of the foetus from the sperm and the blood of menstruation; and how He created the testicles and veins entering into them from the spine, which is the resting place of the semen; and how water flows in the woman from the thorax through the veins; and the division of the womb's hollow into the parts, in some the semen forms males and in some it forms females; and the stages of growth: a clot of blood and coagulated blood;[1] then bone, flesh and blood; and how this develops into a head, hands, legs, abdomen, back and the remaining bodily members—you would be overwhelmed by wonder at the varieties of the blessings of God (Exalted is He!) upon you when you were first conceived. Each wonder is a bounty beyond what is obvious to you now! But we only want to provide [an explanation] of the blessings of God (Exalted is He!) in eating, in order not to lengthen the discussion.

The appetite for food, therefore, is one of the motivating factors (*irādāt*).[A] But it is not sufficient for you as perils may assail you from different directions. If anger were not created within you to motivate you against all that opposes and disagrees with you, you would surely be subjected to persistent harm. All the nourishment you acquired would surely be taken from you, because others would covet what is in your hands. You need a motivating factor for repulsing and combating them. It is with the force of anger that you drive back all that opposes and disagrees with you.

Yet, even this is insufficient for you, since appetite and anger are moved only by what is immediately harmful or beneficial. With respect to what is not immediate, however, these factors will not suffice. So God (Exalted is He!) created another factor for you, subservient to the direction of that [part of] the intelligence that has knowledge of consequences; just as God created the appetite and anger subservient to the sensory perception of the immediate situation. In this way, you benefit from intelligence. For, merely knowing that a particular desire is harmful to you does not prevent

[A] We have chosen to translate *irādāt* here as motivating factors though the singular (*irāda*) is usually translated as the 'will.' We feel that this is appropriate here as Ghazālī is describing impulses or very basic applications of the will.

you from indulging it so long as there does not exist an inclination to act on this knowledge. The motivating factor that separates you from the beasts is an honour for the children of Adam, just as the knowledge of consequences makes you distinct. We have called this 'motivating factor' religious impulse (*bāʿith al-dīn*) and we have discussed it in greater detail in the *Book of Patience*.[A]

The Third Example: On the Blessings of God in the Creation of Strength and Bodily Movement

KNOW that the senses are only of benefit for perception, while the will has no purpose except to choose between going towards or retreating [from something]. These [alone] are insufficient without there being in you an instrument for going forward or retreating. How many a sick person yearns for something far from him, [which he can] perceive, but cannot get to because of the loss of his legs, or he cannot take it because of the loss of his hand, either due to paralysis or numbness in both [the leg and the hand]. There must be instruments of movement and an ability for movement in these instruments in accordance with the demands of appetite and in accordance with [the urges] of repulsion in retreating. This is why God (Exalted is He!) has created for you bodily members whose visible appearance you see but whose mysteries you do not know. Among them are those for seeking and retreating—such as the legs of a man, the wings of a bird, the legs of an animal. Among them are [limbs] for defence; weapons for man and horns for the animal. In this, animals differ greatly, some of them have numerous enemies and their food is distant. Hence they need speed of movement, so wings were created for [birds] to fly rapidly. Some of them were created with four legs; others have two legs; yet others crawl. It would be lengthy to list them here.

[A] The discussion of the 'religious impulse' begins in *K. asrār al-ṣalat* (*Iḥyā'*, IV.62ff.).

Chapter Thirteen

Let us mention only the limbs by which eating is fulfilled, to allow us to compare other things to it. We say, your seeing food from a distance and your movement towards it are insufficient unless you are capable of taking the food. You need an instrument capable of grasping. So God (Exalted is He!) blessed you with the creation of two arms. They are long, [capable of] extending towards objects, and include many joints for movement to either side, to reach forward and bend back towards you. They are not like a rigid [piece of] wood. He made the base of the hand wide, by creating the palm. He divided the top of the palm into five parts, which are the fingers. He aligned them in two ways: the thumb, on one side, turns toward the remaining fingers. Were they stuck or attached together, you would not be able to achieve your goal. He has positioned them so that if you extend them they act as a shovel and if you cup them they act as a ladle. If you fold the [fingers] together, they are an instrument for striking. If you open and then close them, they are an instrument for grasping [things]. Then He created fingernails to protect the tips of the fingers from injury. Delicate things, which the fingers cannot grasp, can be picked up by the tips of your fingernails.

Suppose then that you take up food with your hands, how would this suffice if the food could not reach the stomach? There has to be an external opening that leads to it so that food can enter. He made the mouth an access to the stomach, [that is] aside from the abundance of wisdom in it beyond accessing the stomach.

When you put food in your mouth in one piece, it is not easy to swallow it; you need a mill to grind the food. So He created for you jaws from two bones on which he placed the teeth. He set the upper molars over the lower for grinding the food completely between them. Sometimes the food needs breaking; other times, cutting, then it needs grinding. So the teeth are divided into wide teeth, such as the molars; cutters, such as the incisors; and what is good for breaking, such as the canine teeth. Then He made a hinge for the jaw; it moves back and forth and around, enabling the lower jaw to move backwards and forwards. It turns on the upper jaw like a millstone. Were it not for that, certainly one jaw would only hit the other, like the clapping of two hands, and a grinding process would not be achieved. The lower jaw was made to move in circular motion and the upper jaw is fixed and unmoving.

Observe the miraculous work of God (Exalted is He!)! Every millstone made by human beings has a fixed lower stone and an upper which turns on it. Not this millstone that God (Exalted is He!) has made! It is the lower one that moves against the upper. Praise be to Him! How sublime is He! Mighty is His power, complete is the proof of His wisdom and numerous are His favours!

Suppose that you put food into the cavity of the mouth. How, then, does the food move beneath the teeth; how do the teeth pull it towards them; what happens to the food once it is deposited by the hand inside the mouth? Observe how God has blessed you by creating the tongue! It moves about the sides of the mouth, returning the food to the teeth according to need, like a shovel that returns the food to the millstone. This is in addition to the benefit of taste and the wonders of the power of speech, and other wisdom [in the tongue] which we will not go into.

Suppose then, that you cut the food, grind it, and it is dry. You will not be able to swallow it unless it slides down the throat with some moisture. Observe how God (Exalted is He!) created a spring underneath the tongue from which saliva gushes and pours out, according to need, in order for the food to mix with it. Observe how He made it subservient to this purpose. If you see the food from a distance, the lower jaw is stirred into service and saliva pours out until the corners of your mouth water, while the food is still far from you.

Then, what causes this [now] ground, doughy food to reach the stomach when it is in the mouth and you cannot push it down by hand and there is no hand in the stomach to extend and draw down the food. Observe how God (Exalted is He!) made ready the oesophagus and the larynx and placed layers at the top that can be opened to take food. Thereupon, the layers close over and pressure is applied to the food until it is compressed by the pressure. Then it slides down into the stomach through the oesophagus.

When the food reaches the stomach as chewed up bread or fruit, it still cannot, in this form, benefit the flesh, bones and blood. Rather, it needs to be fully 'cooked', to homogenise its parts. So God (Exalted is He!) created the stomach in the form of a cooking pot into which food passes. It holds the food and shuts its doors, and [the food] remains in the stomach until digestion is completed. It is cooked well in the heat that surrounds the stomach from the internal organs—on its right side is the liver, on the left side is the spleen; in front is the thorax and behind is the flesh of the spinal column. Heat passes to it from these organs on all sides until the food is cooked [into] a homogeneous fluid suitable for absorption into the cavities of the veins. At that point it resembles the water of barley, in terms of its parts and homogeneity.

But it is not yet beneficial as nourishment. Therefore, God (Exalted is He!) created passages of veins between the stomach and the liver, and made many openings for food to pour into them and terminate in the liver. The liver is made from the substance of blood; it is like blood itself. Within it are many hair-like capillaries that spread throughout the liver. The homogenised soft food is poured through them and spreads into the liver's parts until the power of the liver takes possession of it and dyes it the colour of blood. It [the food] settles in these parts where another development occurs. It becomes pure blood, good for nourishing the organs. It is the heat of the liver that ripens this blood. From this blood two residual substances are generated, just as all that is 'cooked' is generated. The first of the two [substances] is similar to sediment turbidity; it is black bile. The other is similar to froth; it is yellow bile. If the two excretions were not separated from it [the blood], the physical condition of the organs would deteriorate. Therefore, God (Exalted is He!) created the gall bladder, the spleen and a duct for each of them extending into the cavity of the liver. The gall bladder draws out the yellowish residue and the spleen draws out the blackish sediment, so that the blood remains pure and is increased in fineness and fluidity through moisture. Were it not so, [the blood] would not flow through these capillaries, nor exit from them, thus ascending to the organs.

So God (Exalted is He!), praise be to Him, also created two kidneys and extended a long duct from each one to the liver. It is a wonder of the wisdom of God (Exalted is He!) how the duct does not enter into the liver! On the contrary, it is connected by veins that ascend from the curvature of the liver and draw out what follows them from the capillaries in the liver. Were it to be drawn out before that, the blood would be thick and would not pass through the veins. When [impure] liquids are separated from it, the blood becomes pure of the three residues, pure from all that spoils the nutrients.

Moreover, God (Exalted is He!) caused veins to extend out from the liver. After their exit, they are divided into parts and each part is divided into branches. This [network of blood vessels] is extended all over the body, from head to foot, [some] visible and [some] invisible. Pure blood flows in them to the rest of the organs. The capillaries, which are divided into branches, are webbed, like the veins of leaves and [the roots of] trees in a way that is not discernible to the eyes. Nourishment goes through them to the rest of the organs by filtration.

If a malfunction were to occur in the gall bladder and the yellowish residue were not drawn out, the blood would become impure. Bilious diseases would result from this, such as jaundice, pustules, and erysipelas. If a malfunction occurred in the spleen and the black bile were not drawn out, blackish diseases would occur, such as vitiligo alba, elephantiasis, melancholia and others. If the [impure] liquids do not pass to the kidneys, dropsy and other [diseases] would occur. So observe the wisdom of the All-Wise Creator, how He has arranged facilities for these impure residues! The gall bladder draws with one of two ducts and discards with the other duct into the intestines so that the roughage from food acquires a lubricating moisture. A combustion occurs in the intestines which causes them to evacuate; they contract until the roughage is expelled. The bile is yellow because of this. The spleen discharges its residue through a transformation which causes acidity and contraction. It sends some of it to the top of the stomach every day so the appetite is set in motion by its acidity, and is stimulated and agitated by it. The remainder [of the residue] is expelled with the roughage. As for the kidneys, they are nourished by the watery fluid from blood and [they] send the remainder to the bladder.

Let us limit [ourselves] to this exposition of the blessings of God (Exalted is He!) in the means provided for eating. It would lengthen our discussion to mention how the liver needs the heart and the brain; how each of these major organs needs its companions; how the arteries branch off from the heart to the rest of the body, interlocking the faculties of sense through them; how motionless veins cause nutrients to move from the liver to the rest of the body; and how the organs and the numerous bones, muscles, veins, tendons, ligaments and cartilage are arranged—all of which are needed for eating and other similar matters.

Furthermore, in a human body there are thousands of muscles, veins and nerves, differing in smallness and largeness, thinness and thickness, multiplicity or singularity. All of them have an [underlying] wisdom, or two, or three, or four, or ten or more. All are of the blessings of God (Exalted is He!) upon you! If a pulsating artery were to stop or a vein start to haemorrhage, surely you, pitiful thing, would perish!

Observe then first the blessings of God (Exalted is He!) upon you, that you may be able to give thanks! [Without this observation] all you will acknowledge of the blessings of God (Exalted is He!) is [the blessing of] food, and that is the least of them! You will know nothing of them [the blessings] save that you hunger and you eat. You only know when you are hungry and eat. The donkey also knows that it is hungry; it eats, tires, sleeps, feels an urge, copulates, awakens, gets up and gallops away. If you do not know yourself any more than the donkey knows [itself], then how can you rise up in thankfulness for God's blessing upon you?

In sum, all we have alluded to is only a drop in one of the oceans of God's blessings. You can measure by this what we have overlooked of all that we know, mindful of a lengthy [discussion]. All that we and all creatures know, in addition to what we do not know of the blessings of God (Exalted is He!), is less than a drop in an ocean. Except that whoever knows something of this understands one of the meanings of the words of God (Exalted is He!), *If you count the blessings of God, never will you be able to number them.*[1]

Now, observe how God bound [together] the main support of these organs and the main support of their benefits, their perceptions and their powers by a gentle vapour, which ascends from the four humours. Its resting place is the heart. It circulates throughout the body by means of the arteries. Whenever it reaches a part of the body, it brings to it sensation, perception, power of movement and other [powers]. It is like a lamp that is taken round the parts of the house. When the lamp reaches a part, light is shed by it on that part of the house. [The light] is the creation and invention of God, but, in His wisdom, He makes the lamp its cause. This gentle vapour is what the physicians call the spirit. Its place is in the heart, and it is like the body of the flame of the lamp. The heart is like its lamp; the black blood in the depth of the heart is like its wick; the sustenance is like its oil; and the visible life in the rest of the limbs of the body is like the light by which the lamp illuminates the whole house. And, just as the lamp is extinguished when its oil is cut off, so the lamp of the spirit is put out whenever its nourishment is cut off. And, just as the wick is consumed by fire and becomes ash, such that it cannot absorb the oil, the lamp will go out due to an excess of oil. Likewise, the blood to which this vapour clings in the heart may burn out with the excess of heat in the heart and thereby be put out, in spite of the presence of nourishment. For it no longer accepts the nourishment through which the spirit persists, just as ashes do not accept the oil in a manner that keeps the fire lit. And just as the lamp is sometimes put out by an internal cause and sometimes by an external cause, such as a stormy wind, so the spirit is sometimes extinguished by an internal cause and sometimes by an external cause, such as killing. And, just as the lamp is extinguished when the oil is exhausted, or the wick fails, or by a stormy wind or by a person putting it out, [this only occurs] through predestined causes in the knowledge of God and a predestined time, so also is the extinguishing of the spirit. Just as the extinguishing of a lamp is the end of the period of its existence, this being its allotted time in the Book [of destiny], so is the extinguishing of the spirit. Just as the lamp, when it is put out, causes the whole house to grow dark, so the spirit, when extinguished, leaves all the body dark. For the light, by which it benefited in its sensations, capacities, drives, and the rest of what is included in the meaning of the word life, has departed. This, therefore, is a concise allusion to another of the worlds of the blessings of God (Exalted is He!) and the wonders of His creation and His wisdom, in order that you may know, *If the ocean were ink (wherewith to write out) the words of my Lord, sooner would the ocean be exhausted than would the words of my Lord.*[2] He who denies God, is truly wretched! May he never succeed! Away with whoever denies His blessings, away with him!

You may say: You have described the spirit and given an analogy of it, whereas when the Messenger of God (may God bless him and grant him peace) was asked about the spirit, he did not go beyond what God said, *Say, the Spirit is of the command of my Lord.*[3] He did not describe it in this [your] manner. Know that this [question] is ignorance as to the multiple applications of the term 'spirit' (*rūḥ*). For spirit applies to many meanings that we will not mention here. We have described only a small portion of its totality, what the physicians call 'spirit'. They know its quality, existence, and the manner it spreads in the organs, and how the organs gain sensation and strength through it, such that if some of the organs become numb, they know that something obstructs the flow of this spirit. They do not treat the place of the numbness, but the sources of the nerves and location of the blockage. They treat [the organs] with what will open the blockage. For the body, in all its complexity, is infiltrated by a network of nerves and by means of them [the spirit] spreads from the heart to the rest of the organs. That which can be understood by the knowledge of physicians is easy.

But as to the Spirit which is the source, and which, if corrupted, corrupts the rest of the body, this is one of the mysteries of God (Exalted is He!) that we have not described. We are only permitted to describe it as a divine command, just as God said, *Say, the Spirit is of the command of my Lord.* The intellects [of people] do not have the capacity to describe Lordly matters, rather the minds of most human beings are perplexed by them. Visualisation and imagination are necessarily deficient here in the same way that sight is incapable of discerning sound. They falter at the mention of the principles of [the Spirit's] description. The complexities of the intellects [of people] are limited in their essentials; they are imprisoned within their set bounds. Consequently, the description of [the Spirit] is not grasped by reason, but by another light [which is] higher and more honourable than reason. That light shines in the world of prophethood and sainthood and its relation to reason is the relation of reason to visualisation and imagination.

God (Exalted is He!) created human beings at different levels. Just as the child understands sensory things but does not grasp theoretical [concepts] because he has not yet reached that stage, so the individual [who has reached] puberty perceives theoretical [concepts] but does not know what lies beyond them because he has not yet reached that level. For this is a noble station, a sweet drinking place and a high degree. In it, the presence of God can be perceived through the light of faith and certainty. This drinking-place is too noble to be accessible to every passerby; rather it is accessible to only to a few. The presence of God has a 'foreground' (*ṣadr*) and at the front of this foreground is a space, a large arena (*maydān*), and at the start of the arena is a threshold and this is the abode of that Lordly command. He who is not permitted to reach the threshold or to view the keeper of the threshold, can never reach the arena. So how can it be possible [for him] to reach the lofty views beyond? This is why it has been said, 'He who does not know himself does not know his Lord.'[4]

Where is this to be found in the library of the physicians, and how is the physician able to observe it? Rather, the meaning of the word designated by the physician as spirit, in addition to the Lordly command, is like a ball which the polo mallet sets in motion in relation to the king [who hits it]. He who knows the medical [definition of the] spirit and presumes to understand the Lordly command is like one who sees the ball which the king's mallet sets in motion and presumes that he saw the king. There is no doubt that his mistake is gross. But more gross than this is when the intellect, by which one becomes cognisant of moral obligations and through which one perceives the good of this world, is incapable of observing that God Himself (Exalted is He!) did not permit His Messenger (may God bless him and grant him peace) to discuss it [the Lordly command], rather He commanded him to address people at the level of their intellects.[5] God (Exalted is He!) did not say anything in His book of the reality [of the Spirit]. Rather, He mentioned its relationship [to Him] and His action, but He did not say anything about its essence. As to its relationship, it is in His statement, *of the command of My Lord*; while the action is mentioned in His words, *O soul at peace, return unto your Lord, well-pleased, well-pleasing! Enter among My servants! Enter My Paradise!*[6]

Let us return now to the matter! What we seek is remembrance of the blessings of God (Exalted is He!) in food. We have [now] mentioned some of the blessings of God (Exalted is He!) in the instruments of eating.

The Fourth Example: On the Blessings of God in the Creation of the Means by which We Acquire Food

KNOW that there are many [types of] foods, and in God's creation of them there are innumerable wonders and endlessly related causes. It would be too lengthy to go into this for each [type of] food. For foods may be medicaments (*adwiya*), fruits (*fawākih*) or staples (*aghdhiya*). Let us take [the example of] the staples, as they are the source; and, from among them, let us consider a grain of wheat and disregard all the rest of the staples.

We say, if you were to find just a few grains and eat them, you would remain weak and hungry. You are dependent on the grain itself growing, increasing and doubling, until it completely fulfils your need! God (Exalted is He!) created in the grain of wheat the power by which people are nourished, just as He created you. Indeed, the plant is distinguished from you only in [its lack of] sensation and movement, but it does not differ in nourishment, because it is fed with water. It draws [water] into its viscera by means of roots, just as you feed and absorb nourishment.

We will not expand on the ways the plant attracts nourishment to itself. But we will indicate its nourishment. We say that just as wood and soil cannot nourish you because you need special food, so the grain cannot be fed by everything, but needs particular things. The proof [of this is that] if you left it in the house, it will not prosper because nothing surrounds it except air. Air alone is insufficient for its nourishment. Were you to leave it in water, it would [still] not prosper. Were you to leave it in the ground without water, it would not prosper. It needs soil with water; the water must be mixed with the earth to become mud. This is indicated by His words, *Let man consider his nourishment. We poured out the rains abundantly; then We split the earth in furrows and therein caused the grains to grow, and vines and reeds and olives and palms.*[7]

But water and soil are insufficient. If the plant is left in moist, compacted, hard-packed ground, it will not sprout because of lack of air. It needs to be left in soft, loose ground through which air can penetrate. But the air would not move towards it on its own, it needs wind to move the air, and to strike the earth with force and violence to penetrate the ground. God (Exalted is He!) pointed to this in, *And we loose the winds that fertilise.*[8] Pollination occurs only in the harmonious combination of air, water and soil. But none of this would set you free from want, if there were excessive cold and a severe winter. You need the heat of spring and summer. It is evident [now] that [plants] are in need of these four [factors] for their nourishment.

Observe, then, what each plant needs. In the cultivation of land, vegetation needs water, to be drawn from seas, rivers, springs and streams. Observe how God created the seas, brings forth springs and causes the rivers to flow from them. When the land is at an altitude and water cannot rise to it, observe, then, how God (Exalted is He!) creates the clouds, and how He causes the winds to exert pressure on them, and how, by His leave, the full and heavy-laden clouds are driven to the ends of the earth! Then observe how He sends over the land pouring rains in spring and autumn according to need! See how He created mountains, preserving water, from which the springs gradually gush forth. If they were to flow all at once, the land would be submerged and the crops and livestock would be destroyed. It is impossible to enumerate God's blessings in the mountains, clouds, seas and rains.

No heat can be generated between water and earth because both are cold. So consider how He subjugated the sun and how He created it, despite its distance from earth, to heat the earth during one season but not the other, to provide cold when cold is required and warmth when warmth is required. This is some of the wisdom of [God] with regards to the sun; but the wisdom in it is more than can be enumerated.

Plants that grow high from the ground yield fruits that harden. They need moisture to ripen. Observe how He created the moon and made moisture[A] its special contribution, just as He made heat the special property of the sun! So it ripens the fruit and gives it colour as predetermined by the Creator, the All-Wise. And because of this, if trees remain in the shade, and the rays of the sun, moon and other heavenly bodies are prevented from reaching the fruit, it would spoil and not ripen. Even a small tree would spoil in the shade of a large tree. You will know the moisture of the moon if you uncover your head at night, the moisture

[A] Meaning dew.

resulting from it condenses on your head, causing the common cold. Whatever wets your head, [also] wets the fruit [trees]. We shall not elaborate on what does not need thorough examination.

We say, every celestial body serves some kind of benefit, just as the sun serves to heat and the moon causes moisture. They are all bound by many wise decrees, which the power of human nature cannot enumerate. Were it not so, their creation surely would have been for sport and vanity and His words would not be true, *Our Lord, you have not created this in vain*;[9] And His statement, Almighty and Majestic, *We created not the heavens and earth, and everything between them in jest.*[10] And, just as every organ in your body has a beneficial purpose, so every 'organ' in the body of the whole world has a beneficial purpose. The whole universe is as one body. Within it, the individual bodies are like the organs; they help each other just like the organs in your body help each other. An explanation of [all of] this would be lengthy.

You should not think that the belief in the stars, the sun and the moon, which are subservient to the command of God, praise be to Him, and have roles [i.e., universal laws] that are decreed for them by [God's] wisdom, is contrary to the law because of what was narrated about the prohibition of believing in the astrologers and astrology.[11] Rather, what is forbidden concerning the stars are two matters. The first is believing that they are agents with effects of their own, entirely independent and that they are not subservient to an order or a Creator [Who] created and subjugated them. This is unbelief. The second forbidden [matter] is to believe the astrologers in the details of what they say about events that are not known to everyone; the astrologers speak this in ignorance. For knowledge of the wisdom of the stars was a miracle of some of the prophets (peace be upon them). This knowledge was then obliterated and there remains of it only a confusion: that which is correct in it cannot be distinguished from that which is erroneous.

Therefore, the belief that the celestial bodies are the causes for effects that take place in God's creation on earth, in plants and in animals, does not violate religion. On the contrary, it is truth. But to claim knowledge about the details of these effects is a violation of religion. For example, if you have a garment you washed and you want it to dry, and another says to you, 'Take the garment outside and spread it out, for the sun has risen; the day and the air have become warm.' You must not consider this false, or deny it, because he concluded that the air has become warm because of the rising of the sun. [Likewise] if you asked about a man's change of complexion and he replied, 'The sun shone on me on the road, and my face was tanned,' you must not think him false in this [statement]. This is how you should consider all effects [of the celestial bodies]; though some effects are known and some are unknown. In those that are unknown, one must not claim knowledge. As to those that are known, some are known to all men, such as the occurrence of light and heat with the rising of the sun, and some are known to a few people, such as the possibility of catching a cold with the rising of the moon.

Thus celestial bodies were not created in sport; they contain much wisdom which cannot be enumerated. This is why the Messenger of God (may God bless him and grant him peace) looked up at the sky and recited His (Exalted is He!) words, *Our Lord, You have not created this in vain. Glory be to You! Guard us against the punishment of the Fire.*[12] Then he (may God bless him and grant him peace) said, 'Woe to the one who recites this verse, and then smooths his moustache!'[13] Meaning that he recites without meditating [upon the verses] and his understanding of the kingdom of the heavens is limited to knowing the colour of the sky and the light of the celestial bodies. That is what the beasts also know. Therefore, he who is content only with this knowledge is the one referred to as he who 'smooths his moustache.'

For God (Exalted is He!), in the kingdom of the heavens, in the horizons, in humans and in animals has wonders whose knowledge the lovers of God (Exalted is He!) seek. He who loves a [particular] scholar is always preoccupied with searching for his books, to increase his love for him by contemplating the wonders of his knowledge. Such is the matter with the wonders of the creation of God (Exalted is He!). The whole world is His composition. Furthermore, the author's composition is His composition, as [God] composed it through the hearts of His servants. Therefore, if you marvel at a composition, do not marvel at the author, but at He who facilitated the composition for the author with His blessings, guidance, direction and instruction. This is the same as when you see the puppets of the puppeteer [who] dance and move, rhythmically balanced and complementary to each other. Do not marvel at the puppets, for they are rags that are moved, and cannot move [on their own], but marvel at the intelligence of the puppeteer [who] moves them by fine, delicate strings hidden from sight.

Finally, the intention [is to show that] the nourishment of the plant is only complete with water, air, sun, moon and celestial bodies. This [process] is complete only through the orbits in which the celestial bodies are stationed. The orbits of the celestial bodies are not complete except in their movements; and their movements are not complete except by the heavenly angels who operate them.[A] Similarly, this process extends to distant causes which we did not mention. You can build on what we have mentioned over and above what we have neglected. Let us be content [here] with the mention of the means of nourishment of plants.

The Fifth Example: On the Blessings of God in the Methods through which Food Reaches Us

KNOW that not all foods are found in every place. Their specific conditions are found in some places but not in others. People are scattered over the surface of the earth, and some foods may be distant from them; the oceans and the desert lands may come between them. Observe how God (Exalted is He!) makes use of merchants and allows love of wealth and the desire for profit

[A] This passage indicates that in philosophical terms Ghazālī adhered to the Ptolemaic theory of the universe, as did his contemporaries in the eastern lands.

to dominate them even though in most cases this does not avail them. They gather together [products], then, either the ships are sunk [with the goods on board], or highway robbers take them by force or they die in a foreign country and the sultan confiscates the goods. Their best lot is when their inheritors take them [the goods]. If they only knew that [commerce] is their worst enemy.

Observe how God causes ignorance and heedlessness to dominate them, so that they struggle with difficulties in their quest for profit, they embark on risky undertakings and rush headlong into human perils sailing the seas! Thus, they carry foods and various kinds of necessities to you from the farthest reaches of the East and West.

Consider how God (Exalted is He!) taught them how to build ships and to travel [the seas] in them! Take note how He created the animals and facilitated them for riding and carrying [things] through desert lands! Observe the camels, how they were created; the horse, how it was given speed; the donkey, how it was made patient for work; the camels, how they cross the desert lands and traverse [the earth] under heavy burdens famished and thirsty! Observe how God (Exalted is He!) leads the merchants by ships and animals, on dry land and by sea, carrying to you foodstuffs and other necessities. Consider what subsistence, supplies and food the animals need; and what the ships need! God (Exalted is He!) has created all this to the measure of need and beyond need. The enumeration of that is impossible, as it leads into matters that are beyond limit, and we see that we must leave this for the sake of brevity.

The Sixth Example: On the Preparation of Foods

KNOW that what grows in the earth as plants and what is derived from animals is unsuitable for eating as it is. It must be prepared, cooked, dressed and cleaned; one part is thrown out, another is retained and countless other things [are done to it]. Examining this for every food would be a lengthy [undertaking], so let us concentrate on one loaf of bread and see what it requires, from the time that the seeds are sown in the ground until it becomes a finished loaf, good for eating.

First a ploughman is needed to sow and prepare the ground; then an ox to till the ground, [in addition to] the plough and all of its tools; then after that [someone] to undertake frequent watering of the ground for a period; then the weeding; and, finally, harvesting the crop. Then [comes] the husking and sifting, then the milling, then [making] dough, and then the baking of bread.

So consider all these actions we have mentioned and all those we did not mention, the number of persons employed in them, and the number of instruments we need, of iron, wood, stone and other materials! Observe the work of the producers of tools for cultivation, milling and baking—from the carpenter to the blacksmith, and others! Observe the need of the blacksmith for iron, lead and brass. Observe how God (Exalted is He!) created the mountains, rocks and metals and how He divided the earth into different, adjacent regions![14] O pitiable one, if you examine [it closely] you will understand that one loaf does not become suitable for eating until more than a thousand craftsmen worked on it. The beginning lies with the King Who drives the clouds[15] to bring down rainwater; then it continues until the last of the work of the angels; then it passes to the work of man. Hence, the welfare [of people] turns on almost seven thousand craftsmen, each craftsman a source of industry on which the production depends.

And consider again the multiplicity of activities of men in those instruments—indeed, even the needle, a small instrument, has a purpose for the tailor [in sewing] clothing which wards off the cold for you. Its form, a piece of iron, is not complete for a needle until it is modified twenty-five times by the hands of the needle-maker, and he exerts [himself] each time differently on it.

Had God (Exalted is He!) not united the lands and not made available the servants and had deprived you, for example, of the work of the scythe, which harvests the wheat after it is ripe, you would have perished and you would have been incapable [of harvesting].

Do you not see how God (Exalted is He!) guides His servant, whom He has created from an impure drop of sperm,[16] so that he might do this marvellous work and extraordinary production?

Look at the scissors, for example, shears corresponding to each other, they grasp something and cut it with speed. Had God (Exalted is He!), with His bounty and goodness, not disclosed a way of manufacturing them to those who came before us, it would have been necessary for us to discover this invention by our own thinking, from how to mine the iron from stone, to produce the tools by which the scissors are made. If one had Noah's lifespan and the most perfect of minds, his lifespan surely would be too short to discover how to invent this one tool, let alone others like it!

Praise be to Him, therefore, Who guided the blind through those who can see and praise be to Him Who forbade any exposition after the Bayān.[A] Observe now, had your land been devoid of, say, the miller, blacksmith, cupper—who is the least specialised of workmen—the tailor or of any one of the craftsmen, what trouble you would have and how stricken you would be in all your affairs![17] Praise be to Him Who facilitates [the work of] some servants for others, so that His will may be executed, and His wisdom be fulfilled! Let us be brief with the statement in this category also, for our object is to attend to the blessing without [detailed] investigation.

The Seventh Example: On the Guidance of those who Hold Responsibility

KNOW that if those skilled in the preparation of food, and in other things, disagreed in their opinions and clashed by their natures like the clashing of the beasts, then they would surely be scattered and become distant from one another, unable to benefit from each other. Furthermore, they would be like wild beasts that no one place could contain, nor a single purpose unite.

[A] A name of the Qur'ān.

Observe how God unites their hearts and causes intimacy and love to overpower them! *Had you expended all that is in the earth, you could not have brought their hearts together, but God brought their hearts together.*[18] Through intimacy and fellowship, human spirits come together to build cities and towns; organise dwellings and houses near each other; organise markets, shops and various other things too many to describe. This love fades away when there are motives that cause [people] to jostle each other and compete. For rancour, envy and rivalry are in the nature of man, and lead to fighting and hostility.

Observe, therefore, how God (Exalted is He!) lets rulers dominate and how He furnishes them with power, preparedness and means. He places fear of them in the hearts of their subjects so that they submit willingly or unwillingly. [And note] how He guides rulers in the way to improve [their] countries and to even organise parts of their districts as if they were the parts of one person, cooperating for a single objective by which one part benefits from the others. Thus, they appoint leaders, judges, prison wardens and commissioners of the markets. They compel people [to follow] the rules of justice and force them to assist each other and cooperate. In this way, the blacksmith benefits from the butcher, the baker and other people in the country all benefit from the blacksmith. The cupper benefits from the ploughman and the ploughman from the cupper. Everyone benefits from everyone else because of their organisation, assembly and discipline under the arrangement and unity of the ruler, just as all the organs of the body cooperate and benefit from each other.

Consider how He sent the prophets (peace be upon them) to reform the rulers [who] reform their subjects. They taught them the regulations of the canonical law (*sharʿ*), the preservation of justice between people and the political ordinances through which to regulate them [the subjects]. They revealed the guiding principles of leadership, kingship and jurisprudence that help them [the rulers] reform this world. This is in addition to the guidance that [the rulers] received from [the prophets] in the furtherance of religion. Take note how God (Exalted is He!) guided the prophets through the angels, and how He guided the angels one through another until you ultimately arrive at the closest angel,[A] between God and whom there is no intermediary.

So the baker bakes the dough; the miller grinds the grain fine for the flour; the ploughman makes it ready for the harvest; the blacksmith prepares the tools used in cultivation; and the carpenter prepares the tools of the blacksmith. Likewise, all those skilled in the manufacturing of the tools for food [do their work]. The ruler guides the craftsmen; the prophets guide the scholars, who are their heirs;[19] the scholars guide the rulers; and the angels guide the prophets until you arrive at the Lordly presence which is the spring of all order, the origin of all goodness and beauty, and the fountainhead of all organisation and composition.

All of these are blessings from the Lord of lords, the Cause of causes. Were it not for His bounty and His generosity as He (Exalted is He!) said, *But those who strive in Our cause, surely We shall guide them in Our ways,*[20] we surely would not have been guided to the knowledge of this facet of the blessings of God (Exalted is He!). If He had not stopped us from aspiring to encompass, through greed, knowledge of the essence of His blessings, we would long to seek everything, even what cannot be counted. But He (Exalted is He!) released us, however, by the wise decrees of coercion and power. For He (Exalted is He!) said, *If you count God's blessings, you will never number them.*[21] Thus when we speak [about certain matters] it is because He has given us permission to do so, and when we are silent it is He Who subdues and restrains us. No one can grant what He restricts and no one can restrict what He gives. In every moment of our lives before death, we listen with the hearing of our hearts to the call of the King, the Almighty, *Whose is the Kingdom today? God's, the One, the Omnipotent.*[22] Therefore, praise be to God Who set us apart from the non-believers and caused us to hear this call before the end of [our] lives.

[A] An allusion to Gabriel. Cf. Q.II.97, LXVI.4.

The Eighth Example: An Exposition of the Blessing of God in the Creation of the Angels (peace be upon them)

THE PREVIOUSLY mentioned blessing of God in His creation of the angels for the advancement and guidance of the prophets (peace be upon them) and for the transmission of the revelations should now be clear to you. But do not think that they are limited in their deeds to this activity [only]. Despite their number and the organisation of their ranks, the angels are divided into three classes: earthly angels, heavenly [angels], and the bearers of the throne (*ḥamalat al-ʿarsh*).[23]

Observe how God (Exalted is He!) entrusted you to them in the matters of eating and sustenance, which we have mentioned [above]. Beyond these is guidance, counsel, and other things. Know that every part of your body, even every part of a plant, is nourished by seven angels who are given responsibility in the matter. But this is the fewest, for they may be ten or one hundred [angels] or even more. The meaning of nourishment is that some food takes the place of another which has been used up, until this nourishment becomes blood, then flesh and bone. When it has become flesh and bone, your nourishment is complete. The blood and flesh are substances that have no power, knowledge or choice, for they neither move nor change by themselves. Their nature is not sufficient for their transformation. Just as wheat, by itself, does not become flour, then a round baked loaf, except by a craftsman. Likewise, blood does not become flesh, bone, veins and nerves except by a craftsman. The craftsmen of the body are the angels, just as craftsmen in the visible [world] are the people of the land.

God (Exalted is He!) has bestowed ample blessings upon you, visible and invisible. You must not be heedless of His invisible blessings. Thus I say, there must be an angel to draw nourishment into the flesh and bone, for nourishment does not move by itself. There must be another angel to retain the nourishment in its [particular] part; there must be a third to extract the form of blood from it; a fourth to clothe it with the form of flesh, veins or bone; a fifth to discard the surplus that goes beyond the required sustenance; a sixth to connect what takes on the quality of bone with bone, and what takes on the quality of flesh with flesh until they are inseparable; and, assuredly, a seventh [angel] to supervise the balance in the connections, and convey to that which is tubular what will keep it tubular, to that which is wide what will keep it wide, and to that which is hollow what will not ruin its hollowness, and preserve each one according to its need.

If, for example, the nourishment that is stored in the thigh were conveyed to the nose of the young boy, the nose would become enlarged, its cavities would become blocked and its shape and form would become deformed. Therefore, it is imperative that the eyelids in all their thinness, the pupils in their clearness, the thighs in their thickness and the bones in their hardness should each receive what is suitable to them in respect of quantity and form; otherwise, the form would be unsound, and some bodily parts would be augmented and others weakened. Again, had this angel not supervised the just division and distribution of the bodily sustenance, and [had he] conveyed nourishment to the head of the boy and, for example, given to the rest of his body what it needs to grow, with the exception of one leg, that leg would remain as it was during childhood while the rest of the body grew larger. Then you would see a person with the build of a man, with one leg like that of a boy; and it would not be of any use whatsoever. The supervision of this symmetry in these [bodily] parts is the responsibility of one of the angels. Surely, you do not think that the blood, by its nature, constructs its form itself! Anyone who assigns these matters to nature [alone] is ignorant and does not know what he speaks of!

These are the earthly angels. They are busy with you when you rest in sleep and when you waver in and out of consciousness. They provide nourishment internally, without your knowledge; and likewise for every part of you which cannot be divided. Some of the parts [of your body], like the eye and the heart, are dependent on more than one hundred angels. We will omit the details of this process for the sake of brevity.

The earthly angels are supported by the heavenly angels in a distinct order whose substance is known only by God (Exalted is He!). The heavenly angels are supported by the bearers of the throne. He Who blesses them all with support, guidance and direction is the All-Preserver, the Most-Holy, He Who is Unique in the invisible and visible [worlds], the Mighty One Who reigns supreme in the heavens and the earth, the King of the dominion, the Possessor of majesty and glory. The traditions related about the angels entrusted with the heavens and the earth, the parts of plants and animals, even each drop of rain and every cloud that moves from place to place,[24] are more than can be counted, so we will leave mention of them.

You may say, 'Why are seven angels entrusted with these acts instead of one?' Does not wheat first need someone to mill it; second, someone to separate the grain and remove the husk; third, someone to pour water over it; fourth, someone to knead [it]; fifth, someone to cut the round balls of dough; sixth, another to flatten the dough into wide loaves of bread; and seventh, to bake it in the oven. [However,] it is possible for one man to deal with all that. Therefore, are the activities of the angels inwardly like the activities of mankind outwardly?

Know that the creation of the angels differs from the creation of mankind; they are each made up of a single attribute. They are not at all complex or composite. There is only one kind of action for each one of them. This is indicated in His (Exalted is He!) statement, *Every one there has a known station.*[25] This is why there is no rivalry and struggle between them. The assignment of each [angel's] station and role is similar to the assignment of the five senses. For sight does not compete with hearing in the perception of sounds; nor does smell compete with them; and neither disputes with smell. It is not like the hand and the leg. You may strike a weak blow with the toes of the foot, which is then in competition with the hand. [Or,] you may strike another with your head, thus competing with the hand which is the instrument of striking. This is not like the one man who alone is occupied with the milling, the dough and the baking. Indeed, there is a kind of crookedness and abandonment of balance caused by the differing attributes of man and the divergence of his motives. For he is not made up of only one attribute, so he cannot do just a single action. Hence, we find that man sometimes obeys God and other times disobeys Him because of the variety of his motives and his qualities.

This is not possible in the nature of the angels. Angels are in fact moulded for obedience; disobedience is not possible for them. This is surely why they do not disobey God's commands and they do what they have been commanded[26] and give praise night and day without end.[27] Their bowing is never-ending; their prostration and their standing are everlasting; there is neither deviation nor lassitude in their acts. Every one has a designated station beyond which he cannot go. They obey God because it is not possible for them to disobey. You may compare this to the obedience of your limbs to you. Once you resolve to open your eyelids, there is no possibility for a healthy eyelid to delay, nor to obey you once, and disobey you another time. It is as if it awaits your command to open or shut, in conformity with your indication. This response resembles [that of the angels] in one way, but differs from it in another way, since the eyelid has no knowledge of the opening and closing, whereas the angels are living beings who know what they do.

This, then, is God's blessing upon you in the earthly and the heavenly angels and your need for them in the sole matter of eating, aside from all the other movements and needs. We will not belabour the point, for this is just another of the classes of blessings, [which] together with all the classes, cannot be enumerated, let alone the individual [blessings] that come under the main classifications. Indeed, God (Exalted is He!) has bestowed His blessings, both visible and invisible, amply upon you. He said, *Eschew all sin, open or secret.*[28] Abandoning inner sin that others cannot see, like envy, suspicion, innovation, malicious intentions towards men and other sins of the human heart, is thankfulness for the invisible blessings. Abandoning the outward sin of the limbs of the body is thankfulness for the visible blessing. Moreover, I say, everyone who disobeys God (Exalted is He!) even in the batting of an eye, for example, in looking up when he should have looked down in modesty, denies every blessing of God (Exalted is He!) upon him in the heavens and earth and what is between them! For all that God (Exalted is He!) created—all the angels, heavens, earth, animals and plants—is a blessing upon every servant and a means of benefit for him, even when it benefits others too.

In each blink of the eye, God (Exalted is He!) grants two blessings in the very eyelid. For He created inside every eyelid muscles which have tendons and ligaments connected with the nerves of the brain by which the upper eyelid is lowered and the lower eyelid is raised. Black hairs exist on each eyelid, and the blessing of God (Exalted is He!) with respect to their blackness is that they collect the light of the eye, since whiteness diffuses the light and blackness gathers it. God's blessing in arranging [the lashes] in a row is that they prevent insects from entering the inside of the eye and prevent foreign bodies flying about the air from sticking to it. There are two blessings in each eyelash—it is soft and yet straight. The greatest blessing, though, is in the interlocking of the eyelashes. For dust in the wind can prevent one from opening the eyes and, when the eyelids are closed, you cannot see. But it is possible to bring the eyelids together until the eyelashes interlock and look from behind the screen of the lashes. This screen of lashes blocks dirt from entering and does not prevent sight from within.

Then [to prevent] specks of dust entering [the eye], He created the edges of the eyelids to close over the pupil like the burnishing tool for the mirror. In shutting once or twice, the dust is polished from the pupil. The specks of dirt are removed to the corners of the eyes and eyelids. As the fly has no eyelid for its pupil, He created it with two hands, so you see it using [them] continually to rub its two eyes, brushing away the dust. We will omit the extensive details of the blessings, which would require a protracted discussion that would go beyond the purpose of this book. If time grants a respite and [God] grants success, we may dedicate a book to it and call it *The Wonders of God's Creation* (*ʿAjā'ib ṣunʿ Allāh*).

So let us return to our objective. We say: he who gazes at a forbidden thing has denied, by raising his eyes [to it], the blessing that God (Exalted is He!) grants in the eyelids. The eyelids exist only for the eye; the eye only for the head; the head for the whole of the body; the body through food; food through water, earth, wind, rain, clouds, sun and moon. None of these can exist without the heavens and the heavens only [exist] by the angels. Indeed, the whole [process] is like one thing whose parts are bound together like the connection of the organs of the body with one another. Thus, [the transgressor] denies every blessing in existence from the farthest reaches of the universe to the deepest depths of the earth. There is no star, no angel, no animal, no plant and no substance that does not curse him.

It has been recorded in the Traditions that the very plot [of earth] on which people gather, once they depart, either curses them or asks [God] to pardon them.[29] Likewise, it has been recorded that everything, even the fish of the sea, seek forgiveness for a scholar.[30] While the angels curse the disobedient.[31] And there are countless other examples. All this indicates that the disobedient person, just with the movement of an eye, commits sin against everything in the visible and the invisible worlds. He destroys himself, unless he follows the sin with a good deed that obliterates it [the sin]; and he exchanges the curse for a pardon. Perhaps then, God will forgive him and pardon him. God (Exalted is He!) revealed to Job (peace be upon him), 'O Job, every servant of mine among human beings has two angels. If he thanks Me for my blessings, the two angels will say, "Almighty God, grant him blessings upon blessings, for You are worthy of praise and thankfulness." So adhere to the thankful for theirs is truly a high level with Me. I praise their thankfulness! My angels supplicate for them. The places [they reside in] love them and the traces [they leave behind] weep over them!'[32]

And just as you know that in every blink of an eye there are many blessings, know that every inhalation and exhalation has two blessings. By exhaling, the spent vapour of the heart goes out. If it did not go out, the servant would surely perish. By inhaling, the essence of the air is brought to the heart and, were his breathing blocked, his heart would surely burn up, cut off from the essence of the air and its coolness, and he would perish. Furthermore, the day and night are twenty-four hours, and in every hour there are nearly one thousand breaths, and every breath takes nearly ten seconds.

So then, there are thousands and thousands of blessings upon you in every part of your body. And, in every part of the world! Look then and see if it is possible to enumerate all these or not. When the reality of the words of God (Exalted is He!), *If you count God's blessing, you will never number them*,[33] were revealed to Moses (peace be upon him), he said, 'My God, how can I thank you when [even] in every hair of my body you have granted two blessings: making its origin supple and covering up its root?'[34]

Thus, it has been set down in the Traditions that he who does not know God's blessing except in his food and drink, his knowledge is scant and his punishment is prepared. All that we have mentioned about food and drink is a measure of how you should consider all the other blessings. For the eye of the person with insight does not notice anything in the world, nor does his thought become familiar with [any] existing [thing], except that he confirms that God has granted him a blessing in it. But we will refrain from an exhaustive listing and detailed explanation, for it is to long for the unattainable.

CHAPTER FOURTEEN
An Exposition of the Causes which Turn People Away from Thankfulness

KNOW that that which turns people away from thankfulness for blessings is ignorance (*jahl*) and heedlessness (*ghafla*). They are prevented by ignorance and heedlessness from recognising the blessings; for one can only be thankful for a blessing that one recognises. Then, when [people] do recognise a blessing, they assume that being thankful for it is only to verbally say, 'Praise be to God! Thanks be to God!' They do not know that the meaning of thankfulness is to use the blessing to perfect the wisdom intended by it and that this is obedience to God, Almighty and Majestic. Nothing prevents thankfulness after the attainment of these two insights except the victory of the appetite and the conquest of Satan.

As for heedlessness, there are many causes. One cause is that people, in their ignorance, do not recognise that what is general to mankind, and granted to them in all their states, is a blessing. They are not thankful, therefore, for all the blessings we have mentioned because these blessings are for all people and are given to them in all of their states. Each person does not see [something] special for himself, so he does not reckon it a blessing. You do not see people thanking God for the substance of the air. Yet if they were grasped by their throats for a moment, until the air was cut off, they would die. If they are imprisoned in a bathhouse full of hot air, or in a well containing air heavy with moisture, they would die in distress. If a disaster such as this were to befall one of them, and he were saved, perhaps he would regard it as a blessing and thank God for it. This is the utmost limit of ignorance, since their thankfulness is deferred until the blessing is withheld from them and then, sometimes, restored to them. Being thankful in all the states is preferred to [being thankful] in only some of them. You do not see the person with sight thankful for the health of his eyes until his eyes are blinded. If, then, his sight is restored to him, he becomes aware of it [as a blessing] and is thankful and reckons it a blessing.

Because the mercy of God encompasses mankind as a whole, and He gives to them generously in all situations, the ignorant person does not reckon it a blessing. This ignorant person is like the unruly servant who always deserves to be beaten—when his beating is left off for an hour, a favour has been granted to him. If his beating were set aside permanently, insolence would overtake him and he would put aside gratitude [altogether].

People today give thanks for wealth, which gains them access to privileges, [whether it be] much or little. They forget all the blessings of God (Exalted is He!) upon them. One such [person] complained of his poverty to a person of insight, and displayed how intensely unhappy he was. So he [his friend] asked him, 'Would it please you, to be blind and to have ten thousand dirhams?' He replied, 'No.' Then he asked, 'Would it please you to be mute and to have ten thousand dirhams?' He replied, 'No.' Then he asked, 'Would it please you to be without hands and legs and to have twenty thousand [dirhams]?' He replied, 'No.' Then he asked, 'Would it please you to be insane and to have ten thousand dirhams?' He replied, 'No.' Then he said, 'Are you not ashamed to complain about your Lord and He has given you goods worth fifty thousand?'[1]

It was said that a reciter [of the Qur'ān] was so oppressed by poverty that he could not bear it. He had a vision in his sleep of someone speaking to him, saying, 'Would you like me to cause you to forget Sūrat al-Anʿām from the Qur'ān and there will be a thousand dinars for you?' He replied, 'No.' The man asked, 'Then Sūrat Hūd?' He replied, 'No.' Then he asked, 'Sūrat Yūsuf?'

He replied, 'No.' The man enumerated all the chapters [of the Qur'ān] and then said, 'You have the value of one hundred thousand dinars and you complain!' When [the reciter] woke up he was relieved.[2]

Ibn al-Sammāk visited one of the caliphs, who was holding in his hand a jug of water and drinking from it. The caliph said to him, 'Give me advice!' He replied, 'If you were not given this drink unless you gave up all your wealth, or you would remain thirsty, would you give it up?' The caliph replied, 'Yes.' Then he asked, 'If you were not given this drink unless [you gave up] all your kingdom, would you leave it?' The caliph said, 'Yes.' [Ibn al-Sammāk] said, 'Then take no joy in a kingdom that does not equal even a drink of water!' This shows that the blessing that God (Exalted is He!) grants the servant in a drink of water when he is thirsty is greater than sovereignty over all the earth!

Because [people] are inclined, by nature, to consider specific blessings rather than general blessings—we have [already] mentioned general blessings—we will now give a brief indication of the specific blessings. We say, every servant who closely examines his condition will find a blessing from God, or many blessings, which are specific to him and which are not shared by everyone. He may share them with a few people but they may [also] be his alone. Every servant can acknowledge this fact in three respects: intellect (*ʿaql*), character (*khuluq*) and knowledge (*ʿilm*).

As for intellect, every servant of God (Exalted is He!) is pleased with God for his intellect: he believes that he is the most intelligent of men. Few are those who ask God for [more] intelligence. Indeed, it is because of the distinction of the intellect that whoever is devoid of it is pleased, just as whoever possesses it is pleased. Therefore, if he is convinced that he is the most intelligent of men, he must be thankful for it. Because if it is so, thankfulness is a duty for him. But if he is not and yet he thinks that he is, then it is a blessing for him. He who buries a treasure in the ground delights in it and is thankful for it. If the treasure is stolen without his knowledge, he will still be happy because of his conviction and his thankfulness remains just as if [the treasure] were still there.

As for character, every servant sees faults that he dislikes in others, and character traits that he finds blameworthy. He criticises these because he considers himself devoid of them. Instead of busying himself with criticising others, he should be occupied with thankfulness to God (Exalted is He!), since He has an good character and another is afflicted with bad character.

As for knowledge, each knows his innermost concerns and his hidden thoughts and what he keeps to himself. If these were revealed, such that someone can look upon them, he would surely be shamed—even more if all men were to look! So if every servant knows of a private matter that he does not share with another of God's servants, why is he not thankful for the beautiful veil that God has sent him, which reveals the commendable and covers up the reprehensible and conceals this from the eyes of people, making knowledge of it specific to him, such that no one looks upon it. These three then are among the specific blessings that every servant can acknowledge, either entirely or in part.

Let us descend from this level to a slightly more general one. We say, there is no servant but God (Exalted is He!) has provided him things, in his [bodily] form, his personality, his character, his qualities, family, children, dwelling, country, companions, relatives, strength, prominence and the rest of what is dear to him, such that, if they were taken away from him and given to another, he surely would not be pleased. For example, He has made him a believer, not a non-believer; a living being, not an inanimate body; a person, not an animal; a male, not a female; a healthy not a sick person; and sound, not disabled. All these are particular [characteristics], despite being general to others. Were these states exchanged for their opposites, he would not be pleased with them.

Furthermore, [each servant] also has other matters that he does not [want to] exchange with the states of other people. That is, either because he will not exchange with another person what is specific to himself, or he will not exchange with most men what is specific to himself. If he will not exchange the state of his soul for the state of another, then his state must be better than the state of the other. If he cannot find anyone whose state he would prefer to his own, whether as a whole or in a specific aspect, then God (Exalted is He!) has granted him blessings that He has not granted to any of His other servants. If he is willing to exchange his own state with that of some but not of others, then let him observe the number of those whom he envies and he will find that they are inevitably few in number in comparison to the others. He will find that those who are beneath his state are many more than those who are above him.

Why, then, does he concern himself with looking at those above him in order to make little of the blessings of God (Exalted is He!) upon himself? And why does he not look beneath himself in order to regard as great the blessings of God upon him? Why does he not use the same measures for the world [that he uses] for his religion? When his soul blames him for a sin, does he not [find] excuses for himself, [saying] there are many sinners? So, he always looks to someone below him in religion, not above him. Why does he not view the world in the same way? For, when the state of most people in religion is worse than his, and his state in the world is better than most people, how does this not compel him to gratitude? About this, he (may God bless him and grant him peace) said, 'He who looks in this world to who is below him and looks in his religion to who is above, God will record that he is patient and thankful. He who looks in this world to who is above him and looks in his religion to who is below him, God will not record that he is patient and thankful.'[3]

Therefore everyone who considers his own state and searches for what is unique to him will find that God (Exalted is He!) [has granted him] many blessings, especially in respect of the Sunna, faith, knowledge, the Qur'ān; but also leisure, health, security, and other [things]. For this, it is said,

> He who wishes a comfortable living by which to increase
> his success in religion and in worldly matters

> Let him consider those above him in piety, and let him consider those below him in wealth.[4]

He [the Prophet] (may God bless him and grant him peace) said, 'He who does not find his sufficiency in the verses of God [the Qur'ān], God has not enriched him.'[5] This is an allusion to the blessing of knowledge. He [also] said, 'The Qur'ān is wealth beyond which there is no wealth, and with which there is no poverty.'[6] He (may God bless him and grant him peace) said, 'The man to whom God has given the Qur'ān and who supposes that another is richer than himself mocks the verses of God;'[7] and he (may God bless him and grant him peace) said, 'He is not one of us who has not been enriched by the Qur'ān;'[8] and he (may God bless him and grant him peace) said, 'It is enough to have certainty (*yaqīn*) as wealth.'[9]

One of the Predecessors said, 'God (Exalted is He!) says, in one of the revealed books, "Truly, I have completed my blessing upon the servant to whom I have spared three things: the visit of the sultan, the need for the physician, and what is with his brother."'[10A]

The poet expressed this thus,

> As food comes to you,
> So come health and security.
> Once you become a brother of sorrow,
> Then sorrow will not from you depart.[11]

Moreover, the most concise advice and the most eloquent of words in the eloquent Arabic language,[B] was expressed by [the Prophet] (may God bless him and grant him peace!) when he said,

[A] 'What is with his brother' here means: the burdens that others have to bear.

[B] Lit., 'to pronounce the *ḍāḍ*.' The Arabic language is often referred to as 'the language of the letter *ḍāḍ*.' Zabīdī quotes the celebrated tradition of the Prophet, 'I am the most eloquent of those who pronounce the letter *ḍāḍ*' (Zabīdī, IX.133); it is also cited in Shawkānī, p. 327, and in Lane, *Lexicon*, v.1759.

'He who awakens healthy in his body, secure in his home, with enough provision for his day, it is as if he were given the world in its entirety.'[12]

If you consider, you will find that all people complain and suffer from matters that return to these three. They see the burden in them and they do not thank God for the blessing in these three. [Nor] are they thankful for God's blessing upon them in faith, through which they attain the abiding favour of God and the great kingdom [i.e., Heaven]. The insightful should only rejoice in wisdom, [inner] certainty and faith.

Furthermore, we ourselves know that among the scholars is he who, if he were offered all that comes under the control of the kings of the earth, from East to West, of wealth, followers and companions and it was said to him, 'Take this in exchange for your knowledge, or even for one percent of your knowledge,' he would not take it. That is because of his hope that the blessing of knowledge will lead him to nearness to God (Exalted is He!) in the Hereafter. If it were said to him, 'You will have all that you hope for in the Hereafter in full. So take these pleasures in this world instead of your pleasure in knowledge and your delight in it in this world.' He would not take it, because he knows that the pleasure in knowledge is continual not ephemeral, permanent not liable to be stolen, it cannot be taken away by force, cannot be vied for and it is pure and unsullied. Whereas the pleasures of this world are all flawed, sullied and unclear. Desire for them is not free from fear, their pleasure is not free from pain and their happiness from sorrow. They have always been thus and so shall they remain till the end of time.

The pleasures of this world were created so that deficient minds may clamour after them and be deceived. Even when they are deceived and bound by them, [the pleasures] deny and resist them. It is like an outwardly beautiful woman who adorns herself for the lustful and rich youth, then when his heart is bound to her, she scorns him and avoids him. He thus remains ever-troubled and in continual strife. All this is due to his enthralment with the pleasure of looking at her even for a moment. If he came to his senses and lowered his gaze, making little of that pleasure, he would be safe for the rest of his life. It is thus that the worldly fall into the net and the traps of this world.

We should not say that he who turns away from the world is grieved by the patience it demands. For he who seeks [this world] is also grieved by his patience, and his need to retain it, to acquire it and to protect it from thieves. The suffering of he who turns away [from the world] leads to pleasure in the Hereafter, while the suffering of he who seeks it leads to pain in the Hereafter. Let the one who turns away from this world recite to himself the saying of the Exalted, *Do not flag in your pursuit of the enemy; if you suffer, they too suffer, but you hope from God what they cannot hope.*[13] Therefore, the way of thankfulness is obstructed for everyone due to their ignorance of the kinds of blessings, visible and invisible, specific and general.

You may ask, 'What is the treatment for these heedless hearts, [to make them] aware of the blessings of God (Exalted is He!) so that they may become thankful?' I will reply that the treatment for those hearts that are capable of insight is the contemplation of the [already] alluded to general blessings of God (Exalted is He!). As for those hearts that are not capable of insight, which do not reckon a blessing to be a blessing unless it is unique to them or [until] they are afflicted by calamity, the remedy for them is to always look at those beneath them. They should do what one Sufi used to do: each day he visited the hospital, the cemetery and the places where legal punishments are meted out. He went to the hospital to witness the forms of afflictions of God (Exalted is He!), so he may then reflect on his own health and safety. His heart would feel the blessing of health when he saw the afflictions of disease, and he would thank God (Exalted is He!). He witnessed the criminals who are killed, those whose limbs are severed and those who are punished by [a variety] of punishments, that he may thank God (Exalted is He!) for His protection from crime and from these punishments, and that he may thank God (Exalted is He!) for the blessing of safety. He visited the cemetery, knowing that what the dead desire most is that they be returned to this world, if only for a day.

[Knowing this] the one who is disobedient to God will redress himself, and the one who is obedient will increase his obedience. For the Day of the Resurrection is the day of mutual disillusion.[14] The obedient will be disillusioned when he sees the rewards of his obedience. He will say, 'I was able to do more than these acts of obedience. How great was my inadvertence, I wasted opportunities in things permitted.'[A] The deception of the disobedient, on the other hand, is apparent. For if he sees the graves with his own eyes and knows that what [the dead] most desire is to recover what life he still has, he will spend the remainder of his life in what the people of the graves long to return to; and this will be a reminder to him of the blessings of God (Exalted is He!) for the rest of his life, and even in the respite that is granted to him in every breath he takes. And, if [the servant] knows this blessing, he gives thanks that he will spend his life for what it was created for: to provide [for oneself] from this world for the Hereafter. This is the treatment for the heedless hearts, to make them aware of the blessings of God (Exalted is He!); that they may become thankful.

Al-Rabīaᶜ b. Khaytham, despite the fullness of his inner vision (*istibṣār*), sought support in this way to affirm [his] gnosis (*maᶜrifa*). He dug a grave in the courtyard of his home, [each night] he put a chain around his neck and slept in this grave. He used to recite *Lord, let me return; that I may do good.*[15] On waking he would say, 'O Rabīaᶜ! You have been granted what you asked for, so do good before [the day when] you will ask to return and it will not be granted!'[16]

Part of what will cure those hearts far removed from thankfulness is to know that the blessing, if [one does] not thank [God] for it, will vanish and not return. Thus, al-Fuḍayl b. ᶜIyāḍ (may

[A] As opposed to busying himself with acts that gain merit and reward in the Hereafter.

the mercy of God be upon him) used to say, 'It is incumbent upon you to persevere in thankfulness for blessings. It is rare that a blessing is withdrawn from and then returned to a people.'[17]

One of the Predecessors said, 'Blessings are unrestrained.[A] Therefore, tie them down with thankfulness.'

And in the narration, 'No sooner does the blessing of God (Exalted is He!) become great upon a servant than people turn to him in need. He who scorns them risks losing that blessing.'[18]

God, praise be to Him (Exalted is He!) said, *God does not change what is with a people, until they change what is in themselves.*[19] This is the end of this section.

[A] *Waḥshiyya*, literally, 'wild' or 'like the wild beasts.'

SECTION THREE
ON WHAT PATIENCE AND THANKFULNESS SHARE AND WHAT LINKS ONE WITH THE OTHER

CHAPTER FIFTEEN
An Exposition of that which Unites Patience and Thankfulness

YOU MAY say that what I have mentioned about blessings indicates that there is a blessing from God (Exalted is He!) in every existing thing. This would mean that tribulation does not essentially exist. What, then, does patience mean? And if tribulation does exist, what does thankfulness for tribulation mean? [Also] there are those who claim, 'We are thankful for both tribulation and blessing.' Yet how is thankfulness imaginable for tribulation? And how can one be thankful for what one endures patiently, for patience in tribulation is accompanied by pain and thankfulness is accompanied by joy—are they then not mutually contradictory? What [then] is the meaning of our statement that God (Exalted is He!) has a blessing for His servants in all that He has created?

Know that tribulation exists, just as the blessing exists. To affirm the existence of the blessing necessitates the affirmation of the existence of tribulation, because they are mutually contradictory. To be free of tribulation is blessing and to be free of blessing is tribulation. [We have mentioned] earlier that blessings are divided into the blessing that is absolute in every respect—whether in the Hereafter, such as the happiness of the servant in being granted proximity to God (Exalted is He!), or in this world, such as faith, good character and what helps in their attainment. And into the relative blessing that is good in one respect but not in another, such as wealth, which can benefit religion in one respect and can spoil it in another. Likewise tribulation is divided into absolute and relative. As for the absolute: in the Hereafter, it is distance from God (Exalted is He!), either for a period of time or forever; in this world, it is unbelief, disobedience and bad character traits, which lead to absolute tribulation. As for the relative [tribulations], such as poverty, disease, fear and other varieties of tribulation, these are not tribulations in religion but in this world.

Absolute thankfulness, therefore, is for an absolute blessing. As for the absolute tribulations of this world, one is not commanded to be patient with them. It is senseless to say that one should be patient with the tribulations of unbelief and disobedience.

It is incumbent on the non-believer to leave his unbelief; as it is incumbent on the disobedient [to become obedient]. Indeed, the non-believer may not know that he is a non-believer; he then resembles someone who has an illness, but who is not in any discomfort from faintness or other [symptoms], so no patience is required. He who is disobedient knows that he is disobedient; it is incumbent upon him to put aside disobedience. In fact, man is not commanded to bear patiently any tribulation that he is able to dispel. If someone leaves water until his thirst causes him great suffering, he is not commanded to bear it with patience, rather he is commanded to relieve the suffering. Patience in suffering is applicable only when the suffering cannot be alleviated.

Thus, patience in this world refers to what is not an absolute tribulation, but to what can also be considered a blessing. This is why it is possible for the functions of patience and thankfulness to be combined in it. For example, wealth may be the cause of a man's destruction, he can be a target because of his money; he and his children could [even] be killed. Health too [can be considered] in the same way. Every worldly blessing, in addition to [being a blessing], can also become a tribulation. While every [worldly] tribulation, in addition to [being a tribulation], can also become a blessing.

It may be that poverty and illness are what is best for a servant. If his body were healthy and his wealth manifold, he may behave with pride and insolence. God has said, *Were God to expand His provision to [all] his servants, they would act insolently on earth*;[1] and He (Exalted is He!) said, *No indeed, surely man is insolent, for he thinks himself self-sufficient*.[2] The Prophet (may God bless him and grant him peace) said, 'When God loves a believing servant, He protects him from the world just as any of you protects his sick one,'[3] and his wife, children and kinsmen.

Everything we have mentioned in the sixteen divisions of blessings, apart from faith and good character, may become a tribulation for some people; and their opposite would be a blessing for them. Earlier, knowledge was defined as a perfection and a blessing, being an attribute of God (Exalted is He!). However, in some circumstances, it may be a tribulation for the servant and its loss a blessing. For example, a man's ignorance of when he will die is a blessing for him, since, if he knew, he may lose any pleasure in life and may become overwhelmed with grief. Likewise, his ignorance of what [ill thoughts] his acquaintances and kinsmen harbour against him may be a blessing for him; if the veil were lifted and he were able to observe this, he may become overwhelmed with pain, resentment and envy and occupy himself with revenge.

Similarly, [the servant's] ignorance of the blameworthy qualities of another is a blessing for him. Were he to know them, he would detest the other and harm him, and that would have deleterious consequences in this world and the Hereafter. His ignorance of the praiseworthy qualities of another may also be a blessing for him. For the latter may be a saint of God (Exalted is He!), and he may be obliged to harm him and to insult him. If he knew this and harmed [the saint], his sin would inevitably be greater.

For he who has harmed a prophet or a saint knowingly is not [in the same position] as he who has harmed him unknowingly. The same [applies to] the concealment by God (Exalted is He!) of the Resurrection, His concealment of the Night of Power (*laylat al-qadr*),[A] and of the hour [in which prayers are accepted] on Friday, and His concealment of some of the grave sins. All of this is a blessing, because ignorance [of them] increases your incentive to seek and strive. So these are aspects of the blessings of God (Exalted is He!) with regards to ignorance.

What then [of the blessings of God with regard to] knowledge? It is true when we say that God (Exalted is He!) has placed a blessing in every existent thing. This is invariably so for everyone. No exception to this can be supposed, except the sufferings that He created in some people. Yet even these can be a blessing for the one suffering them. Yet, these are not a blessing for him if the pain occurs from disobedience, such as cutting off one's own hand and tattooing one's skin; for he feels pain through his own disobedience. And the pain of the non-believers in the Fire is a blessing, but for other servants and not for them; 'for the disasters (*maṣā'ib*) of one people have benefits (*fawā'id*) for another people.'[4] If God (Exalted is He!) had not created punishment and punished a portion of the people by it, those who live within His blessing surely would not know the extent of His blessings, nor the abundance of their joy because of it. For the joy of the people of Paradise will be amplified when they reflect on the suffering of the people of the Fire.

So you can [now] see that the joy of the people of this world in sunlight does not increase, despite their essential need for it, because it is universal and given to everyone. Nor does their joy become more intense from gazing at the adornment of the heavens, which is better than any garden they have on earth that

[A] The night in which the Qur'ān was revealed. It is considered by Muslims to be the holiest night of the year and is said to fall in the last ten nights of the month of Ramaḍān.

they labour to beautify. Because the adornment of the heavens is universal, they do not feel it and they do not rejoice because of it. What we have [previously] mentioned, therefore, is true: God (Exalted is He!) did not create anything except with wisdom within it. Nor did He create anything without a blessing in it, either for all His servants or for some of them. So in His creation of tribulation, there is also a blessing, either for the one afflicted or for the one not afflicted. Therefore, for the servant, every state that is not described as an absolute tribulation or an absolute blessing combines two functions: patience and thankfulness.

You may say that these are mutually exclusive, so how can they be united when there is no patience but in affliction, and no thankfulness but in joy? Know that [the servant] may be distressed by something and delighted with it from another aspect. Patience is in distress and thankfulness is in joy. In every indigence, illness, fear and tribulation in this world there are five matters for which the intelligent should rejoice and give thanks. First, for every misfortune and disease there is one that is even worse, for what God (Exalted is He!) decrees has no end and if God (Exalted is He!) doubles these and increases them, what can stop Him or turn Him back? So be thankful that there are not greater [misfortunes] in this world.

Second, the misfortune could be in his religion. A man said to Sahl [al-Tustarī] (may God be pleased with him), 'A thief entered my house and took my furniture.' Sahl replied, 'Be thankful to God (Exalted is He!). Had Satan entered your heart, he would have corrupted your belief in the unity of God. What would you have done then?'[5]

Likewise, Jesus (may the blessings and peace of God be upon him) sought refuge in his supplication, saying, 'Almighty God, do not cause my misfortune to be in my religion.'[6]

ʿUmar b. al-Khaṭṭāb (may God be pleased with him) said, 'There is not a trial with which God (Exalted is He!) has afflicted me without [giving me] four blessings [through it]: that it was not in my religion; that it was not greater than it was; that I was not prevented from accepting it; and that I aspired to a reward for it.'[7]

A Sufi had a friend whom the ruler imprisoned. The prisoner sent for him [his friend], told him [of his situation] and complained to him. [The Sufi] said to him, 'Be thankful to God!' The prisoner struck him. Later, he sent for [the Sufi] again, told him [of his situation] and complained. The Sufi said, 'Be thankful to God!' A Zoroastrian, who was afflicted with a stomach disorder, was imprisoned with him. The prisoner was then put in chains; one of the fetters was placed around his ankle and the other around the ankle of the Zoroastrian. So he sent for [the Sufi], who said to him, 'Be thankful to God!' The Zoroastrian had to get up numerous times and he had to get up with him and stand by him while he relieved himself. He wrote about this [to the Sufi], who replied, 'Be thankful to God!' The prisoner asked, 'How long will this last and what trial is greater than this?' [The Sufi] replied, 'If the fetters were around his waist, what would you have done?'[8]

Therefore, if every person who suffers tribulation reflects carefully on the truth regarding his bad conduct, both open and concealed, in relation to his Lord, surely he would see that he deserves more than what befalls him, both now and in the future. He who has the right to give you one hundred lashes and lessens the punishment by ten deserves thanks. And he who has the right to cut off both your hands and leaves one, deserves thanks.

A religious teacher passed by a street and a basin of ashes was dumped on his head. He prostrated to God (Exalted is He!) in a prostration of thankfulness. He was asked, 'What is this prostration for?' He replied, 'I was expecting fire to be poured on me, that it was restricted to ash is a blessing.'[9]

It was said to one of them [the Sufis], 'Will you not come out to pray for rain, for the rains have been held back?' He replied, 'You think that the rain has been held back, [while I think the that] the stones have been held back!'[10]

You may ask, 'How can I rejoice when I see that there are others whose disobedience has surpassed my disobedience and who have not been afflicted with what has afflicted me, although they are non-believers?' Know that for the non-believer what has been held back for him is [even] greater; he has been granted a respite only so that he may add to his sins and that his punishment is lengthened. As He (Exalted is He!) said, *We grant them indulgence only that they may increase in sin.*[11]

As for disobedience, how do you know that there are others in the world who are more disobedient [than you]? An iniquitous thought regarding God (Exalted is He!) or His attributes may be a greater and more serious matter than the drinking of wine, fornication and other acts of disobedience [committed by] the limbs. For this, God (Exalted is He!) gave an example, *And you reckoned it a light thing, but with God it was a mighty thing.*[12] And how do you know that another is more disobedient than you? Perhaps his punishment has been delayed until the Hereafter, whereas your punishment has been hastened in this world. Why are you not thankful to God (Exalted is He!) for this?

This is the third aspect in thankfulness: it is possible for every punishment to be delayed until the Hereafter. The afflictions of this world can be alleviated through other causes and their impact can be made easier, while the misfortune of the Hereafter is continuous. Even if it were not continuous, there would be no way of diminishing it through consolation, since in the Hereafter the means of consolation is completely cut off from those being punished. He whose punishment is hastened in this world is not punished a second time. As the Messenger of God (may God bless him and grant him peace) said, 'Truly, if the servant commits a sin and distress and tribulation befall him in this world, God is more generous than to punish him a second time.'[13]

The fourth [aspect] is that a misfortune or trial were preordained (*maktūb*) for him in *Umm al-Kitāb*.[A] For there is surely no

[A] *Umm al-Kitāb* (Q.III.7; XIII.39 and XLIII.4) is synonymous with the *lawḥ maḥfūẓ* ('Preserved Tablet') (Q.LXXXV.22). It is where all that is predestined is recorded.

escape from it. When the [trial] arrives and it is over and he has found relief from part or all of it, then this is a blessing.

The fifth [aspect] is that the reward [for misfortune] is greater [than the tribulation]. For the misfortunes of this world are roads to the Hereafter in two ways. The first [way] is similar to the blessing of disagreeable medicine for the sick man, or when the means of play are withheld from a child as a blessing for him. For were he to be free to play, it would prevent him from [acquiring] knowledge and good manners and he would lose throughout his life. Likewise, wealth, family, kinsmen, limbs, even the eye, which is the most precious of things, might be a means for the destruction of a man in some circumstances. Equally, the intellect, which is the most esteemed of things, might be a means for his destruction. The atheists will one day wish that they were insane or mere children[A] and that they had not used their intellects in opposition to the religion of God (Exalted is He!).

Everything that is within the means of the servant is potentially of religious benefit to him. It is incumbent on him to think well of God (Exalted is He!) and consider it a benefit and be thankful to Him. For the wisdom of God is vast and He knows even more than the servants what is good for His servants. The servants will one day thank Him for tribulations, when they see God's reward for tribulations. Just as a boy thanks his teacher and his father, once he has attained to [full] intelligence and maturity, for spanking him and disciplining him; for he has understood the fruit of what he gained from the discipline. The tribulation of God (Exalted is He!) is a discipline, and His care for His servants is more complete and abundant than the care of fathers for their children.

It has been reported that a man said to the Messenger of God (may God bless him and grant him peace), 'Counsel me.' He replied, 'Do not accuse God in anything He has decreed for you.'[14] He (may God bless him and grant him peace) looked up towards

[A] The intelligence of the insane is impaired and that of children is incomplete, therefore neither are held responsible under the law.

the heavens and laughed. He was asked why. He replied, 'I marvel at the decrees of God (Exalted is He!) for the believer. When He decrees good fortune for him, he is content and it is good for him. When He decrees hardship for him, he is content, and it is good for him.'[15]

The second way [in which misfortunes of this world are roads to the Hereafter] is that all sins leading to perdition are to be found in the love of this world, [while] all of the means of deliverance are to be found in turning the heart away from the abode of vanities. Were blessings to be granted according to the desires [of each], without mixing [them with] tribulation and misfortune, the heart would find itself at home in this world and in its means, until it becomes as a Paradise for it. Thus [the person's] tribulation is great at death because of his separation [from the world]. However, if misfortunes multiply for him, his heart is disturbed by this world, he is not at peace with it, he does not 'feel at home' in it, and it becomes a prison for him. His deliverance from it is the utmost delight, just as [if it were] a release from prison. For this, the [Messenger of God] (may God bless him and grant him peace) said, 'This world is the prison of the believer and the Paradise of the non-believer.'[16]

The non-believer is he who turns away from God (Exalted is He!) and wants only the life of this world; he is satisfied with it and is at home in it. The believer is he who cuts himself off from this world in his heart, intensely desiring to leave it. Unbelief is partly visible and partly invisible. To the extent that love of this world is in the heart, the hidden association [of other things with God] moves within it. The absolute monotheist is he who loves only the One, the Truth. There are, therefore, blessings in tribulation in this respect, and one must rejoice in them, even when the pain is, necessarily, there. This fact is comparable to your joy at the need for cupping by one who does your cupping without charge or gives you a beneficial and unpleasant medicine to drink, free. For you suffer and rejoice; you are patient with the pain and you thank him for the means of joy. The analogy for every tribulation in worldly affairs, therefore, is the medicine that causes pain in the present and benefits in the Hereafter.

Take someone who enters the hall of a king to see its splendour, knowing for certain that he must leave it. He sees a beautiful person who cannot leave the palace with him. This will result in trouble and tribulation for him because it causes him to become attached to a residence in which he cannot remain. However, if there is danger during his stay, for example, because the king comes upon him and punishes him, then he will experience something he dislikes, and flee from that place. That would be a blessing for him. This world is a dwelling that people enter through the door of the womb and exit through the door of the tomb. Thus all that causes their attachment to the dwelling is a tribulation. And all that disquiets the heart, breaking its attachment to it, is a blessing. Whoever knows this should be thankful for tribulations. But whoever does not know this blessing in tribulation, cannot be expected to be thankful, because thankfulness follows the knowledge of blessing as a matter of course. It cannot be imagined that one who does not believe that the reward of misfortune is greater than the misfortune will be thankful for misfortune.

It is said that a bedouin went to offer his condolences to Ibn ʿAbbās at the death of his father. He said,

> Be patient! And let us be patient with you.
> Truly, the patience of the followers is only after the patience of the leader.
> Your reward for separation from him is better than al-ʿAbbās himself.
> And God is better for al-ʿAbbās than you.

Ibn ʿAbbās then said, 'Nothing comforted me more than his condolence.'[17]

There are many traditions that pertain to patience in misfortunes. The Messenger of God (may God bless him and grant him peace) said, 'God afflicts those whom He wishes well.'[18]

He (may God bless him and grant him peace) said, 'God

(Exalted is He!) said, "If I sent one of my servants a misfortune in his body, his wealth or his children and he receives it with goodly patience, I would be embarrassed to weigh his actions or bring up an accounting for him on the Day of Judgement."'[19]

He (peace be upon him) said, 'Every servant who is afflicted with a trial and says, as God commanded him, "*Surely we belong to God, and to Him we return*,[20] Almighty God, reward me for my misfortune and may good follow after it,"—God verily grants him this.'[21]

And he (may God bless him and grant him peace) said, 'God (Exalted is He!) said, "The reward of the one whose eyes I take away is eternal residence in My abode, and looking on My countenance."'[22]

A man is said to have uttered, 'O Messenger of God, my wealth is gone and my body ails.' He (may God bless him and grant him peace) replied, 'There is no good in a servant whose wealth does not go and whose body is not ailing. Truly, when God loves a servant, He tests him. And as He tests him, He gives him patience.'[23]

The Messenger of God (may God bless him and grant him peace) said, 'Indeed, a man may not be able to attain to a rank with God (Exalted is He!) through actions. He is then afflicted with a misfortune in his body and he attains to it [this rank] through this.'[24]

Khabbāb b. al-Aratt reported, 'We came to the Messenger of God (may God bless him and grant him peace), who was reclining in the shade of the Kaʿba. We complained to him and said, "O Messenger of God, would you not pray to God, asking assistance of Him [against the unbelieving Meccans] for us?" Then he sat up; he reddened and said, "Truly, among those who came before you a man would be brought and a ditch dug in the ground for him. A saw would be brought and it would be placed on his head and he would be sawn in two. Yet that would not cause him to run away from his religion!"'[25]

It was said, on the authority of ʿAlī (may God ennoble his face), 'Whenever a man is imprisoned unjustly by the ruler and dies, he is a martyr. If the man is struck and he dies, he is a martyr.'[26]

He (peace be upon him) said, 'It is out of reverence for God and knowledge of His right that you should not complain about your pain, nor mention your misfortune.'[27]

Abū 'l-Dardā' (may God be pleased with him) said, 'You are born for death, you live for ruin, you labour for what passes away, and you throw away that which endures. You would do well [to remember] the three hateful things: poverty, disease and death.'[28]

Anas said that the Messenger of God (may God bless him and grant him peace) said, 'When God wills a servant well and wishes to purify him, He showers him with tribulation, and it flows copiously over him. If the servant supplicates Him, the angels say, "It is a recognised voice." If he supplicates a second time and says "O Lord!" He (Exalted is He!) says, "I am present, my servant, here at your service. Ask Me for anything and I shall give it to you, or I shall put aside that which is good that I may keep for you with Me that which is better." Then, on the Day of Resurrection, the people of good deeds—the people of prayer, fasting, charity and pilgrimage—will be brought forth and they will be rewarded for their actions according to justice. Then the people of tribulation will be brought forth and for them there will be no weighing or accounting of actions. Just as tribulation was poured out abundantly upon them, so will the reward be poured out abundantly upon them. Those who were without affliction in this world will then wish that their bodies were but cut with scissors when they see what reward the people of affliction have gained.'[29] For this, He (Exalted is He!) stated, *Surely the patient shall be given their reward in full without reckoning*.[30]

On the authority of Ibn ʿAbbās (may God be pleased with both of them), he said, 'One of the prophets (peace be upon him) complained to his Lord. He said, "O Lord, the believing servant obeys You and desists from what You have prohibited, [yet] You distance the world from him and you present tribulation for him. The unbelieving person does not obey You and defies You and Your prohibitions and You distance tribulation from him and You spread this world out before him." God (Exalted is He!)

then revealed to the prophet, "Truly, the servants are Mine and the tribulation is Mine. Everything shall extol My praise. The believer will have committed sins; so I distance this world from him and present tribulation to him as an atonement for his sins, until he meets Me, then I shall reward him for his good deeds. The non-believer will have acquired good deeds; I make easy his sustenance and distance tribulation from him that I may reward his good deeds in this world, until he meets Me, then I recompense him for his sins.'[31]

It was related that when He (Exalted is He!) revealed [the verse] *Whosoever does evil shall be recompensed for it,*[32] Abū Bakr al-Ṣiddīq (may God be pleased with him) said, 'How can there be joy after this verse?' The Messenger of God (may God bless him and grant him peace) replied, 'May God forgive you, O Abū Bakr, do you not sicken? Does harm not come to you? Do you not grieve? This is how you are recompensed.'[33] This means that all of what afflicts you is an atonement for your sins.

On the authority of ʿUqba b. ʿĀmir, the Prophet (may God bless him and grant him peace) said, 'If you see a man to whom God grants the things he loves and he is persistent in his disobedience, then know that God is luring him to his destruction.' Then he recited His (Exalted is He!) statement, '*So, when they forgot what they were reminded of, we opened unto them the gates of all [good] things.*'[34] This means that when they renounce what they are commanded to do, We open the gates of plenty for them—*until they rejoice in what they receive*[35]—that is, what good they were given, *We shall take them by surprise.*

Al-Ḥasan al-Baṣrī (may God have mercy on him) reported that one of the Companions saw a woman whom he knew from the pre-Islamic era. He spoke to her and then left her but kept turning towards her as he walked away. He struck a wall and it left a mark on his face. He went to the Prophet (may God bless him and grant him peace) and informed him. He (may God bless him and grant him peace) said, 'If God wills good for a servant, He hastens the punishment for his sin in this world.'[36]

ʿAlī (may God ennoble his face) said, 'Shall I not inform you of the most hopeful verse in the Qur'ān?' They replied, 'Yes, indeed.' He recited to them, *Whatever affliction may visit you is for what your own hands have earned, and He pardons much.*[37]

The misfortunes of this world, therefore, are acquired through sins. If God punishes [someone] in this world, God is more gracious than to punish him a second time. If He pardons him in this world, God is more gracious than to punish him on the Day of Resurrection.

On the authority of Anas (may God be pleased with him), the Prophet (may God bless him and grant him peace) said, 'A servant does not drink two draughts more beloved to God than a draught of rage where he responds with clemency and a draught of misfortune in which he is patient. There is no drop more loved of God than a drop of blood spilt in the way of God, or a tear drop in the darkness of the night while the servant is prostrated in prayer and none sees it but God. A servant does not walk two steps more loved by God (Exalted is He!) than a step toward the obligatory prayer and a step toward the close ties of kinship.'[38]

[On the authority of] Abū 'l-Dardā', [the Prophet] (may God bless him and grant him peace) said, 'A son of Solomon, son of David (peace be upon them both), died and [Solomon] grieved for him intensely. Then, two angels appeared and knelt before him in the guise of two disputants. One of them said, "I sowed seed and when it was ready for harvest, this one passed by and spoiled it." [Solomon] asked the other, "What do you say?" He replied, "I took to the main road and I came to the crop. I looked to the right and to the left but the road passed through it." Solomon (peace be upon him) asked [the first], "Why did you sow seed on the road? Did you not know that people must use the road?" The first replied, "Why did you mourn your son? Did you not know that death is the path to the Hereafter?" Thereupon Solomon turned to his Lord in repentance and did not mourn for any of his children after that.'

ʿUmar b. ʿAbd al-ʿAzīz went to visit a son who was ill. He said,

'O my son, it is more beloved to me that you were in my scale [mourning your loss] than that I am in your scale [mourning my loss]. He replied, 'O my father, may that which you love be more loved by me than what I love.'[39]

When the death of his daughter was announced to him, Ibn ʿAbbas (may God be pleased with them both) said the following words, *We belong to God and to Him we shall return.*[40] He continued, 'She [my daughter] was a weakness [for me] and He has provided for it. She was a burden[A] which God has taken away. And [her death] will be a reward that God has granted.' Then he offered two units [of prayer] and he said, 'We have done what God (Exalted is He!) has commanded. For God has said, *Seek (God's) help with patient perseverance and prayer.*'[41]

[It is reported] that a son of Ibn al-Mubārak died and a Zoroastrian who knew him consoled him. [The Zoroastrian] said to him, 'The intelligent must do what the ignorant [man] does after five days.'[B] Ibn al-Mubārak replied, 'All of you write this statement down!'

A scholar said, 'Truly, God will test the servant with one tribulation after another until he walks the earth without sin.'[42]

Al-Fuḍayl said, 'God, Almighty and Majestic, promises to try His believing servant with tribulations, just as a man promises his family good [provision].'[43]

Ḥātim al-Aṣamm said, 'Truly, God, Almighty and Majestic, will judge men on the Day of Resurrection according to four categories related to four persons: Solomon for the rich; Christ for the poor; Joseph for the slaves; and Job for the sick (may God bless them all).'

It was reported that when Zachariah (peace be upon him) fled from the unbelieving Israelites, he hid in a tree. They found out

[A] Meaning that she was a responsibility and that he was accountable to God for her.

[B] Meaning that he should conduct himself now as others do after the initial grief is passed.

and brought a saw. They cut into the tree until the saw reached Zachariah's head. He let out a moan. God (Exalted is He!) revealed to him, saying, 'O Zachariah! if you let out a second moan, surely I will erase you from the register of the prophets.' Thereupon Zachariah (peace be upon him) bit his finger until it was cut in two.

Abū Masʿūd al-Balkhī said, 'He who is struck by misfortune and tears his garment or strikes his chest, acts as if he takes a spear intending to fight God, Almighty and Majestic.'

Luqmān[A] (may God have mercy on him) said to his son, 'O my son, gold is tested by fire, and the righteous servant is tested by tribulation. When God loves a people, He tests them. He who is content with it will have God's contentment, and he who is enraged by it will have [God's] wrath.'[44]

Aḥnaf b. Qays said, 'One morning I had a toothache. I said to my uncle, "I could not sleep last night because of the pain in my tooth." I said it three times. He replied, "You go on because your tooth hurt you for one night. I lost this eye thirty years ago and no one has known of it!"'[45]

God (Exalted is He!) revealed to ʿUzayr,[B] (peace be upon him) 'If I send you a trial, do not complain of Me to My servants but complain to Me, for I do not complain to the angels when your sins and shameful acts rise up [to Me].'[46]

We ask God to grant us His great kindness and generosity, His beautiful concealment [of sins] in this world and in the Hereafter.

[A] B. Heller, in his article 'Lukmān' (*SEI*, pp. 289–290) traces this figure in pre-Islamic, Qur'ānic and post-Qur'ānic sources.

[B] Cf. B. Heller ʿUzair,' *SEI*, p. 617.

CHAPTER SIXTEEN
An Exposition of the Merit of Blessing over Tribulation

PERHAPS you will say that these traditions are proof that tribulation in this world is better than blessing. So is it for us to ask God for tribulation? I say there is no reason for that because of what has been reported of the Messenger of God (may God bless him and grant him peace). He used to seek protection from tribulation in this world and tribulations in the Hereafter in his supplications.[1] He and the other prophets used to say, *Our Lord, give us good in this world and good in the Hereafter.*[2] They used to seek refuge from the gloating of an enemy, among other things.[3]

ʿAlī (may God ennoble his face) said, 'Almighty God, I ask you for patience.'[4] He (may God bless him and grant him peace) said, 'You have asked God for tribulation. Ask him for well-being (*ʿāfiya*).'[5A]

Abū Bakr al-Ṣiddīq reported that the Messenger of God (may God bless him and grant him peace) said, 'Ask God for sound health (*ʿāfiya*). For none was given anything better than sound health save [inner] certainty.'[6] By certainty he meant the health of the heart against the sickness of ignorance and doubt; the health of the heart being more important than the health of the body.

Al-Ḥasan (may God have mercy on him) said, 'The good that has no evil in it is sound health with thankfulness, for many are blessed but are not thankful.'[7]

[A] Lane gives *ʿāfiya* as 'health and safety' (*Lexicon*, v.2095). We have chosen to translate it as 'well-being,' 'sound health' or just 'health,' depending on the context.

Muṭarrif b. ʿAbd Allāh said, 'That I be given sound health and am thankful is preferable than that I be tested and be patient.'[8]

He (may God bless him and grant him peace) said in his supplication, '. . . [To be granted] well-being from You is more beloved to me.'[9A]

All this is clear and does not require evidence and testimony. For tribulation becomes a blessing for two reasons. One reason is that [tribulation] is measured against what is worse than it, either in this world, or in religion. The other is that it is measured against the reward for which the servant hopes. We must, therefore, ask God [to grant us] the perfect blessing in this world and to repel what tribulation lies beyond it. We must ask Him for reward in the Hereafter because of [our] thankfulness for his blessing. Indeed, God is able to give, for thanks, what He does not give for patience.

You may say that some have said, 'I desire to be a bridge, over the Fire, upon which all creation will cross. Then they will be saved and I will be in the Fire.'

And Sumnūn (may God have mercy on him) said,

> I have no share in anything other than You,
> Then try me in whatever way You wish.[10]

[One can] conclude from this that they have asked for tribulation. Know that it was reported that Sumnūn al-Muḥibb (may God have mercy on him) after writing this line of poetry, was afflicted with [urine] retention. And subsequently, he used to go around to the Qur'ān schools and say to the boys [studying there], 'Pray for your uncle, the liar!'[11]

As for the love of a person to be in the Fire apart from the rest of mankind, it is impossible. Love, however, may overwhelm the heart to the point that the lover thinks there is a love within himself such as that. He who drinks the cup of love becomes drunk; and he who is drunk is loose in speech. When his drunkenness leaves him,

[A] Part of the Prophet's prayer at Ṭā'if.

he knows that what overcame him was a state with no reality to it. What you hear of this sort, therefore, is the speech of passionate lovers, those whose love is excessive. People enjoy hearing the speech of passionate lovers, but it should not be relied upon.

It was said, 'A ring-dove kept enticing his spouse [to love-making] and she would deny him. He said, "What is it that keeps you from me? If you desired it, I would overturn the two universes and the kingdom of Solomon back to front for your sake." Solomon (peace be upon him) heard him, summoned him and rebuked him. The [ring-dove] replied, "O Prophet of God, the speech of lovers should not be repeated."'[12] And it is as he said.

The poet spoke,

> I desire his union and he desires my parting,
> So, I shall leave what I desire for what he desires.

This [love] too is impossible! It means that I desire what I do not desire; for he who desires union, does not desire parting. So, how can he desire parting when he did not desire it. This statement cannot be believed, except through two interpretations. First, that this may be so in certain situations so that the favour [of the beloved] is gained, and through it he reaches the desired union at a future time. Therefore, parting becomes a means of access to favour; favour becomes a means of access to union with the beloved; and what leads to the beloved is beloved. An example of this is that of a person [who] loves money. He invests one dirham, though he loves it, so as to acquire more because of his love of more.

The second interpretation is that his favour becomes his goal solely because it is the favour [of the beloved]. He then delights in his consciousness of the favour of his beloved for him. For him, this delight is greater than observing [the beloved] while knowing that he is not favoured. This is why it is possible to imagine that [all] that he desires is the favour of [the beloved]. This is the state that some lovers come to; their delight in affliction with the knowledge of the favour of God for them is greater than their delight in well-being without the awareness of favour. They esteem His favour in tribulation and, therefore, they cherish the tribulation more than well-being. This state is possible in the throes of love, yet it does not last. And even if it were to last, for example, would it be a true state or would it be a state which is necessitated by another state that has occurred in the heart and which has unbalanced it? This needs looking into, [but] discussion of its reality is not appropriate to the matter at hand. As we stated before, well-being is better than tribulation. We ask God (Exalted is He!), therefore, to graciously bestow pardon (*ʿafw*), and well-being (*ʿāfiya*)[A] through His bounty upon all of His creatures in [their] religion, in this world and in the Hereafter, to us and to all Muslims.

[A] *ʿAfw* and *ʿāfiya* derive from the same root *ʿ-f-w*.

CHAPTER SEVENTEEN
Exposition of which is Better: Patience or Thankfulness?

KNOW that people differ in this [what they consider to be better: patience or thankfulness]. Some say that patience is better than thankfulness; others that thankfulness is better; and [yet] others that they are equal. Still others say that it differs according to different circumstances. Each group tries to prove its point with highly emotive and far-fetched language. There is no point in repeating the arguments; presenting the truth is better.

We say that this exposition has two stations. The first station is that of facilitating understanding [of the matter]. Here, we concentrate on what is obvious in the matter without delving into its substance. This is the exposition with which the general public are addressed because their understanding is insufficient to grasp the hidden realities. This manner of address should be adopted by preachers because the purpose of their speech with the public is to reform [them]. A compassionate wet nurse does not prepare fowl and various sweets as food for an infant, but uses suitable milk. She must delay giving the infant the most delicious foods until he is strong enough to accept them—when he has left behind the weakness of his infancy.

So, we say that this station in the exposition [of which is better] puts aside research and detail. All that is required of it is that it look at the literal meaning of the sources of the law. This necessarily gives preference to patience. For while there are many traditions regarding the excellence of thankfulness, if to these is added what has been said about the excellence of patience, the virtues of patience would be greater. Furthermore, there are explicit references to its preference, such as what he (may God bless him and grant him peace) said, 'Among the lesser [gifts of God] that you have been granted are certainty (*yaqīn*) and resolute patience (*ʿazīmat al-ṣabr*).'[1] There is the tradition, '[On the Day of Judgement], the person who was most thankful on earth will be brought forward and God will reward him with the rewards of the thankful. The person who was most patient on earth will be brought forward and will be asked, "Are you satisfied that we should reward you just as we have rewarded this thankful one?" He will reply, "Yes, O Lord." And God (Exalted is He!) will say, "Not at all! I bestowed favour upon him, and he was thankful. I tested you and you were patient. I will surely redouble your reward over his." Thus, he will be given several times the reward of the thankful.'[2] God (Exalted is He!) has said, *Surely the patient shall be given their reward in full without reckoning*.[3]

As for the Prophet's saying, 'He who eats and gives thanks is equal to he who fasts and is patient,'[4] it is an indication that the excellence of patience is emphasised and that it raises [with it] the rank of thankfulness. So he linked [thankfulness] with patience, which becomes the highest rank. Were it not that it—the lofty rank of patience—is affirmed by revelation, relating thankfulness to it would not be an elevation for thankfulness. This is similar to the saying of the Prophet (may God bless him and grant him peace), 'Friday is the pilgrimage of the poor, and the *jihād* of woman is devotedness,'[5] and as the Prophet (may God bless him and grant him peace) said, 'The drinker of wine is like the worshipper of idols.'[6]

It is evident that the object to which you compare something ought to be of a higher rank. Hence the saying of the Prophet (may God bless him and grant him peace), 'Patience is half of faith.'[7] This does not mean that thankfulness is like it. Similarly, may God bless him and grant him peace said, 'Fasting is half of patience.'[8] For everything [that can be] divided into two, each of its parts is called a half, even if there is disparity between them. [For example,] it is said that faith is knowledge and action; action is thus half of faith. But this does not mean that action is equal to knowledge. And the tradition of the Prophet (may God bless him and grant him peace) states, 'The last of the prophets to enter Paradise will be Solomon the son of David (peace be upon them both) because of the extent of his kingdom; and the last of my Companions to enter Paradise will be ʿAbd al-Raḥmān b. ʿAwf, because of his wealth.'[9] In another tradition, 'Solomon will enter after the prophets by forty autumns.'[10] And in the tradition, 'All of the gates of Paradise are two-leaved [i.e., double] doors, except the door of patience, which is one-leafed.[A] The first to enter it are the people of tribulation and leading them will be Job (peace be upon him).'[11]

Everything that has been said about the excellence of poverty[B] points to the excellence of patience, because patience is the state of the poor man, while thankfulness is the state of the rich man. This is the station that befits the public and is sufficient for them in terms of suitable preaching and instruction as to how to improve their religious [practice].

The second station of the exposition [of which is better: patience or thankfulness] is the one we intend for the people of knowledge and insight, [and it concerns] the realities of matters by way of unveiling (*kashf*) and clarifying. For we say: It is not possible to judge between two unknowns as long as they remain unknown and as long as the reality of each is not exposed. Every known thing is made up of divisions; [however] it is not possible to balance between the totality [of the parts of one known thing] and the totality [of the parts of another]. Rather, the individual parts must be isolated and compared in order to ascertain which is superior. Patience and thankfulness are made up of numerous

[A] Meaning a narrower door, as fewer people will enter through it.

[B] See *K. al-faqr wa'l-zuhd*; book XXXIV of the *Iḥyāʾ*.

divisions and branches; and it is not possible to ascertain which is superior and which inferior through the totality.

So we say, we mentioned earlier that these stations are organised into three matters: knowledge, states and actions. And this applies to thankfulness, patience and the rest of the stations [of the spiritual life]. If these three are measured against each other, it will appear to those who view the outer nature of things that knowledge is desired for the states, the states are desired for the actions, and that the actions are [therefore] the most excellent. But for the people of perception, the matter is quite the opposite. Actions are desired for the states, and the states are desired for knowledge. The most excellent is knowledge, then the states, and then the actions, because everything that is required [to gain] something else, that something else is inevitably more excellent than it.

[Let us consider] these three individually. Actions can be equal or, when some [actions] are added to others, can vary [in degree]. The same applies to the individual states whenever some are added to others. Likewise, the individual [forms] of knowledge. The most elevated form of knowledge is the knowledge by unveiling (*mukāshafa*); it is more elevated than the sciences of practical transactions (*muʿāmala*). The sciences of practical transactions are [themselves] beneath commercial transactions because they are required for them; they support the perfection of [these] transactions. A person who possesses the sciences of practical transactions may be better than a person who [only] worships if his knowledge is beneficial to others as it is [then] preferred to an action limited [to one person]. However, knowledge [of practical transactions] without action is not better than action alone.

Therefore, we say: The benefit of improving [one's] actions is to improve the state of the heart. And the benefit in improving the state of the heart is so that the majesty of God (Exalted is He!) in His essence, His attributes and His acts is unveiled to us. The highest level in the knowledge by unveiling is the knowledge of God, praise be to Him; it is the goal that is sought after for itself [alone] because happiness is obtained through it. Moreover, it is the essence of happiness. The heart may not sense that it is the essence of happiness in this world; it will sense it in the Hereafter. It is pure knowledge which has no bounds, for it is not bound by anything else. All other forms of knowledge are like slaves and servants in relation to it because they are sought for its sake. As they are sought for its sake, they are [considered] beneficial according to the degree that they lead to the knowledge of God (Exalted is He!). Some forms of spiritual knowledge lead to others, either by one means or by many. The fewer the means between man and the knowledge of God (Exalted is He!) the better.

As for the states, we mean by them the states of the heart when it is purified and cleansed from the stains of this world and the distractions of creation. Once [the heart] is cleansed and purified the reality of the Truth [God] is clear. The excellence of the states is in their influence in the improvement of the heart, its cleansing and its preparation to obtain the knowledge by unveiling. Just as the polishing of a mirror undergoes certain stages in the [process] of its completion, some of which are closer to a reflective [stage] than others; such are the states of the heart. The state that is close to, or that brings closer, the purity of the heart is certainly better than that which is beneath it and this is because of its proximity to the goal.

Actions are similarly ordered. Their effect is to reinforce the purity of the heart and to draw the states to it. Each action either draws to it a state which obstructs unveiling, which darkens the heart and which attracts the vanities of this world, or it draws to [the heart] a state which prepares it for unveiling, which purifies it and which severs its relations with this world. The name of the first is disobedience, the name of the second is obedience. The [acts of] disobedience from the standpoint of their ability to darken and harden the heart are of varying degrees. Likewise are [the acts] of obedience [in their ability] to illuminate and purify the heart. Their degrees depend on the degrees of their influence, and differ with the variety of states. In general terms, we can say that one supererogatory canonical prayer (*ṣalāt al-nāfila*) is better than all other supererogatory worship, and that pilgrimage is better than voluntary almsgiving (*ṣadaqa*), and that night-time [supererogatory] prayer [*qiyām al-layl*] is better than other [supererogatory prayers].[A] However, the fact of the matter is that for the rich man who has wealth, but who is overcome by avarice and love of money, spending his money is better for him than waking up at night for prayers and fasting during the day.[B]

Fasting is appropriate for he who is overcome by gluttony and who wants to break its grip [on him]; or for he who, due to satiety, cannot concentrate clearly on the knowledge by unveiling and who wishes to purify the heart through hunger. As to he whose state is not such, [either] he cannot be harmed by gluttony or he is not engaged in a kind of reflection which can be deflected by satiety. To busy himself with fasting would take him from his state to another state. He is then like a sick man who complains of a stomach pain and then uses medicine for a headache, which fails to benefit him. Rather, his duty is that he should look into the illness that has gripped him.

Avarice that is succumbed to is considered among the mortal vices (*muhlikāt*). To fast a hundred years or to get up a thousand nights to pray would not diminish it by a particle. For the only thing that will eradicate it is donating money. It is incumbent upon him, therefore, to donate from what he has. We have elaborated on this in the quarter on moral vices (*rubʿ al-muhlikāt*).[C] Let [the reader] refer to it.

Therefore, [the actions] differ according to the states. He who has insight knows that a standard answer [to all cases] is an error. It is as though someone were to say to us: Is bread better than water?

[A] Ghazālī is here emphasising the importance of acts of worship decreed by God (the canonical prayer and the pilgrimage) and those highly recommended by the Prophet (night-time prayer) over other voluntary acts of worship.

[B] Meaning that overcoming faults of character is more meritorious because it is harder than performing voluntary acts of worship. The fasting here does not refer to the fasting of the month of Ramaḍān, which is obligatory.

[C] The third quarter of the *Iḥyā'*, books XXI through XXX.

There would be no other true response but [to say]: Bread is better for the hungry and water is better for the thirsty. If both occur together, then let him look to what is more urgent. If thirst is more urgent, then water is better. If hunger is more urgent, then bread is better. If they are equal, [the necessity for] both is equal.

Similarly, if someone were to ask, 'Which is better: oxymel[A] (*sakanjabīn*) or a drink of *laynawfar*?'[B] There can be no right answer to this at all. Instead, if we were asked, 'Which is better: oxymel or the absence of yellow bile?' We would reply, 'The absence of yellow bile.' Oxymel is required for this, and that which is required for something else is invariably beneath this thing. Therefore, giving money away is an action, called charity, through which a state is achieved: the retreat of avarice and exodus of the love of this world from the heart. Through the exodus of the love of this world from the heart, it will be prepared for the knowledge and love of God (Exalted is He!). Thus, knowledge is best, followed by the state, and then by the acts.

You will say: the law has urged us to act and has gone to great lengths in mentioning the virtues of action; it has also urged the giving of alms through His statement, *Who is he that will lend God a good loan*,[12] and He (Exalted is He!) says, [*God accepts repentence from His servants*] *and takes alms.*[13] How then can action and giving alms not be the best? Know that when the physician commends a medication, this does not mean that the medication is desired for itself, nor that it is better than the health and the healing which result from it. Acts are the remedy for the diseases of the heart. And the diseases of the heart are most often not detected. They are similar to leprosy on the face of he who has no mirror. He is unaware of

[A] A mixture of vinegar and honey.

[B] Zabīdī comments that 'it is a plant that grows near ponds and rivers at the flooding of water. It has a flower called *nujūnī*. The drink taken from it is cooling and refreshing, useful for a cough, pain in the bowels, or a throbbing artery, and for pleurisy. It strengthens the heart, quenches thirst, causes sleeplessness due to a relieving fever and is therefore soothing to physical health.' (Zabīdī, IX.156) it. If it is mentioned to him, he does not believe it. The only way to [cure him is] to convince him of, for example, the virtues of washing the face with rose water, if rose water can make the leprosy disappear. Persistent praise will prompt him to be assiduous in this and his disease will vanish. If he were told that 'the reason is to eliminate leprosy from your face,' perhaps he would leave the treatment and claim that his face has no blemish on it.

Let us give a more familiar example than this. We say, take someone with a son, to whom he teaches knowledge and the Qur'ān. He wants this [knowledge] to become fixed in his son's memory and not vanish. He knows that if he orders his son to repeat and study it so that he would remember it, [his son] would say that he remembers it and that he is not in need of repetition and study because he thinks that what he remembers now will remain with him forever. The [father] has servants and he commands the son to instruct the servants. In addition, he promises to reward him so that he becomes more motivated in repetition and teaching. The pitiable boy may then think that the aim is the instruction of the servants in the Qur'ān and that he has been employed for their instruction; he may become doubtful about the matter. He may say, 'Why have I been employed for the sake of the servants, when I am greater than they are and dearer in the eyes of my father? I know that if my father desired the instruction of the servants, he could surely do it without delegating it to me. I know that my father would not even notice these servants were it not for the fact that they are ignorant of the Qur'ān.' This pitiable one may become indolent and may abandon their instruction, relying on his father's lack of need [for the servants] and his generosity in forgiving him. So, he forgets the knowledge and the Qur'ān and falls behind and becomes deprived without even being conscious of it.

There are those who have been deceived by a similar fantasy, and they have taken to permitting what [God] has prohibited. They say, 'God (Exalted is He!) can do without our worship and He is above asking us for a loan. [We do not understand] the meaning of His statement, *Who is he that will lend God a good loan?*'[14] And [they say], 'If God wills that the poor be fed, He would surely feed them [Himself]. Therefore, there is no need for us to spend our money on them.' He (Exalted is He!) said, regarding the statements of the non-believers, *And when it is said to them, 'Expend of what God has provided you with,' the non-believers say to the believers, 'What, shall we feed such a one whom, if God willed, He would feed?'*[15] And they said again, *Had God willed we would not have been idolaters, neither our fathers.*[16] Observe how they were truthful in their speech and how they perished by their truth! Praise be to He Who, if He wills it, can cause one to perish [who speaks] the truth; and if He wills it, makes many [people] happy in ignorance. *He deludes many by it and guides many by it.*[17]

Those who think that they are not required to serve the unfortunate and the poor, or [to serve] for the sake of God (Exalted is He!), and said, 'We cannot benefit the poor, nor do we benefit God, in spending or retaining our possessions,' they will perish, just as the boy will come to ruin if he thinks that his parent seeks his employment for the sake of the servants, and he is not aware that his father wants his knowledge to be confirmed and fixed in his heart, this being the means to his happiness in this world. The father only favours it in order to draw his son towards what would bring him happiness.

This example shows you the error of those who err in this way. Therefore, the poor person who takes from your wealth, helps to eliminate the evil of avarice and the love of this world from your inner self by means of money. He 'harms' you in the same way that the cupper who draws blood from you in order to remove the destructive illness through the removal of the blood, does. But the cupper is your servant, you are not his servant. The cupper does not cease to be a servant because his purpose is to do [something else] with the blood [more than removing the ailment].

Since alms (*ṣadaqāt*) cleanse the inner [self] and purify it against impure qualities, the Messenger of God (may God bless him and grant him peace) did not partake of them and refrained from them. He also forbade the cupper from earning [money from cupping].[18] He called them [alms] 'the filth in the wealth of men.' He honoured his household by protecting them from it [taking alms].[19] What is intended here is that actions influence the heart, as has been mentioned in the quarter on mortal vices. Depending on their effect, the heart is capable of receiving guidance and the light of knowledge. This is the definitive statement and the fundamental law that should be referred to for knowledge about the virtues of actions, states and knowledge.

Let us now return to our particular concern with patience and thankfulness. We say, each contains knowledge, states and actions. It is not possible to compare knowledge in one with the state or the action of the other. Rather, each one should be compared with its equivalent so that what is common to both becomes apparent. After what is common [becomes apparent], what is better will become apparent.

When comparing the knowledge of the thankful with the knowledge of the patient [you may find that] their origin is the same knowledge. For example, the knowledge of the thankful is in comprehending that the blessing of the eyes is from God (Exalted is He!); while the knowledge of the patient is comprehending that blindness is from God. When considered from [the point of view] of tribulation and misfortune, both [forms of] knowledge are similar and equal. We have explained that patience can be applied to obedience and against disobedience. Here, patience and thankfulness are united because patience in obedience is the essence of thankfulness in obedience. Thankfulness means using the blessing of God (Exalted is He!) according to the wisdom it was intended for; and patience means the constancy of the religious impulse in confronting the impulse of passion. Patience and thankfulness are thus two names for the one idea but considered from two different points of view. The constancy of the religious impulse in its opposition to the impulse of passion is called patience when it is considered from the point of view of the impulse of passion; it is called thankfulness when considered from the point of view of the religious impulse. The religious impulse is created for this wisdom, that it should strive against the impulse of appetite, and fulfil what is intended by wisdom. Therefore, they [patience and thankfulness] are two expressions for a single idea. And how can a thing be preferred over itself?

Thus, the applications of patience are to three: obedience, disobedience and tribulation. Their application to obedience and disobedience has been mentioned. As to tribulation, it consists of the loss of a blessing. The blessing is either an indispensable one, such as the eyes; or one of a need, such as the increase of wealth to reach a sufficient amount of money. As for the eyes [i.e., the indispensable blessing], the patience of the blind is in refraining from complaint, openly accepting the decree of God (Exalted in He!), and not permitting oneself liberties in acts of disobedience because of one's blindness. The thankfulness of he who has sight is twofold: one is that he does not exploit [his sight] in the way of disobedience; the other is that he employs it in obedience. Neither of the two matters is devoid of patience. The blind man has been spared [the need for] patience in the face of [the temptation of] beautiful things because he does not see them. While, for he who can see, if his vision falls upon a beautiful thing and he is patient, he is thus thankful for the blessing of the eyes. Were he to pursue what he sees, he would have denied the blessing of sight. Thus, [for he who is obedient] patience is part of his thankfulness. Equally, if he relies on his eyes in obedience, there will always be a need for patience in obedience. Moreover, he may be thankful for sight when contemplating the wonders of God's creation in order to reach the knowledge of God (Exalted is He!). This thankfulness would be better than patience. If it were not so, then, for example, from among the prophets the rank of Shuʿayb (peace be upon him), who was blind, would be above that of Moses (peace be upon him) and other prophets, because he was patient at the loss of sight while Moses (peace be upon him) did not have to be patient. Surely, perfection is not in depriving a man of all his limbs, leaving him like meat on a butcher's block. That is most absurd, because every one of these limbs is an instrument [to be utilised] in religion; with its loss, the accomplishment of a part of religion is lost. Its thankfulness is in its use as an instrument of religion, and that can only be through patience.

As for what can be categorised as a need, such as the increase of wealth to reach a sufficient amount of money, if one is only given the bare necessity [to live] and one needs what is beyond it, then patience in this is a struggle (*mujāhada*); it is the struggle (*jihād*) of poverty. The existence of surplus [wealth] is a blessing. Its thankfulness is in spending it in good deeds and not using it in disobedience. If patience is added to thankfulness, such as when spending [wealth only] on permissible things, then thankfulness is better [than patience in poverty] because it incorporates patience. In it also is joy in the blessing of God (Exalted is He!); and in it is the endurance of the pain of spending on the poor and putting aside what could be spent on [what is] permitted (*mubāḥ*).

The conclusion of this is that two things are better than one thing, and the whole is of higher rank than the part. [Yet] there is a flaw in this, since it is not right to compare the whole with its parts. If his [the servant's] thankfulness is that he does not use [wealth] as an aid in disobedience but spends it on permitted pleasures, then patience [of the poor] at this point is better than thankfulness. The poor person who is patient is better than the rich person who clings to his wealth and spends it on himself for permissible [things], but not [better] than the rich person [who spends] his wealth on good deeds. For the poor one has struggled with himself, has broken his craving and has cheerfully accepted the tribulation of God (Exalted is He!). This state inevitably calls for strength. While the rich person may follow his craving and obey his appetite, although he limits himself to permitted things. The things permitted are a choice over that which is forbidden (*ḥarām*). Thus there must also be a strength in the patience against what is forbidden. Except that the strength for the patience of the poor is higher and more complete than the strength which restricts enjoyment to permitted pleasures. The place of honour goes to that strength which is apparent in actions. For actions are desired only for the states of the heart. And this strength is a state of the heart that differs in accordance with the strength of certainty and faith. That which indicates an increase of strength in faith is inevitably better.

All the verses [of the Qur'ān] and all the traditions that indicate the preference of the reward of patience over the reward of thankfulness refer to this degree in particular. This is because what first comes to people's minds regarding blessing and wealth is that it enriches them. And what first comes to mind regarding thankfulness is that a person should say, 'Praise be to God' [*al-ḥamd li-Llāh*] and that he should not use the blessing in disobedience, and [it does not come to mind] to spend it in obedience. Thus patience is better than thankfulness, that is, the patience which the public understands. Junayd (may God have mercy on him) pointed to this particular meaning when he was asked which of the two was better: patience or thankfulness? He replied, 'The preference of the rich man is not because of the presence [of wealth], nor is the preference of the poor man in the absence [of wealth], but what is laudable is in each upholding the conditions of [the state] they find themselves in. The conditions that the rich man finds himself in are in conformity with him [being a rich man] and are accompanied by things which conform with his situation and which are enjoyable and delightful. The conditions that the poor man finds himself in are in conformity with him [being a poor man] and are accompanied by things which are oppressive and disquieting. If each upholds, for the sake of God (Exalted is He!), the conditions [imposed upon] him, he who suffers pain and disquiet in his state is more complete than he who enjoys and delights in his state.'[20] The matter is as he described it. It is truly among the divisions of patience and thankfulness in the last division that we mentioned and he intended nothing else by it.

It was said that Abū 'l-ʿAbbās Ibn ʿAṭā had contradicted [Junayd] in that and said, 'The rich man who is thankful is better than the poor man who is patient.' Then Junayd cursed him[A] and

[A] The meaning here is that Junayd intended this as a lesson to benefit Ibn ʿAṭā' spiritually.

he was struck with the tribulation of the death of his children, the destruction of his possessions and the loss of his mind for fourteen years. He used to say, 'The curse of Junayd fell upon me.' And he returned to favouring the poor man who is patient over the rich man who is thankful.[21]

If you have understood the definitions we gave, you will know that each of the two statements is applicable depending on the situation. Many a poor man who is patient is better than a rich man who is thankful, just as discussed. And many a rich man who is thankful is better than a poor man who is patient. That is, the rich man who sees himself as poor, holding no wealth for himself, except what is necessary, while the rest he spends in good deeds, or he holds on to it with the conviction that he is the trustee for the needy and the miserable. He awaits a need to occur, so that he can spend on it. Also, what he spends is done not in pursuit of prominence and good repute, nor to bestow favour, but it is done for the sake of God (Exalted is He!) through the ways in which He tests His servants, and this is better than being poor and patient.

You may say that [the above situation] does not weigh heavily on the soul, whereas poverty weighs heavily upon the poor man. For the former [the rich man] experiences the pleasure of ability, and the latter experiences the pain of patience. If he [the rich man] is pained by parting from wealth, he is restored by his pleasure in the ability to give. Know that he who spends his wealth voluntarily and out of goodness of soul is of a higher state than he who spends it in a miserly fashion and can only be separated from it forcibly. We have elaborated on this in the *Book of Repentance*.[A] For the suffering of the soul is not sought for its own sake, but for disciplining [the soul]. This is similar to disciplining the hunting dog; a well-trained dog is better than a dog that needs to be disciplined, even if it is patient during the discipline. Therefore, there is need for suffering and struggle at the beginning, but not at the end. Rather, at the end, that which was [previously] painful for

[A] *K. al-tawba*, book XXXI of the *Iḥyāʾ*.

him becomes a delight; just as learning becomes a delight for the boy when he matures, although it was painful for him at first.

Indeed, all of mankind, except for a few, are [like children] at the beginning or not even at the beginning.[A] This is why Junayd designated those who suffer as of a better quality. What he said is sound in describing the general public. But, if you do not qualify his [Junayd's] answer, and you apply it to everyone, then the statement designates that patience is better than thankfulness and it is true in that this is what is first understood by most [people]. However, if you seek the reality [of the matter] then you must qualify [it]. For in patience there are degrees, the least of which is refraining from complaint about what is disliked, and above it is contentment (*riḍā*), a station beyond patience, and above contentment is thankfulness for tribulation (*al-shukr ʿalā 'l-balā'*). Patience in suffering and contentment are possible when there is neither pain nor joy.[B] However, thankfulness is not possible except in what is loved and what gladdens.

Thankfulness also has many degrees. We have mentioned the most important, but others come under them. For the bashfulness of the servant because of the succession of God's blessings upon him is thankfulness; his knowledge of his deficiency with respect to thankfulness is thankfulness; the apology for the paucity of the thankfulness is thankfulness; the knowledge of the greatness of God's clemency and His concealment [of our faults] is thankfulness; the recognition that blessings originate from God (Exalted is He!) without being merited is thankfulness; the knowledge that thankfulness itself is one of the blessings of God and a gift from Him is thankfulness; proper humility and self-abasement [in relation to] the blessings is thankfulness; and thankfulness to the means [by which blessings are acquired] is thankfulness—for the Prophet (may God bless him and grant him peace) said, 'He who

[A] Meaning that the majority of people are immature.

[B] That is, it is possible to be patient without pain and to be content without joy.

is not thankful to people is not thankful to God'[22] (we have mentioned the reality of this in the *Book of the Mysteries of Zakāt*);[A] to desist from objecting and [maintaining] proper behaviour towards the Bestower is thankfulness; and receiving blessings graciously and considering small ones great is thankfulness.

The individual actions and states that are classified under thankfulness and patience cannot be compared; they are of differing degrees. Therefore, how can there be unanimity in preferring one over the other [i.e., patience over thankfulness or vice versa] except when wishing to speak in general terms, as is found in the traditions of the Prophet and his Companions.

It is narrated that one of them [the Sufis] said, 'On one of my journeys, I saw an old man who had become very advanced in years. I asked him about his state and he replied, "At the beginning of my life, I fell in love with a cousin of mine and she also loved me. He [the uncle] agreed that she could marry me. On the wedding night I said, 'Come! that we may live this night in thankfulness to God (Exalted is He!) for bringing us together.' We prayed that night and neither one of us had time for the other. When the second night came, we said the same; and we prayed the length of the night. Now, for the past seventy or eighty years we have remained in that state every night. Is it not so, O wife?" The old woman replied, "It is as he says."'[23] Observe these two! Had God not joined them and they had borne the trial of separation patiently, what would this patience in separation have been to the thankfulness of such a union! It should be clear to you that this thankfulness is better. Thus one can only know the true nature of the precedence of one thing over another through the definitions of preference given above. And God knows best.

[A] *K. asrār al-zakāt*, book v of the *Iḥyā'*.

NOTES

Prologue

1 ʿIrāqī states that this is cited by Daylamī, *Musnad*, on the authority of Anas b. Mālik through Yazīd, who is considered a weak narrator.

Chapter 1

1 ʿAbd al-Bāqī lists 102 references (*al-Muʿjam*, II.399–401).

2 Q.XXXII.24.

3 Q.VII.137.

4 Q.XVI.96.

5 Q.XXVIII.54.

6 Q.XXXIX.10.

7 Ibn Ḥanbal, *Musnad*, IV.260, 363.

8 Ibn Ḥanbal, *Musnad*, I.446; Nasāʾī, *Sunan*, IV.162. See also *K. asrār al-ṣawm* (*Iḥyāʾ*, I.6).

9 Q.VIII.46.

10 Q.III.125.

11 Q.II.157.

12 *Maʾthūr*, II.575.

13 ʿIrāqī gives no reference for this tradition (*Mughnī*, IV.60). Ghazālī may have obtained it from Makkī; cf. *Qūt*, I.194. Suyūṭī offers the *ṭarf* (opening phrase) of this tradition with variation (cf. Suyūṭī, *Jāmiʿ al-aḥādith li'l-masānīd wa'l-marāsīl*, V.295).

14 Q.XVI.96.

15 Ibn Abī Dunyā, *Makārim al-akhlāq*, p. 13; Ibn Ḥanbal, *Musnad*, IV.385; Ṭabarānī, *Makārim al-akhlāq*, p. 47.

16 ʿIrāqī gives no reference for this tradition (*Mughnī*, IV.60). In his commentary on the *Iḥyāʾ*, Zabīdī suggests that the last word of the tradition should not be *janna* but *khayr*, and that it can be traced back to al-Ḥasan al-Baṣrī (Zabīdī, IX.5).

17 *Maʾthūr*, II.575.

18 Abū Dāwūd, *Sunan*, II.485; *Maʾthūr*, II.240.

19 Ibn Abī Dunyā, *Kitāb muḥāsabat al-nafs*, p. 123.

20 Cited in Qushayrī, I.401.

21 ʿIrāqī gives no reference for this tradition (*Mughnī*, IV.61). This tradition appears in *Qūt*, I.194.

22 Ibn Ḥanbal, *Musnad*, I.307.

23 *Qūt*, I.194.

24 *Maʾthūr*, III.387.

25 See *Qūt*, I.194, where it is given as a definition of *islām*.

26 Zabīdī says it is from *Qūt*, and in Bayhaqī (*Shuʿab*) on the authority of ʿAlī (Zabīdī, IX.7).

27 Zabīdī says it is from *Qūt*, and cited by Saʿīd b. Manṣūr, Ibn al-Mundhir, al-Ḥākim, Bayhaqī and

Ibn Abī Dunya (Zabīdī, IX.7).

28 Q.II.157.

29 Q.XXXVIII.44.

30 Zabīdī says it is from *Qūt* and Abū Nuʿaym (Zabīdī, IX.7).

Chapter 2

1 ʿAjlūnī, *Kashf al-khafāʾ*, II.279; Shawkānī, *al-Fawāʾid al-majmūʿa fī ʾl-aḥadīth al-mawḍūʿa*, p. 267.

2 Q.VI.94.

3 Q.XVII.14.

4 Allusion to Q.XCIX.1.

5 Allusion to Q.LXIX.14.

6 Allusion to Q.LXXVII.10.

7 Allusion to Q.LXXXI.1.

8 Allusion to Q.LXXXI.2.

9 Allusion to Q.LV.37.

10 Allusion to Q.LXXXII.3.

11 Allusion to Q.LXXV.29.

12 Allusion to Q.LXXXI.4.

13 Allusion to Q.LXXXIV.3–4.

14 Allusion to Q.LXXXVI.7.

15 Allusion to Q.XXIII.13.

16 Allusion to Q.XXIII.14.

17 Q.XXXI.28.

18 Q.LVI.61.

19 *Maʾthūr*, III.337.

20 ʿIrāqī says it is in Tirmidhī, Nasāʾī and Ibn Māja with an alternate wording that does not specify Muḥammad by name. Ibn Māja, *Ḍaʿīf sunan Ibn Māja*, p. 123, this version substitutes *aʿinnī* for *hawwun ʿalā*.

21 Q.XXXVI.49–50.

22 Q.XXXVI.30.

23 Q.XXXVI.31.

24 Q.XXXVI.32.

25 Q.XXXVI.46.

26 Q.XXXVI.9–10.

27 Mālik, *al-Muwaṭṭāʾ*, p. 676; Abū Dāwūd, V.536; Ibn Saʿd, *Kitāb al-ṭabaqāt al-kabīr*, VII.2, 206.

Chapter 4

1 Q.II.177.

2 Q.LXVII.22.

Chapter 5

1 Unidentified saying. Qushayrī has a longer variant of this saying: *al-ṣabr ʿalā ʾl-ṭalab, ʿunwān al-ẓafar*, 'patience in the quest is the announcement of victory' (I.401).

2 Q.XLI.30.

3 Q.LXXXIX.27–28.

4 Q.XXXII.13.

5 Q.LIII.29–30.

6 Ibn Ḥanbal, *Musnad*, IV.124; *Maʾthūr*, III.357.

7 Q.IX.102.

8 Allusion to Q.XXV.44.

9 Mutanabbī, *Dīwān*, p. 492.

10 Q.XCII.5–7.

11 ʿIrāqī, *Mughnī*, IV.67; Ibn Saʿd, II.119–124.

Chapter 6

1 Q.XCVI.6–7.

2 Q.II.280.

3 Q.LXIV.14.

4 *Maʾthūr*, V.145, with Khula bt. Ḥakīm as the transmitter with listings in Ibn Saʿd, IX.70. ʿAjlūnī, *Kashf*, II.339; Jīlānī, *Faḍl Allāh al-Ṣamad fī tawḍīḥ al-adab al-mufrad*, I.159 with ʿAbd Allāh b. Ṣālih the transmitter, and in Wensinck, I.320.

5 Q.VIII.28; LXIV.15.

6 Zabīdī claims in his comments that the tradition is found in the collections of Ibn Ḥanbal, Abū Dāwūd, Tirmidhī, Nasā'ī, Ibn Māja, Abū Yaʿlā, Ibn Khazima, Ibn Ḥibbān, Ḥākim, Bayhaqī, and al-Ḍiyā. It is a tradition of ʿAbd Allāh b. Burīda on the authority of his father (Zabīdī, IX.21). ʿAbd Allāh b. Burīda is mentioned in Ibn Saʿd, VII.115; p. 2, 77, 104.

7 Q.LXXIX.24. Zabīdī does not identify the Sufi who uttered this saying, nor the collection in which it may be found (Zabīdī, IX.22).

8 Q.XLIII.54.

9 Q.XCVIII.5.

10 Q.XI.11.

11 Q.XXIX.58–59

12 Q.XLVII.33.

13 Q.II.264.

14 Q.XVI.90.

15 Q.XVI.90.

16 ʿIrāqī states (*Mughnī*, IV.69), that the first part is listed in Ibn Māja's collection of traditions, while the second part is in that of Nasā'ī. Faḍāla b. ʿUbayd is the transmitter, listed in Ibn Ḥibbān, *Tārīkh al-ṣaḥāba*, p. 205; Ibn Ḥajar, *Tahdhīb al-tahdhīb*, VIII.268.

17 *Ma'thūr*, III.142, with Jābir as transmitter; ʿAjlūnī, *Kashf*, II.81. ʿIrāqī observes (*al-Mughnī*, IV.69) that the tradition is used by Ghazālī in the *K. āfāt al-lisān* (*Iḥyā'*, III.138) with a different wording, with the warning idiom at the beginning (*iyyākum* 'Beware, you (pl.)!), and narrated on the authority of Jābir and Abī Saʿīd, in Ibn Abī Dunyā, *al-Ṣamt*, Ibn Ḥibbān, *al-Ḍuʿafā'* and Ibn Mardawayh in his *tafsīr*.

18 This tradition appears in *Qūt*, I.195, where Makkī takes it as the saying of one of the *ʿulamā'*, not a Companion.

19 Q.XIV.12.

20 ʿIrāqī states that it is a tradition from Ibn Masʿūd, who is listed in Ibn Saʿd, III.106ff (*al-Mughnī*, IV.70). Zabīdī comments that 'he said that the Day of Ḥunayn when he gave al-Aqraʿ (b. Ḥābis) and Uyayna b. Ḥiṣn one hundred camels (each), but he gave less than that to others' (Zabīdī, IX.24). The second is mentioned a number of times in Ibn Saʿd, IX.181. On the division of booty following the Battle of Ḥunayn (January 8/630), Watt notes, 'There was sufficient booty to give every man in the Muslim army four camels or the equivalent. There is said to have been trouble over the distribution and complaints at the delay. . . . Those in the list who did not come into [the] category of allied leaders, notably Mālik b. ʿAwf and perhaps ʿUyayna b. Ḥiṣn and al-Aqraʿ, may have received gifts to reconcile their hearts' (Montgomery Watt, *Muhammad at Medina*, pp. 73, 74).

21 Q.XXXIII.48.

22 Q.LXXIII.10.

23 Q.XV.97–99.

24 Q.III.186.

25 Q.XVI.126.

26 The tradition is listed in Ibn Abī Dunyā, *Makārim al-akhlāq*,

p. 15; Ibn al-Jawzī records the second half of the tradition in *Zād al-masīr*, VIII.253; and in Munāwī (*Fayḍ al-qadīr*, IV.196, 197), Ghazālī's discussion is included in the commentary, though the tradition is a variant from the form employed in this text.

27 Smith does not list this quotation in her commentary on Ghazālī's citations from the canonical Gospels, but Zwemer includes it. Margaret Smith, *Al-Ghazālī the Mystic* (London: Luzac and Co., 1944), pp. 115ff; Samuel M. Zwemer, *A Moslem Seeker After God, The Life and Teaching of Al-Ghazālī* (New York: Fleming H. Revell, 1921), pp. 274–275.

28 In his commentary, Zabīdī credits the tradition to ʿAlī rather than Ibn ʿAbbās, and notes its inclusion in the collections of Ibn Abī Dunyā, Abū 'l-Shaykh, and *Ma'thūr* (Zabīdī, IX.25).

29 This tradition is found in *Qūt*, I.198.

30 This tradition is listed in al-Munāwī, *Fayḍ al-qadīr*, IV.487 and Ghumārī, *Fatḥ al-wahhāb*, II.384, with Anas as transmitter.

31 Dāraquṭnī, *al-Mu'talif wa'l-mukhtalif*, III.1310; ʿAjlūnī, *Kashf*, I.206, and Ghumārī, I.49. The first part of the tradition is listed in Wensinck, VI.481.

32 Q.II.156.

33 This tradition is very close in structure and meaning to one listed in Wensinck, III.432; Ṭayālisī, *al-Musnad*, 192; and Ibn Ḥajar, *Tahdhīb*, XII.471.

34 Daylamī includes a tradition very close in meaning (*Ma'thūr*, II.465). Ibn Ḥibbān has a tradition in which God does not address Gabriel, but says, 'If I took the two eyes and he was patient' (Ibn Ḥibbān, *Ṣaḥīḥ* (IV.257). Wensinck lists two other readings with the same meaning (I.409 and VI.3). ʿIrāqī says that this is narrated in Ṭabarānī, *Awsaṭ*, on the authority of Abī Ẓalāl al-Qasmali, a weak transmitter from Anas; in a shorter version from Bukhārī; and also from Ibn ʿAdiy and Abū Yaʿla with a different wording.

35 Ḥākim, I.349; similarly Ibn Māja, *Ḍaʿīf Sunan*, p. 121, but beginning without God as the speaker. Cf. Wensinck, I.214.

36 Zabīdī comments that this tradition can be found in the collections of Daylamī and Ibn ʿAsākir (Zabīdī, IX.28).

37 Q.XXXIX.10. Zabīdī remarks that this tradition can be found in Abū Nuʿaym, *Ḥilya* (Zabīdī, IX.29).

38 Q.LII.48.

39 Qushayrī includes this tradition without ascribing it to David (cf. I.279).

40 In *al-Mughnī* (IV.71), ʿIrāqī says he could not identify its source. Ibn Abī Dunyā, however, transmitted it in *al-Maraḍ* from the transmission of Sufyān on the authority of a jurisprudent: He said, 'It is because of patience that you do not discuss your misfortune, your pain, or the purification of your soul.' The first phrase is listed in Wensinck, I.352.

41 Reported by Ibn al-Mubārak, according to Ibn Ḥajar, *Tahdhīb*, v.382.

42 Q.II.156.

43 ʿIrāqī says (*al-Mughnī*, IV.72), that this tradition is also found in Abū Nuʿaym, *Ḥilya*, on the authority of Anas b. Mālik, who is listed in Ibn Ḥanbal, *Musnad*, IV.347. Cf. Wensinck, 'Anas', *SEI*, p. 43. Wensinck lists a tradition very similar to this one (I.200).

44 Zabīdī comments that this tradition is found in Ṭabarānī and Abū Nuʿaym (*Ḥilya*), as well as the two *Ṣaḥīḥ*s of Bukhārī and Muslim (Zabīdī, IX.30).

45 Zabīdī comments that it was reported by Jābr ʿAbd Allāh al-Ansārī, Zabīdī, IX.30.

46 *Qūt*, I.195.

47 Allusion to Q.VII.12; Q.LV.14; Q.XV.26, 28, 33.

48 Q.VII.12.

49 Q.XLIII:36.

50 Zabīdī comments that the version Ghazālī employs is found in the *Ḥilya* of Abū Nuʿaym (Zabīdī, IX.33). Cf. Shawkānī, *al-Fawā'id*, p. 147. A very similar tradition is listed in Wensinck, I.200, but at the close it reads, 'the stupid among men' (*al-balīd min al-rijāl*), in place of 'the idle youth,' cf. in *Ma'thūr*, I.193, with ʿAbd Allāh b. ʿAmr as the transmitter.

51 The question was asked by Aḥmad b. Fatib. Louis Massignon and Paul Kraus, *Akhbār al-Ḥallāj*, p. 97 (Arabic text), p.101 (French translation).

Chapter 7

1 Allusion to a tradition of the Prophet. Cf. Ibn Ḥibbān, *Ṣaḥīḥ*, VII.621; Baghawī, *Maṣābīḥ al-sunna*, III, no. 3510.

2 Cf. Zabīdī.IX.34. The tradition is found in *Ma'thūr*, V.44; al-Ḥākim al-Nīsābūrī, *al-Mustadrak ʿalā 'l-Ṣaḥīhayn*, IV.314; Ibn Saʿd, IX.53; Ghumārī, I.265. Ghazālī quotes it in full earlier in *K. asrār al-ṣawm* (*Iḥyā'*, I.6), p. 241.

3 Listed in *Ma'thūr*, III.52, and Ṭabarānī, *al-Muʿjam al-ṣaghīr*, I.188. Ibn al-Athīr comments that *wijā'* is 'people opposing an enemy' (*al-Nihāya*, V.159). This tradition is also found in Wensinck, I.229.

4 Qushayrī phrases it 'the good of patience (*ḥasan al-ṣabr*)' and lists it as the last of the three virtues: trust (*tawakkul*), contentment (*riḍā*), and patience, where it is cited under *taqwā* (I.279).

5 This tradition was cited in the Arabic text on pages 60 and 65.

6 Q.XXVI.42.

7 This tradition is listed in Munāwī, *Fayḍ al-qadīr*, II.505, and in Wensinck, I.229, with a slight variation. Muḥammad b. Maslama, with listings in Ibn Saʿd, IX.215 and Ibn Ḥibbān, *Ṣaḥāba*, p. 226. See also Watt, *Muhammad at Medina*, p. 160f.

8 Q.LI.22.

9 Q.XV.9.

10 Q.XIV.52; Q.XXXVIII.29.

11 Q.LIV.17.

12 Cf. Qushayrī, I.397–398.

13 Q.XVII.85.

14 Allusion to Q.xxi.37.

15 This is the second half of the tradition that occurs in Arabic text, page 66, note 14). The full *ḥadīth* reads: 'The wise man is he who judges himself and works for what is after death, while the stupid man is he who lets his soul follow its own passions and presumes upon God!'

16 Q.lxxv.20–21.

17 Q.lxxvi.27.

18 Q.liii.29–30.

19 Q.ix.38.

20 Allusion to the Qur'ānic verse xxxii.17.

21 This is actually a tradition. Cf. Ibn Abī Dunyā, *Dhamm al-dunyā*, p. 51; with listings in Ibn Saʿd, ix.250.

22 Q.x.24.

23 Q.xviii.45.

24 Q.iv.97.

25 The tradition is listed in Ghumārī, ii.242; Munāwī, *Fayḍ al-qadīr*, ii.544; and Wensinck, vii.263.

26 ʿAjlūnī, *Kashf*, ii.285; listed in Ibn Saʿd, ix.24. In these collections it is given in the imperfect indicative and the third person with *man*. It is also listed in Wensinck, iii.76.

27 Cf. Qushayrī, i.399–400.

28 Q.iii.200.

29 Cf. Qushayrī, i.401.

30 These verses on patience appear in Qushayrī, i.401. Neither Qushayrī nor Zabīdī identify the poet. In the second verse, Zabīdī uses *yuḥmad* (is praiseworthy) in place of *yujmal* (is beautiful).

Chapter 8

1 Q.xxix.45.

2 Q.ii.152.

3 Q.iv.147.

4 Q.iii.145.

5 Q.vii.16.

6 Q.vii.17.

7 Q.xxxiv.13.

8 Q.xiv.7.

9 Q.ix.28.

10 Q.vi.41.

11 Q.ii.212.

12 Q.iv.48.

13 Q.ix.15.

14 Q.lxiv.17.

15 Q.xxxix.74.

16 Q.x.10.

17 This tradition is listed in Dārimī, *Sunan*, ii.95; Ḥākim, i.422. It is also listed in Ibn Ḥibbān, *Ṣaḥīḥ*, i.267; Bayhaqī, *al-Sunan al-ṣughrā*, iv.306; Wensinck, *Concordance*, iii.241.

18 ʿIrāqī remarked that the tradition is listed in the collections of Ibn Ḥibbān and Muslim (*al-Mughnī*, iv.79). The concluding quotation is from Q.ii.164.

19 Q.ii.24.

20 Note Qushayrī, i.383. A similar reference to Moses appears in Numbers, 20:1–11.

21 ʿIrāqī says, 'It is in the tradition collection of Ṭabarānī, Abū Nuʿaym (*Ḥilya*), and Bayhaqī (*Shuʿab*) from a tradition of Ibn ʿAbbās and Qays b. al-Rabīʿa. A later collection keeps this tradition with a slight variation' (*al-Mughnī*, iv.79). Cf. Shawkānī, *al-Fawā'id*, p. 384.

22 *Qūt*, I.206.

23 *Qūt*, I.205, and much later in ʿAjlūnī, *Kashf*, I.369.

24 *Qūt*, I.203.

25 *Qūt*, I.204.

26 Cf. Ṭabarānī, *Ṣaghīr*, II.45; Aḥmad al-Buṣīrī, *Miṣbāḥ al-zujāja fī zawāʾid Ibn Māja*, I.665; Ghumārī, II.127, where it is an appeal to God in prayer by the Prophet, beginning with *Allahuma*; and Munāwī, *Fayḍ al-qadīr*, V.350. Wensinck notes that the first part of the tradition is found in Ibn Ḥanbal (*Concordance*, VI.307).

27 Cf. *Maʾthūr*, I.149, and *Qūt*, I.203.

Chapter 9

1 Ibn Ḥibbān, *Ṣaḥīḥ*, II.97; also found in Wensinck, *Concordance*, II.394.

2 Ibn Abī Dunyā, *Kitāb al-shukr*, p. 21 with *dhikr* and *duʿāʾ* reversed in the first and second clauses of the tradition. Cf. Ibn Ḥanbal, *Musnad*, II.302, 310, 371, 375, and 515; Ibn Ḥibbān, *Ṣaḥīḥ*, II.104; *Maʾthūr*, I.431; Munāwī, *Fayḍ al-qadīr*, II.33; and Wensinck, *Concordance*, II.181 and repeated in V.164.

3 ʿIrāqī comments that Ibn Abī Dunyā reports it in *Kitāb al-shukr* on the authority of Ibrāhīm al-Nakhʿī (*al-Mughnī*, IV.80). Ibn Ḥajar, *Tahdhīb*, I.126.

4 Allusion to Q.VII.54.

5 Qushayrī, I.386.

6 Qushayrī, I.386.

7 Qushayrī, I.386.

8 Zabīdī identifies the poet who wrote these lines as Mutanabbī (Zabīdī, IX.52).

9 This tradition is found in Suyūṭī, *Jāmiʿ*, V.70. The opening part of this tradition is listed in Ṭabarānī, *al-Muʿjam al-awsaṭ*, X.243. Cf. Wensinck, *Concordance*, III.233.

10 Q.XXIX.17.

11 Q.VII.194.

12 Zabīdī comments that the incident as reported goes back to a tradition of Sahl b. Abī Hathma (Zabīdī, IX.53). He is listed in Ibn Ḥajar, *Tahdhīb*, IV.248 and Ibn Ḥanbal, *Musnad*, IV.2. This tradition is included in Abū Dāwūd, IV.655; Ibn Hanbal, *Musnad*, IV.2, 3 and Qushayrī, I.389, where it appears verbatim.

13 Qushayrī, I.384.

14 Qushayrī, I.384.

15 Qushayrī, I.385.

Chapter 10

1 Cf. *Qūt*, I.204.

2 Cf. *Qūt*, I.204.

3 Cf. *Qūt*, I.204.

4 Cf. *Qūt*, I.204.

5 Allusion to Q.VI.108; X.46 and 70; XI.4; XXIX.8; and XXXIX.7, with *marjiʿukum*.

6 Q.XXXVIII.44; this verse alludes to Job, who is mentioned in verse 41.

7 Zabīdī does not cite a collection, where the incident may be found (Zabīdī, IX.56).

8 Q.V.54.

9 Q.LXXXIII.29–33.

10 Q.LXXXIII.34–35.

11 Q.XI.38.

12 Q.LV.26–27.

13 Allusion to Q.XXXVII.35.

14 Q.XXXIX.3.

15 Zabīdī does not identify the poet (Zabīdī, IX.58).

16 Q.XCVI.19

17 This second petition of prayers is found in Ṭabarānī, *Awsaṭ*, X.54.

18 Q.XXVIII.88.

19 This tradition is listed in Abū Dāwūd, *Sunan*, II.177; Ḥākim, I.511.

20 This tradition is listed in Muslim, Bukhārī, Nasā'ī, *Sunan*, III.219; Ibn Abī Dunyā, *Shukr*, p. 16; and also, Wensinck, *Concordance*, IV.529.

21 Q.XIV.7.

22 Q.XCV:4–6.

23 Munāwī, *Fayḍ al-qadīr*, II.12, lists it with Ibn ʿAbbās and ʿUmrān b. Ḥuṣīn (Ibn Saʿd with listings in IX.171). It is also in Wensinck, *Concordance*, IV.375, as cited here.

24 Q.XV.43.

25 Allusion to Q.LXXVI.4.

26 Q.XL.16.

Chapter 11

1 Allusion to Q.LXXVIII.8–11.

2 Q.LXXX.25–28.

3 Q.XXXVII.6.

4 Q.XVII.85.

5 Q.LI.56–57.

6 Q.IX.34.

7 Dārimī, II.121; Ibn al-Jawzī, *Zād al-masīr*, V.316; Ṭabarānī, *Ṣaghīr*, I.115; Abū Yaʿlā, *Musnad*, XII.3089, with Umm Salama as transmitter with listings in Ibn Saʿd, IX.100; Bayhaqī, *Maʿrifat al-sunan wa'l-āthār*, I.562; and in Wensinck's *Concordance*, III.85. It is also an allusion to Q.II.174.

8 ʿAbd Allāh b. ʿUqayl (d. 769/1367) includes the substance of the proverb in the discussion on *ḥarf* in his famous grammatical commentary on the one thousand line poem of Ibn Mālik al-Andalusī (d. 672/1273), where the poet summarises the rules of the Arabic language (*Sharḥ Ibn ʿUqayl ʿalā Alfīya Ibn Mālik*, I.12).

9 Shāfiʿī cites traditions that relate to the problems in this issue. See Majid Khadduri, *Islamic Jurisprudence: Shāfiʿī's al-Risāla*, p. 210.

10 See Munāwī, *Fayḍ al-qadīr*, V.273, for traditions prohibiting hoarding.

11 Q.LXV.1.

12 Q.II.269.

13 Among others, Q.II.269, III.7, XIII.19.

14 ʿIrāqī says this *ḥadīth* is in Ibn Ḥanbal, it was mentioned previously, (*al-Mughnī*, I.233).

15 Q.XLV.13.

16 Allusion to Q.II.164; XVI.65; XXIX.63; XXX.19, 24, 50; XXXV.9; and XLV.5.

17 Allusion to Q.V.112, 114.

18 Q.XLVII.37.

19 Q.XXXIV.13.

20 Q.VII.17.

21 Q.XXI.23.

22 This tradition is listed in Munāwī, *Fayḍ al-qadīr*, I.347; and Wensinck, *Concordance*, VI.221.

23 Zabīdī does not identify the poet (Zabīdī, IX.74).

24 ʿIrāqī (*al-Mughnī*, IV.94–95) says that this tradition is found in Ibn Abī Dunyā, *Kitāb al-yaqīn* and *Ma'thūr*. In his discussion of inner certainty (*yaqīn*), Ibn Abī Dunyā does not refer specifically to this tradition, but he does exhort his readers regarding faith with inner certainty, referring to the Gospel incident of Jesus walking on water (Ibn Abī Dunyā, *al-ʿAql wa-faḍl wa'l-yaqīn*, p. 100).

25 Allusion to Q.XVI.102.

26 Q.LI.56

27 Q.XXXIX.8.

28 Q.VII.16, XXXVIII.82.

29 Q.LI.22.

30 Q.LXV.12.

31 Q.LXV.12.

32 Allusion to Q.III.7.

33 Q.LXV.12.

34 Description given in Q.LXXX.16.

35 ʿIrāqī (*al-Mughnī*, I.6) says this is in Abū Dāwūd, Tirmidhī, Ibn Māja, and in *Ṣaḥīḥ* Ibn Ḥibbān on the authority of Abū 'l-Dardā'.

36 Two traditions very similar to this one in the first passage are listed in Wensinck's *Concordance*, I.104. ʿIrāqī reports a number of variant traditions (*al-Mughnī*, IV.96).

37 There are eight traditions listed there with the same protasis that warn of a time when the leadership of the Muslim community will turn away from the way of the Prophet, though they vary in expression. A similar tradition received by Ibn Māja refers to those in Ibn Ḥanbal's *Musnad*, 'Trials will occur'; 'a man among them will appear a believer, but he will live as an unbeliever save that God gives him an awareness through knowledge' (Ibn Māja, *Sunan*, II.289–290). ʿIrāqī says this is in Muslim on the authority of Umm Salama and in Tirmidhī with a different wording ('There will be imams over you. . . ') (*al-Mughnī*, IV.96).

38 This tradition is also in *Qūt*, II.254, but Ghazālī alters the tradition by omitting *dimā'* (blood) and replacing *afkār* (thoughts) with *abdān* (bodies).

39 A slightly different version of Tustarī's tradition is found in *Qūt*, II.255.

Chapter 12

1 Q.XIV.34 and XVI.18.

2 Q.II.10.

3 Q.XXXVI.70.

4 Q.VIII.42. (*But [it was] so that God might accomplish a matter already decreed.*)

5 Q.LIX.2.

6 Allusion to Q.CIV.6–7.

7 Q.CII.5–6.

8 Q.CII.7.

9 This tradition is listed in Ibn Ḥibbān, *Ṣaḥīḥ*, VII.517; *Qūt*, I.206, who quotes it in the section on thankfulness; Munāwī, *Fayḍ al-qadīr*, II.100; and Wensinck, *Concordance*, IV.449.

10 Alfred Guillaume, *Ibn Isḥāq's*

Life of Muḥammad, p. 450f.; Watt, *Muhammad at Medina*, p. 35f.

11 Guillaume, *Ibn Isḥāq's Life of Muḥammad*, pp. 649–654; Ibn Saʿd, pp. 124–132. Ghazālī quotes a variant of this tradition in the first volume of the *K. asrār al-ḥajj* (*Iḥyā'* I.256).

12 Wensinck lists the first and second parts of this tradition in *Concordance* II.381 and in I.278, respectively.

13 Q.LV.8–9.

14 Q.LIII.39

15 ʿIrāqī (*al-Mughnī*, IV.101) states that the tradition is traceable to the famous general ʿAmr b. al-ʿĀṣ, who is mentioned over thirty times in Wāqidī, *Kitāb al-maghāzī*, I.6ff. Cf. *Ma'thūr*, V.14. Ibn al-Athīr cites this in his discussion of *niʿma* (blessing) (*Nihāya*, V.84). It is also Jīlānī, *Faḍl Allāh al-Ṣamad*, I.392; Ghumārī, II.317; and Wensinck, *Concordance*, III.335 with slight variation. See also Hitti, *History of the Arabs*, pp. 159–168.

16 This tradition is given in *Ma'thūr*, V.13, with *dīn* for *taqwā*; Ghumārī retains it with *taqwā* (*Fatḥ al-wahhāb*, II.318); Ibn Qutayba, *al-Maʿārif*, p. 461 and in Ibn Ḥajar, *Tahdhīb*, IX.473. A tradition similar to this one is listed in Wensinck, *Concordance*, VII.300.

17 This Sufi tradition appears in *Qūt*, I.209.

18 This tradition is listed in ʿUqaylī, *Kitāb al-ḍuʿafā' al-kabīr*, II.146; Jīlānī, *Faḍl Allāh al-Ṣamad*, I.394; Ibn Qutayba, *al-Maʿārif*, p. 268. The second half of the tradition is listed in Wensinck, *Concordance*, I.106. The full tradition is found in Munāwī, *Fayḍ al-qadīr*, VI.68. The clauses, however, are reversed; the tradition is also found in ʿAjlūnī, *Kashf*, II.227.

19 ʿIrāqī could not find the transmission chain of this tradition (*al-Mughnī*, IV.101). He suggests the true tradition in this case is: *al-dunyā matāʿ wa-khayr matāʿ al-dunyā 'l-mar'ata al-sāliḥa*, 'This world is an object of delight and the best delight in it is the pious wife.' It is also found in Ṭabarānī, *Awsaṭ*, X.159. This tradition is also listed in Ghumārī, with Ibn ʿAmr (*Fatḥ al-wahhāb*, II.294).

20 Munāwī preserves the one indicated here, the full text including, '*ṣadaqa jāriya aw ʿilm yuntafaʿu bihi aw walad ṣāliḥ*,' 'ongoing charity, or knowledge which can be made use of, or a good child, [the continuation of the tradition is: '...a good son who will pray for him, or a benefit that continues or knowledge that remains useful in itself [for others].' Munāwī preserves a full text of the one cited here except where *insān* is substituted for *ʿabd*. (*Fayḍ al-qadīr*, I.437). Cf. Abū Yaʿlā, XI.343; Abū Dāwūd, III.300; Ibn al-ʿArabī, *Kitāb al-qabas*, III.1228; Ibn al-Jawzī has *inṣān* in place of *ʿabd* (*Zād al-masīr*, VII.10), with '*banī Ādam*' in VI.111; and Ḥākim, who preserves a positive version, *tabiʿahu* 'there followed him . . .' (*al-Mustadrak*, I.371). ʿIrāqī (*al-Mughnī*, IV.101) says the tradition

goes back to Abū Hurayra. Wensinck lists traditions of a very similar verbal/conditional pattern (*Concordance*, VI.282 and V.430); as does Suyūṭī, *Jāmiʿ*, V.70.

21 Q.II.251.

22 Wensinck lists a tradition that is close in meaning to the first half of this tradition (*Concordance*, I.51 and another to the second half, VII.86).

23 Ghazālī quotes only the first clause of the tradition. Cf. Tayālisī, p. 284; Ibn al-ʿArabī, II.612; Abū Yaʿlā, VII.4032; Bayhaqī, *Maʿrifat* (I.42, IV.9, 59). Cf. Wensinck, *Concordance*, I.92.

24 The first phrase of this tradition '*min akramu 'l-nās*' is closely paralleled in Ḥākim, III.329. The pattern of the tradition appears in the tradition *fa-akramu al-nās, Yūsuf, nabī Allāh* (Wensink, *Concordance*, I.125). ʿIrāqī supplies a second tradition related to this one, 'God chose Kināna from the children of Ismāʿīl; He chose Banī Ḥāshim from the Quraysh; and He chose me from among Banī Hāshim.' A version of this tradition in the first person, '*Anā akram walid ādam ʿalā Rabbī*' (I am the most excellent child of Adam before my Lord), Baghawī, *Maṣābīḥ*, IV.40.

25 This tradition is listed Ḥākim, II.163. The second clause is different. This is found in the late collection of Shawkānī, *Fawā'id*, p. 130. It is also given in Wensinck, *Concordance*, VI.474.

26 It is listed in Zabīdī who mentions that the tradition can be found in Dāraquṭnī. Cf. *Ma'thūr*, Zabīdī, IX.89, and the late collections of Suyūṭī, *Jāmiʿ*, V.379 and Shawkānī, *Fawā'id*, p. 130. It closes, literally, 'a growing place of badness,' or 'a bad smelling growing-place.' Ibn Manẓūr cites this tradition to illustrate *khudār*, and follows it with a sequel to the tradition, 'It can be compared in her case to the flourishing tree in the dung heap of the camels' (*Lisān al-ʿArab* II.1184).

27 ʿIrāqī (*al-Mughnī*, IV.103) mentions that it is a questionable tradition (*gharīb*).

28 The story is attributed to the seventh ʿAbbāsid caliph, al-Ma'mūn (d. 218/833). See Ibn Khallikān, *Wafayāt*, II.519–523; Suyūṭī, *Tārīkh al-khulafā'*, pp. 242–260; Hitti, *History of the Arabs*, pp. 297ff.

29 This tradition is listed in *Ma'thūr*, I.102 and ʿUqaylī, *Kitāb al-ḍuʿafā'*, II.139, 321, IV.100. Cf. Khaldūn al-Aḥdab, *Zawā'id Tārīkh Baghdād*, V.974, VII.1593. It is also listed in ʿAjlūnī, *Kashf*, I.136.

30 Q.II.247.

31 ʿIrāqī states that it is listed in Tirmidhī from a tradition of Kaʿb b. Mālik (*al-Mughnī*, IV.103).

32 Q.LXIV.14.

33 Q.LXIV.15.

34 This tradition is listed in Abū Dāwūd, I.18; Ibn Ḥibbān, *Ṣaḥīḥ*, II.353; Nasā'ī, I.38; Bayhaqī, *Sunan*, I.58; ʿUqaylī, *Kitāb al-ḍuʿafā'*, IV.506; Wensinck, *Concordance*, VII.317.

35 Cf. Wensinck, *Concordance*, VII.90.

36 ʿIrāqī states that it is listed in

Ibn Māja and al-Ḥākim. Wensinck lists a tradition with the same meaning and very close in form, *Concordance*, II.365.

37 ʿIrāqī states that it was narrated by al-Ḥākim on the authority of ʿAbd al-Raḥmān b. ʿAwf and claimed that it was authentic. ʿIrāqī further states that it is a weak tradition due to Khālid b. Abī Mālik, whose narrations are extremely weak, being in the chain. (*al-Mughnī*, IV.105). He is listed in Ibn Ḥajar, *Tahdhīb*, III.126.

38 Q.XX.50.

39 Q.XXIV.21.

40 This tradition is listed in Abū Yaʿlā, XI.115 and Munāwī *Fayḍ al-qadīr*, V.468. Wensinck lists traditions close in meaning (*Concordance*, I.378–379 and II.239). ʿIrāqī claims that the tradition goes back to Abū Hurayra, a second version to ʿĀ'isha and a third to Jābir (*al-Mughnī*, IV.105).

41 Q.XC.10.

42 Q.XLI.17.

43 Q.XXII.46.

44 Q.XLIII.22.

45 Q.XLIII.31.

46 Q.LIV.24.

47 Q.XXIX.69.

48 Q.XLVII.17.

49 Q.II.120 and VI.71.

50 Q.VI.122.

51 Q.XXXIX.22.

52 Q.XXI.51.

53 Q.V.110.

54 Q.XII.24.

55 Q.XIV.38.

Chapter 13

1 Q.XIV.34.

2 Q.XVIII.109.

3 Q.XVII.85.

4 This tradition, though frequently cited by Sufis, is not to be found in any of the collections. Cf. Hujwīrī, *Kashf al-mahjūb*, II.428 (Arabic text) and Nicholson's translation, p. 197. See also William Chittick, *The Heart of Islamic Philosophy*, pp. 118, 121, 164

5 Bukhārī attributes this statement to ʿAlī, with a different wording (ʿAjlūnī, *Kashf*).

6 Q.LXXXIX.27–30.

7 Q.LXXX, 24–29.

8 Q.XV.22.

9 Q.III.191.

10 Q.XLIV.38.

11 A slightly different tradition but with the same prohibition is listed in Wensinck, *Concordance*, VI.362, '*lā tujālisu aṣḥāb al-nujūm*' (you should not sit in the company of astrologers). ʿIrāqī states that this tradition is found in Abū Dāwūd on the authority of Ibn ʿAbbās (*al-Mughnī*, IV.114). He cites a second part or separate tradition which has become a proverb, '*man iktasaba ʿilman min al-nujūm, iktasaba shuʿbatan min al-siḥr*' (He who seeks knowledge from the stars seeks [it from] the twig of sorcery) (Abū Dāwūd, IV.226). He says, 'He went beyond what was beyond [man].' This second tradition is listed in Ṭabarānī's collection as a tradition of Ibn Masʿūd. Thawbān gave even another, '*Idhā dhukira al-nujūm fa*

amsakū' (When the stars are remembered, they desist). However, the certification is weak. A third tradition is that of Muʿāwiya b. al-Ḥakam, who said, 'O Messenger of God, we used to do [many] things in the time of ignorance [before Islam]. We used to do fortune-telling.' Muḥammad replied, 'So then, desist from fortune telling!' ʿIrāqī introduced similar traditions, the first listed in Wensinck, *Concordance*, v.232, the third in vi.71.

12 Q.iii.191.

13 ʿIrāqī comments that it is a tradition of Ibn ʿAbbās with the wording, 'he did not consider it' (*al-Mughnī*, iv.115).

14 Allusion to Q.xiii:31.

15 Allusion to Q.xxiv.43.

16 Allusion to Q.lxxx.19.

17 *Unẓur*. Ghazālī's exhortatory style which began earlier in this series on the blessings of God rises in intensity as the chapter closes, calling the reader to moral and spiritual considerations.

18 Q.viii.63.

19 ʿIrāqī states that this tradition is found in Abū Dāwūd, Tirmidhī and Ibn Māja on the authority of Abū 'l-Dardā' (*al-Mughnī*, i.6).

20 Q.xxix.69.

21 Q.xiv.34 and xvi.18.

22 Q.xl.16.

23 Q.lxix.17.

24 A similar tradition is listed in Wensinck, *Concordance*, vi.265. ʿIrāqī (*al-Mughnī*, iv.118) lists eight additional traditions that pertain to Ghazālī's discussion on the relation of angels to the life of man and his environment.

25 Q.xxxvii.164.

26 Allusion to such Qur'ānic passages as the following: The angels bow before Adam at the command of God (Q.ii.34); they join with God and the believers in cursing the non-believers (Q.iii.87); they support the Muslims at the Battle of Badr (Q.iii.125); they declare that they descend at the command of God (Q.xix.64–65).

27 Allusion to Qur'ānic passages that speak of the angels in worship of God: all the angels worship God together (Q.xv.30); all the angels made prostration, save Iblīs (Q.xxxviii.73–74); for in the presence of your Lord are those who celebrate His praises by day and by night (Q.xli.38).

28 Q.vi.120.

29 ʿIrāqī was unable to trace this tradition (*al-Mughnī*, iv.120), neither could we locate it in Wensinck, *Concordance*.

30 This tradition is listed with a slight variation in Wensinck, *Concordance*, i.524.

31 Ibn Ḥibbān lists the version of this tradition that ʿIrāqī cites from Abū Hurayra, but not the version that Ghazālī quotes (*Ṣaḥīḥ*, vii.574). This tradition is also found in Ṭabarānī, *Awsaṭ*, vi.378. A tradition close in meaning and pattern is listed in Wensinck, *Concordance*, vi.125 and 274.

32 *Qūt*, i.210.

33 Q.xiv.34 and xvi.18.

34 This tradition can be found in Abū Nuʿaym, *Ḥilya* (i.210).

Chapter 14

1 Makkī reports that the incident goes back to a man who complained to the people of Medina (*Qūt*, i.210).

2 *Qūt*, i.210.

3 This tradition is listed in Ghumārī, ii.23 and in ʿAjlūnī, *Kashf*, ii.283. It is also listed in Wensinck, *Concordance*, vi.475.

4 Though Zabīdī does not identify the poet or the poem in his commentary, he does confirm the quotation and it fits well with Ghazālī's discussion in this particular case (Zabīdī, ix.132).

5 ʿIrāqī did not find a source for this *ḥadīth* (*al-Mughnī*, iv.122).

6 This tradition is listed in the *Musnad* of Abū Yaʿlā. ʿIrāqī (*al-Mughnī*, iv.122) states that it can be found in the collections of Abū Yaʿlā and Ṭabarānī. Zabīdī adds that it is also in the collections of Dāraquṭnī, Bayhaqī and Khaṭīb (Zabīdī, ix.132). Cf. Ghumārī, i.243.

7 ʿIrāqī (*al-Mughnī*, iv.122) states that it can be found in Bukhārī's *Tārīkh*.

8 ʿIrāqī mentions that this tradition is listed in Bukhārī on the authority of Abū Hurayra and Bayhaqī, *Maʿrifat*, xiv.150. It is also listed in Wensinck, *Concordance*, v.16, 17 and Munāwī, *Fayḍ al-qadīr*, v.387.

9 Ibn Abī Dunyā, *al-ʿAql*, p. 117; *Ma'thūr*, iii.337. It is also listed as the second half of a longer tradition in Munāwī, *Fayḍ al-qadīr*, v.3 and Ghumārī, ii.353.

10 *Qūt*, i.210.

11 *Qūt*, i.209. Makkī does not cite the name of the poet, nor does Zabīdī (ix.133).

12 See chapter 12, note 18.

13 Q.iv.104.

14 *Yawm al-taghābun*, Q.lxiv.9.

15 Q.xxiii.99–100.

16 Ibn Saʿd does not include this tradition in his collection of traditions regarding al-Rabīaʿ b. Khaytham.

17 *Qūt*, i.209.

18 ʿIrāqī (*al-Mughnī*, iv.124) states that it can be found in Ibn Ḥibbān's collection of traditions *al-Ḍuʿafā'*. In Ghumārī (ii.58) there is the addition of 'except that the provision [or burden] common to man became too great for him.'

19 Q xiii.11.

Chapter 15

1 Q.xlii.27.

2 Q.xcvi.6–7.

3 This tradition is listed in Munāwī, *Fayḍ al-qadīr*, ii.298 and Wensinck, *Concordance*, i.519.

4 The second clause of this sentence is a verbatim quote by Ghazālī of a poem title composed by Mutanabbī, '*maṣā'ibu qawmin ʿinda qawmin fawā'idu*' (*Dīwān*, p. 398f.)

5 Qushayrī, i.387.

6 Zabīdī does not identify the source of this tradition. It is not

listed among the sayings attributed to Jesus in Qushayrī's *Risāla*, nor does it appear to be attributed to him by Makkī in *Qūt*. However, among the supplications of the Prophet regarded as sound is this petition, '*lā tajʿal muṣībatanā fī dīninā*' [and do let our misfortune be in our religion], cf. Munāwī, *Fayḍ al-qadīr*, II.132–133.

7 Zabīdī identifies no source for this tradition. However, there is a tradition very similar to it that accounts for five blessings in trial but it is not credited to ʿUmar b. al-Khaṭṭāb. It is included in *Qūt*, I.211.

8 This Sufi tradition appears in Qushayrī, I.386–387.

9 Zabīdī does not cite a source for this Sufi tradition. It does not appear either in *Qūt* or Qushayrī.

10 Zabīdī comments that in his *Ḥilya*, Abū Nuʿaym credits this tradition to a chain of transmitters which begins with Abū ʿUmar and ʿUthmān b. Muḥammad (Zabīdī, IX.139).

11 Q.III.178.

12 Q.XXIV.15.

13 Various versions of this tradition are given in the following sources: ʿIrāqī (*al-Mughnī*, IV.126) cites Ibn Ḥanbal, *Musnad*, V.313; Ibn Ḥajar, *Tahdhīb*, V.111; Ibn Ḥibbān, *Ṣaḥīḥ*, II.141, and IV.198, with a dependent clause and replacing *adhnaba* with *akhṭa'a*. A different version of this tradition is listed in Ḥākim, *Mustadrak*, IV.388. This version is also listed in Wensinck, *Concordance*, II.187.

14 Wensinck, *Concordance*, VII.227.

15 The beginning of this tradition is listed in Wensinck, *Concordance*, II.548 and the second portion in V.416.

16 Ibn Abī Dunyā, *Dhamm al-Dunyā*, pp. 45–46; *Ma'thūr*, II.352; Munāwī, *Fayḍ al-qadīr*, III.546.

17 *Qūt*, I.211.

18 Baghawī, *Maṣābīḥ*, I.517; Munāwī, *Fayḍ al-qadīr*, VI.243; Ghumārī, I.312. ʿAjlūnī lists a tradition that affirms the first part of the present tradition, but in relation to mankind in general and not just an individual, '*idhā aḥabba Allāh qawman, ibtalāhum*' (If God loves a people, he sends them a tribulation) (*Kashf*, I.77). ʿIrāqī (*al-Mughnī*, IV.128) states that it is in the tradition collection of Ibn Abī Dunyā, *Kitāb al-maraḍ wa'l-kaffārāt*. Zabīdī comments that the same wording is found in Ḥakīm, *al-Nawādir* and *Ma'thūr*. A tradition with a similar meaning is listed in Wensinck, *Concordance*, I.219.

19 ʿIrāqī does not mention this.

20 Q.II.156.

21 The first portion of this tradition is listed in Wensinck, *Concordance*, II.99 and the second portion in I.17. Zabīdī comments that another version of this tradition is listed in Ibn Saʿd, VIII.61. Cf. Zabīdī, IX.142.

22 Ibn Ḥibbān, *Ṣaḥīḥ*, IV.257; ʿUqaylī, *Kitāb al-ḍuʿafā'* with the first

clause but a variation in the second clause. Zabīdī comments that the same reading is found in Ṭabarānī, *Kabīr* and *Awsaṭ* and in a slightly different version in Abū Yaʿlā, Ibn Ḥibbān and al-Ḍiyā' (cf. Zabīdī, IX.142). A tradition close in meaning but using *akhadha* in place of *salaba* in the first clause is listed in Wensinck, *Concordance*, VI.3.

23 ʿIrāqī (*al-Mughnī*, IV.128) says that the whole tradition is found in Ibn Abī Dunyā, *Kitāb al-maraḍ wa'l-kaffārāt*. The middle portion of this tradition is listed in Wensinck, *Concordance*, I.219, but with the plural predicate *qawman* (people). A tradition very close in pattern and meaning to the last section is listed in *Concordance* III.239.

24 Zabīdī mentions that the tradition is found in Bukhārī [presumably his *Tārīkh*], in the biography of Muḥammad b. Khālid, where *daraja* is replaced with *manzila* (IX.143). ʿIrāqī (*al-Mughnī*, IV.128) states that the tradition is found in Abū Yaʿlā, Ṭabarānī, Abū Nuʿaym, Ibn ʿAbd al-Barr and Ibn Munduh. A tradition listed in Wensinck (*Concordance*, I.219) is close in meaning and pattern to the second half.

25 Zabīdī states that this tradition is found in the collection of Abū Nuʿaym in addition to the most recognised collections (Zabīdī, IX.143). Wensinck lists the middle portion of this tradition (*Concordance*, I.480) and the last portion (III.303).

26 Zabīdī merely states that ʿAlī's saying is one of his transmitted sayings (Zabīdī, IX.143).

27 Zabīdī states that this tradition is given by Abū Nuʿaym in the *Ḥilya* (Zabīdī, IX.143).

28 Zabīdī comments that this tradition is also to be found in the *Ḥilya* of Abū Nuʿaym (Zabīdī, IX.143).

29 Wensinck lists the beginning of this tradition (*Concordance*, II.319). ʿAjlūnī lists five traditions that begin with this same conditional pattern and have to do with God's testing of the individual or a people (*Kashf*, I.78).

30 Q.XXXIX.10.

31 Zabīdī does not give a reference for this tradition. However, the anecdote appears to paraphrase some passages of the Qur'ān (Q.VIII.17 and XIV.6).

32 Q.IV.123.

33 This tradition is listed in *Ma'thūr*, III.125; Ibn Ḥibbān, *Ṣaḥīḥ*, IV.249. The opening words of this tradition are found in Wensinck, *Concordance*, IV.529 and a good part of the remainder in VI.198.

34 Q.VI.44. This tradition appears with a slight variation in Munāwī, *Fayḍ al-qadīr*, I.354.

35 Q.VI:44.

36 This tradition is listed in Ibn Abī Dunyā, *Makārim al-akhlāq*, p. 31; *Ma'thūr*, I.301; and Munāwī, *Fayḍ al-qadīr*, I.258. It is one of ten traditions listed that begin with the same conditional pattern and with the same root verb. Cf. Wensinck, *Concordance*, II.319.

37 Q.XLII.30. Zabīdī, IX.145.

38 Jīlānī, *Faḍl Allāh al-Ṣamad,* I.130, and Wensinck, *Concordance*, I.338, is very close in pattern and meaning to the first clause; there is also a second tradition that corresponds to the second clause in II.50.

39 Zabīdī notes that this Sufi tradition can be found in Abū Nuʿaym's *Ḥilya* (Zabīdī, IX.146).

40 Q.II.151.

41 Q.II.45. Zabīdī cites no sources.

42 Zabīdī comments that this quote may be found in Ṭabarānī (Zabīdī, IX.146).

43 Cf. Zabīdī, IX.146.

44 Cf. Wensinck, *Concordance*, I.406.

45 Cf. Zabīdī, IX.147.

46 According to Zabīdī (IX.147) this tradition can be found in Daylamī.

Chapter 16

1 A tradition with the same supplication using the fifth form of the root verb (*ʿawadha*) is listed in Munāwi, *Fayḍ al-qadīr*, V.201, but omits *balā' al-ākhira*. This tradition with some variation is listed in Wensinck, *Concordance*, IV.431.

2 Q.II:201. Abū Yaʿlā, VI.31; Ibn Ḥibbān, *Ṣaḥīḥ*, VI.51; Ḥākim, *Mustadrak*, I.455, and II.277; Suyūṭī, *Jāmiʿ*, V.178; and in Wensinck, *Concordance*, I.468.

3 On the supplication, see note 1 of this chapter. A similar reading is listed in Wensinck, *Concordance*, III.174.

4 Zabīdī holds that this saying of ʿAlī was spoken on an occasion of illness (Zabīdī, IX.148).

5 Cf. Wensinck, *Concordance*, IV.288.

6 This reading of the tradition is very close to Abū Yaʿlā, I.49, 75–76, 87, 112, 123. All of these are variations of the same tradition with the last seven, p. 123, being the closest to Ghazālī's quotation. Part of Abū Bakr's response included in ʿIrāqī's listing is found in Mundhirī, *Kitāb al-targhīb*. It is also found in Suyūtī, *Jāmiʿ*, V.524; Wensinck, *Concordance*, V.168, 447 and IV.286.

7 *Qūt*, I.206.

8 *Qūt*, I.206.

9 ʿIrāqī (*al-Mughnī*, IV.131) states that Ibn Isḥāq in his biography of the Prophet mentions that this was part of the prayer of the Prophet when he visited Ṭā'if at the beginning of his mission. It is also to be found in Ibn Abī Dunyā.

10 Zabīdī (IX.149) includes the full text of Sumnūn's poem (eight verses). Ghazālī quotes only the first line.

11 Qushayrī, I.122. The statement that Sumnūn called himself 'the Liar' was cited earlier by Sulamī in *Kitāb ṭabaqāt al-ṣūfiyya*, p. 195. This incident also appears in the later collection of Farīd al-Dīn ʿAṭṭār, *Tadhkirāt al-awliyā'*, translated by Arberry as *Muslim Saints and Mystics*, p. 241.

12 Qushayrī, II.625.

Chapter 17

1 This tradition was given earlier in the exposition on patience. See Chapter One, note 13.

2 *Qūt*, I.195.

3 Q.XXXIX.10.

4 Abū Yaʿlā, XI.459; Ibn Ḥibbān, *Ṣaḥīḥ*, I.267; Baghawī, *Maṣābīḥ*, III.159 with *ka* in place of *bi*; Munāwī, *Fayḍ al-qadīr*, IV.285.

5 Munāwī, *Fayḍ al-qadīr*, III.359; Shawkānī, *al-Fawā'id*, p. 437.

6 Munāwī, *Fayḍ al-qadīr*, IV.153; Wensinck, *Concordance*, IV.106.

7 This tradition was given earlier in the exposition on patience; *Ma'thūr*, II.575.

8 *Ma'thūr*, II.569; Wensinck, *Concordance*, VI.464.

9 ʿIrāqī (*al-Mughnī*, IV.133) says this tradition is found in Ṭabarānī's *Awsaṭ*. The tradition is also quoted in *Qūt*, I.203. The first part of this tradition is listed in Wensinck, *Concordance*, VI.337.

10 ʿIrāqī (*al-Mughnī*, IV.133) says it is also found in Daylamī's *Musnad al-firdaws*. The last part of this tradition is listed in Wensinck, *Concordance*, II.216.

11 *Qūt*, I.195. Cf. Wensinck, *Concordance*, I.220 for the last part.

12 Q.II.245.

13 Q.IX.104.

14 Q.II.245.

15 Q.XXXVI.47.

16 Q.VI.148

17 Q.II.26.

18 Nasā'ī, *Sunan*, V.311; Munāwī, *Fayḍ al-qadīr*, VI.338; and Wensinck, *Concordance*, VI.10.

19 ʿIrāqī (*al-Mughnī*, IV.136) comments that this tradition can be found in Muslim.

20 *Qūt*, I.201.

21 *Qūt*, I.201.

22 Ibn Abī Dunyā, *Shukr*, p. 14; Jīlānī, *Faḍl Allāh al-Ṣamad*, I.303; Ibn Hibbān, *Ṣaḥīḥ*, V.172–173; Abū Yaʿlā, II.365; and Wensinck, *Concordance*, III.166.

23 Qushayrī, I.389.

APPENDIX

PERSONS CITED IN THE TEXT

ᶜABD AL-RAḤMĀN B. ᶜAWF al-Qurashī (d. 31/652). An early Companion of the Prophet, he became Muslim before the Prophet entered the House of Arqam in Mecca (c. 614) and was among eight who came early to Islam. He was one of the wealthiest man in the nascent Islamic community. He emigrated to Abyssinia during the persecution of 615, but returned to Medina. He participated in the battles of Badr, Uḥud and other engagements during the Prophet's lifetime. When the second caliph, ᶜUmar, died ᶜAbd al-Raḥmān was one of the council of six that chose ᶜUthmān b. ᶜAffān as the succeeding caliph. (Ibn Saᶜd, *Ṭabaqāt al-kabīr*, III.1, 87ff; Ibn al-Athīr, *Usd al-ghāba*, v.480ff; Nawawī, *Tahdhīb*, II.300–302; *EI²*, I.84.)

ABŪ BAKR AL-ṢIDDĪQ b. Abī Quḥāfa al-Taymī (d. 13/634). Born in Mecca, Abū Bakr was the first to embrace Islam outside of the Prophet's family. He was a trusted lifelong Companion of the Prophet. When the Prophet was critically ill, Abū Bakr was called upon to conduct the ritual prayers. After the death of the Prophet he became the first caliph (r. 11–13/632–634). (*Mashāhīr*, pp. 4–5; Abū Nuᶜaym, *Ḥilya*, I.28–34; Suyūṭī, *Tārīkh al-khulafā'*, trans. Jarrett, pp. 25–112; *EI²*, I.109–111.)

ABŪ 'L-DARDĀ', ᶜUwaymir al-Khazrajī 'l-Anṣārī (d. 32/652). He did not become a Muslim until after the Battle of Badr. Abū 'l-Dardā''s reputation rested chiefly on his authority in Qur'ān studies and his initiative in assembling it. He settled in Damascus, where he was both a judge and a teacher. He was known as the 'true father of the Damascus school.' (Ibn Ḥanbal, *Musnad*, traditions in which Abū 'l-Dardā' is the transmitter: v.94, VI.440–452; Abū Nuᶜaym, *Ḥilya*, I.208–227; Ibn Ḥajar, *Iṣāba*, III.45–46, 266f; *EI*, I.113–114, 266f.)

ABŪ MASᶜŪD al-Balkhī (Unidentified). Ghazālī quotes him in his discussion of tribulation with patience in relation to thankfulness. This is set in a paragraph in which Balkhī's convictions match those of famous Sufis such as Ibn al-Mubārak, al-Fuḍayl b. ᶜIyāḍ and Ḥātim al-Aṣam. (Ibn Ḥajar, *K. lisān al-mīzān*, VI.436; Zabīdī, IX.147; Le Strange, *Lands*, p. 479.)

ABŪ MŪSĀ 'L-ASHᶜARĪ, ᶜAbd Allāh b. Qays (d. c. 42/622–623). A Companion of the Prophet and a military commander, he was commissioned to go on diplomatic missions and preach to the tribes and cities of Yemen. During the period of the rightly-guided caliphs, ʿUmar appointed Abū Mūsā governor of Basra and Kufa. When ʿAlī was elected caliph, Abū Mūsā pledged his allegiance to him. Abū Mūsā later withdrew from active political life. He was noted not only for his military skills but also for his compassion and recitation of the Qur'ān. (Ibn Ḥibban, *Tārīkh al-ṣaḥāba*, p. 154; Abū Nuʿaym, *Ḥilya*, I.256–268; Nawawī, *Tahdhīb*, II.268–269; Ibn al-Athīr, *Usd al-ghāba*, III.367–369; *EI*[2], I.695–696.)

ABŪ SAʿĪD AL-MAYHANĪ (d. 330/941). Known as Faḍl b. Aḥmad b. Muḥammad, surnamed Ibn Abī 'l-Ḥasan. Abū Saʿīd was a contemporary of Abū 'l-Qāsim, Salmān b. Nāṣir al-Anṣarī and Abū ʿAlī Zāhir b. Aḥmad al-Sarkhaṣī. He is remembered for his *karamāt*. Ḥujwīrī has preserved a number of anecdotes about his life. He passed away in Mayhana. (Hujwīrī, pp. 164–166; Zabīdī, pp. 56–57.)

ABŪ SULAYMAN AL-DĀRĀNĪ, ʿAbd al-Raḥmān (d. 205/820–821 or 215/830–831). We do not hear of him making great journeys or receiving instruction from renown teachers, nevertheless, his pithy aphorisms, maxims and occasional retorts demonstrate a pious man of deep faith. This won him the distinction of being a true ascetic of the Sufi tradition. His affirmation of the need to balance hope and fear of God influenced future generations of Sufi Muslims including Abū Ḥāmid al-Ghazālī. (Sulamī, pp. 75–90; Abū Nuʿaym, *Ḥilya*, IX.254–280; Qushayrī, I.86–88; Ibn Khallikān, *Wafayāt*, II.88–89; Ṣafadī, XV.397.)

ABŪ ṬALḤA, Zayd b. Sahl al-Anṣārī 'l-Khazrajī (d. 34/654). A Companion of the Prophet. His wife was Umm Sulaym bint Milḥam, the mother of Anas b. Mālik. Abū Ṭalḥa was a warrior at the Battle of Badr, one of the archers and a guardian of the Prophet. Muḥammad said of him, 'The voice of Abū Ṭalḥa was better than one hundred men.' He also fought at Uḥud and Ḥunayn. He passed away at the age of seventy in Medina. (Ibn Saʿd, *Ṭabaqāt al-kabīr*, V.53–54; Ibn al-Athīr, *Usd al-ghāba*, pp. 289–290; Nawawī, *Tahdhīb*, II.235–236; Ibn Ḥajar, *Iṣāba*, IV.113–114; Ibn Ḥibbān, *Tārīkh al-ṣaḥāba*, p. 106.)

AḤNAF B. QAYS, Sakhr b. Muʿāwiya al-Tamīmī (d. 67/686–687). One of the Followers, the second generation of Islam, and the first of the tribe of Tamīm to join Islam, he was credited with the conversion of his tribe. He fought in many battles and collected traditions narrated by ʿUmar, ʿUthmān, ʿAlī and Ḥasan al-Baṣrī. He was noted for his aphorisms, maxims and proverbs. He died at Kufa at the age of seventy. (Ibn Saʿd, *Ṭabaqāt al-kabīr*, VII.66–69; *Mashāhīr*, pp. 87–88; *Ṣifat al-ṣafwa*, III.123–125; Ibn al-Athīr, *Usd al-ghāba*, I.68; Ibn Khallikān, *Wafayāt*, I.635–644; *EI*[2], I.304.)

Appendix

ʿĀ'ISHA bint Abī Bakr (d. 58/678). The third and most revered wife of the Prophet. It was with her that the Prophet spent his last days, having taken leave from the other women of the household. Following the death of the Prophet, ʿĀ'isha lived a comparatively quiet life for two decades, becoming an avid reader of Arabic literature and history, writing poetry and gathering traditions. When ʿUthmān faced opposition and finally death at the hands of his enemies, she joined the forces of Ṭalḥa and Zubayr against ʿAlī. Following the Battle of the Camel she was escorted back to Medina where she lived until her death. (Ibn Ḥibbān, *Tārīkh al-ṣaḥāba*, p. 201; Abū Nuʿaym, *Ḥilya*, II.43–50; Ibn Ḥajar, *Iṣāba*, IV.359–361; Bint al-Shāṭī', *Tarājim Sayyidāt*, pp. 252–297; *EI²*, I.307–308.)

ʿALĪ B. ABĪ ṬĀLIB (d. 40/661). The cousin of the Prophet and later son-in-law by his marriage to Fāṭima, daughter of the Prophet. ʿAlī's marriage to Fāṭima took place after the Hijra and she bore him two sons, Ḥasan and Ḥusayn. He took no other wife until her death. ʿAlī took part in the battles of Badr, Uḥud and Khandaq. After ʿUthmān's death he reluctantly accepted the office of caliph. His election was contested by ʿA'isha, Ṭalḥa, Zubayr and Muʿāwiya in Damascus. These protestations led to a long series of insurrections, battles and negotiations, ending in his assassination by the Khawārij. ʿAlī was committed to a life of austerity and piety. Nearly six hundred traditions are ascribed to him as transmitter. He was sixty-two years of age at his death. (*Mashāhīr*, pp. 6–7; Abū Nuʿaym, *Ḥilya*, I.61–87; Ibn al-Athīr, *Usd al-ghāba*, pp. 91–96; Nawawī, *Tahdhīb*, I.344–349; Suyūṭi, *Tārīkh al-khulafā'*, trans. Jarrett, pp. 170–189.)

ʿAMR B. AL-ʿĀṢ al-Sahmī (d. 42/663–664). Born a Qurayshī from the clan of Sahm, he became a Companion of the Prophet, a skilled general and a shrewd politician. He was instrumental in the conquest of Palestine and Egypt, where he established the military garrison city of Fusṭāṭ, later Cairo. He allied himself with Muʿawiya at Ṣiffīn and represented him at the arbitration that followed. When Muʿawiya became the new caliph, ʿAmr resumed his service as the governor of Egypt until his death. (*Mashāhīr*, p. 55; Ibn al-Athīr, *Usd al-ghāba*, IV.244–248; Nawawī, *Tahdhīb*, II.30–31; Ibn Ḥajar, *Iṣāba*, III.2–3; *SEI*, p. 42.)

ANAS b. Mālik b. Naḍr al-Khazrajī (d. 91 or 93/709–710 or 711–712). A well-known Companion of the Prophet. At the age of ten he was given over to the Prophet by his mother, as a servant. He served the Prophet for ten years and after the Prophet's death, he fought in the wars of conquest and served as prayer leader. Traditions which are credited to him can be found in Ṭayālisī, *Musnad* (pp. 1959–2150) and in Ibn Ḥanbal (*Musnad*, III.98–292). He died and was buried in Basra. (Ibn Saʿd, *Ṭabaqāt al-kabīr*, VII.10–16; Ibn Ḥibbān, *Tārīkh al-ṣaḥāba*, pp. 28–29; Ibn al-Athīr, *Usd al-ghāba*, I.151–152; Nawawī, *Tahdhīb*, I.128–129; *EI²*, I.482.)

ʿAṬĀ B. ABĪ RABĀḤ (d. 114–115/732–733). An outstanding representative of the early Meccan school of law, he is ranked with two others of the Followers (the generation that succeeded the Companions of the Prophet): Abū ʿAbd al-Raḥmān Ṭa'ūs al-Yemenī (d. 106/724) and Mujāhid b. Jabr al-Makkī (d. 104/722–723). ʿAṭā was born in Yemen of Nubian parents in the latter part of ʿUthmān b. ʿAffān's caliphate, but was raised in Mecca. He was influenced by four prayer leaders: Ibn ʿUmar, Ibn ʿAbbās, Ibn al-Zubayr and Ibn al-ʿĀṣ. Al-Shāfiʿī said, 'No one among the successors of the Companions was a greater follower of the tradition of the Prophet than ʿAṭā.' (Ibn Saʿd, *Ṭabaqāt al-kabīr*, v.344–346; *Mashāhīr*, p. 81; Abū Nuʿaym, *Ḥilya*, III.310–325; Nawawī, *Tahdhīb*, II.333–334; *EI*², I.730.)

BILĀL b. Rabāḥ al-Habashī 'l-Taymī (d. 17 or 21/638–639 or 642–643). A Companion of the Prophet. He was born into slavery in Mecca. His first master, Umayya b. Khalaf, treated him harshly, particularly after he became a Muslim. He was purchased by Abū Bakr al-Ṣiddīq and became a freeman. After the Hijra, the Prophet asked him to call Muslims to prayer in Medina. Bilāl also took part in military campaigns. After the death of the Prophet, Bilāl joined the Muslim army in Syria, and then returned to serve the caliph Abū Bakr as the caller to prayer. (Ibn Saʿd, *Ṭabaqāt al-kabīr*, III.165–170; Abū Nuʿaym, *Ḥilya*, I.147–150; Ibn al-Athīr, *Usd al-ghāba*, I.243–245; Nawawī, *Tahdhīb*, I.136–137; *EI*², II.1215.)

FATḤ al-Mawṣulī 'l-Zāhid (d. 170/786). His surname was Abū Naṣr. He was a well-known ascetic in Mawṣul and Baghdad. The story in our text indicates how much his wife supported him in his asceticism. We have no death date for her. Al-Khaṭīb al-Baghdādī, in his history, shares stories of his visits to Bishr b. al-Ḥārith, a relative and fellow Sufi in Baghdad. He was noted as one of the renown shaykhs of Mawṣul. (*Tārīkh Baghdād*, XII.381–383.)

FUḌAYL b. ʿIyāḍ (d. 187/803–804). A celebrated ascetic of early Sufism, he had a bold and fearless nature. In his youth and early adult life he was a bandit. Hearing a verse from the Qur'ān at a critical moment in his life (Q.LVII.15), he repented. Giving up a passionate love for a woman, he began a life of devout asceticism. Al-Fuḍayl studied under Sufyān al-Thawrī and Abū Ḥanīfa. He was remembered for his unswerving denial of worldliness and his pithy aphorisms. (Sulamī, pp. 6–15; Abū Nuʿaym, *Ḥilya*, VIII.84–139; Ḥujwīrī, pp. 97–100; ʿAṭṭār, pp. 52–61; Ibn Khallikān, *Wafayāt*, III.478–480; Ṣafadī, XXIV.80–82.)

ḤABĪB b. Abī Ḥabīb al-Bajlī (or Bajalī) (death date unknown). His surnames include Abū ʿAmr, Abū ʿAmīra and Abū Kashutha. Al-Bajlī or al-Bajalī may indicate a *nisba* after an Arab tribe. Ḥabīb transmitted a number of traditions on the authority of Anas b. Mālik. (Ibn Ḥajar, *Tahdhīb al-tahdhīb*, II.180; Zabīdī, IX.7.)

AL-ḤALLĀJ, al-Ḥusayn b. Manṣūr al-Bayḍāwi (d. 309/922). The most dynamic and controversial figure of Sufism in the late second and early third Islamic centuries, he was born (244/857–858) of Persian parents in the village of Ṭūr in the vicinity of Bayḍā', in southwest Iran. His surname was Abū 'l-Mughīth. His father was a wool-carder, as he was occasionally. The family moved from Ṭūr to Wāsiṭ, founded by the Arabs, located near the Tigris. The city's population adhered to Ḥanbalī Islam. At twelve years old, he had memorised the Qur'ān by heart. Later, the young Ḥallāj became a disciple of Saḥl al-Tustarī and then went to Basra, where he made a profession of Sufi Islam, received the Sufi mantle and was a follower of ʿAmr al-Makkī. His divergences from conventional Sufism brought him into conflict with Muslim authorities on several occasions. He was tried and executed under the caliph Muqtadir. (Sulamī, pp. 307–311; *Tārīkh Baghdād*, VIII.112–141; Hujwīrī, pp. 150–152; ʿAṭṭār, pp. 264–271; Ibn Khallikān, *Wafayāt*, I.423–426; *Passion*, p. 1, *EI²*, III.127–128.)

ḤAMDŪN AL-QASSĀR, Ibn Aḥmad al-Nīsābūrī (d. 218/833). A jurist who followed the school of law founded by Sufyān al-Thawrī. He was recognised among the righteous men of Nīsābūr, Khurāsān. He enjoyed a large following among the Sufis and was known for his many aphorisms and exhortations. His followers became known as the Qassārī movement. When Ḥamdūn al-Qassār passed away, he was buried in Hira cemetery in Nīsābūr. (Sulamī, pp. 123–129; Abū Nuʿaym, *Ḥilya*, x.231–232; Qushayrī, I.103–104; Hujwīrī, pp. 125–126, 183–184; Ṣafadī, XIII.165.)

AL-ḤASAN B. ʿALĪ b. Abī Ṭālib (d. c. 50/670–671). The first grandson of the Prophet and second Imam of the Shīʿa. He claimed the caliphate but then renounced it from the mosque minbar in Kufa. He passed away after a long period of ill health and was buried in Medina. (*Mashāhīr*, p. 7; Ibn al-Athīr, *Usd al-ghāba*, II.10–16; Ibn Ḥajar, *Iṣāba*, *EI²*, III.240–243.)

AL-ḤASAN AL-BAṢRĪ, Abū Saʿīd (d. 110/728–729). Of those who succeeded the Companions of the Prophet in early Islam, he was the first great model for Sufism and Muslim theology. Ḥasan was born in Medina. He joined the military campaigns in eastern Iran and settled in Basra, where he earned a reputation for piety and knowledge of the Qur'ān and *ḥadīth*. His funeral brought out the whole city of Basra and his tomb attracts many devout visitors. (Ibn Saʿd, *Ṭabaqāt al-kabīr*, VII.114–129; Abū Nuʿaym, *Ḥilya*, II.131–161; Hujwīrī, pp. 86–87; ʿAṭṭār, pp. 19–26; Ibn Khallikān, *Wafayāt*, I.370–372; *EI²*, III.247–248.)

ḤĀTIM AL-AṢAMM al-Balkhī (d. 237/851–852). A member of the Khurāsānian school of asceticism, he was a disciple of Shaqīq al-Balkhī and adopted many of his ascetic themes. Ḥātim was known as 'the Luqmān of this nation' for his good works, plain speech and memorable aphorisms. (Sulamī, pp. 91–97; Abū Nuʿaym, *Ḥilya*, VIII.73–84; *Tārīkh Baghdād*, VIII.241–245; Qushayrī, I.89–90; Hujwīrī, p. 115; Ṣafadī, XI.233–234; ʿAṭṭār, pp. 150–152.)

AL-ḤUSAYN B. ʿALĪ b. Abī Ṭālib (d. 61/680). The second grandson of the Prophet, he grew up in Medina but did not play a major role in the affairs of the community for the remaining years of the Prophet's life and during the caliphates of Abū Bakr, ʿUmar and ʿUthmān. He recognised the caliphate of Muʿawiya but refused to recognise his son Yazīd as the heir. Having received pledges of support from the Kufans, he marched to Kufa. Ḥusayn's support evaporated and the Kufans met him in battle in Karbala, where he was slain. (*Tārīkh Baghdād*, I.141–143; Ibn al-Athīr, *Usd al-ghāba*, II.18–23; Suyūṭī, *Tārīkh al-khulāfa'*, trans. Jarrett, pp. 210–211; *EI*², III.607–615.)

IBN ʿABBĀS, ʿAbd Allāh al-Hāshimī 'l-Makkī (d. 68/687–688). A close Companion and cousin of the Prophet. In his youth and early adulthood he followed the Muslim armies on several campaigns, gaining first-hand knowledge of events. As he became prominent towards the end of ʿUthmān's caliphate, the caliph charged him with leading the pilgrimage to Mecca. Later Ibn ʿAbbās commanded a section of ʿAlī's troops at the Battle of the Camel (36/656) and Ṣiffīn (37/657). Dissatisfied with political developments, Ibn ʿAbbās retired to Mecca and involved himself occasionally in the interest of the Hāshimī clan. Through all these events Ibn ʿAbbās was highly respected by everyone. He is recognised for his well rounded knowledge. He is acknowledged as 'the father' of Qur'ānic exegesis and prominent narrator of *ḥadīth*. (Ibn Saʿd, *Ṭabaqāt al-kabīr*, II.2, 119–124; Ibn Ḥanbal, *Musnad*, I.214–374; Ibn Ḥibbān, *Tārīkh al-ṣaḥāba*, pp. 148–149; Ibn Ḥajar, *Iṣāba*, II.330–334; Ibn al-Athīr, *Usd al-ghāba*, III.290–294; *EI*², I.40–41.)

IBN ABĪ NAJĪḤ, ʿAbd Allāh (d. 131/748–749). He was known for his piety and gathered many reliable traditions as did his father. He died in Mecca. (Ibn Saʿd, *Ṭabaqāt al-kabīr*, V.355; Nawawī, *Tahdhīb*, II.294; Ibn Ḥajar, *Iṣāba*, IV.199.)

IBN ʿAṬĀ', Abū'l ʿAbbās (d. c. 309/921 or 922) was considered among the more learned of the Sufi shaykhs of his time. He was a disciple of Junayd and counted such contemporary Sufis as Ibn Khafīf and Abū Bakr al-Shiblī among his friends. Ibn ʿAṭā' defended Sufism against criticism, but was eventually put on trial and executed. His works are lost, but the aphorisms and stories about him have been preserved in the writings of Sulamī (pp. 260–268). (Abū Nuʿaym, *Ḥilya*, X.302–305; *Tārīkh Baghdād*, V.26–30; and ʿAṭṭār, pp. 236–238.)

IBN MAS^c^ŪD, ^c^Abd Allāh al-Hudhalī (d. 32–33/652–653 or 653–654). A companion of the Prophet, he liked to call himself 'the sixth of six,' emphasising that he entered Islam early. He emigrated with others to Abyssinia and on his return he joined the Prophet in Medina. The Sufis considered him one of the People of the Veranda (Ahl-al-Ṣuffa). He is remembered for his knowledge of the Qur'ān and the Sunna. He is also credited with collecting eight hundred and forty-eight traditions. (Ibn Sa^c^d, *Ṭabaqāt al-kabīr*, III.106–114; Ibn Ḥanbal, *Musnad*, I.374–466; *Mashāhīr*, p. 10; Abū Nu^c^aym, *Ḥilya*, I.124–139; Ibn al-Athīr, *Usd al-ghāba*, III.384–390; Ṣafadī, XVII.604, 606; Ibn Ḥajar, *Iṣāba*, II.3688–3770; *EI*,[2] I.873–875.)

IBN AL-MUBĀRAK b. Wāḍiḥ al-Ḥanẓalī (d. 181/797–798). A man learned in Islamic traditions and a respected ascetic, Ibn al-Mubārak became a Sufi of exemplary conduct and compassion. He was born in Merv, Khurāsān, and grew up in a rich atmosphere of learning. Later he traveled to Kufa, the Holy Cities, and Damascus, studying under Sufyān al-Thawrī, Mālik b. Anas and Awzā^c^ī of Syria. His feats of memory were celebrated. He could listen to a long sermon and repeat it verbatim upon request. His life came to an end at the age of sixty-three, as a result of wounds suffered in duels with the Byzantines. (*Mashāhīr*, 194f; Abū Nu^c^aym, *Ḥilya*, VIII.162–90; *Tārīkh Baghdād*, X.152–169; Hujwirī, p. 95f; *Ṣifat al-ṣafwa*, IV.109f; ^c^Aṭṭār, pp. 124–128; Ibn Khallikān, *Wafayāt*, II.12f.)

IBN AL-SAMMĀK, Muḥammad b. Ṣabīḥ (d. 183/799–800). He was a Sufi who became a great preacher, ascetic and traditionalist. He studied Qur'ān under Sulayman b. al-^c^Amash and *ḥadīth* under Sufyān al-Thawrī. He came to Baghdad in the days of the caliph Harūn al-Rashīd. Many anecdotes about his life and aphorisms, wit and wisdom have been preserved by his biographers. After spending some time in Baghdad, he returned to Kufa, where he passed away. (Abū Nu^c^aym, *Ḥilya*, VIII.203–217; *Tārīkh Baghdād*, V.368–373; Ibn Khallikān, *Wafayāt*, III.18–20.)

JĀBIR b. ^c^Abd Allāh al-Khazrajī 'l-Anṣārī (d. 68/687–688 or 78/697–698). A Companion and the son of a Companion of the Prophet, he is credited with gathering 1,540 traditions of the Prophet. Jābir was held in high esteem by many Companions and leaders of the succeeding generation. In the late period of the rightly-guided caliphs he fought on the side of ^c^Alī at Ṣiffīn. (Ibn Ḥanbal, *Musnad*, III.292–400; Ibn Ḥibbān, *Tārīkh al-ṣaḥāba*, p. 58; Ibn al-Athīr, *Usd al-ghāba*, pp. 307–308; Nawawī, *Tahdhīb*, I.142–143; Ibn Ḥajar, *Iṣāba*, p. 213.)

AL-JUNAYD, Abū 'l-Qāsim b. Muḥammad (d. 298/910–911). A Sufi scholar of great renown, he was a native of Baghdad. He was the nephew and disciple of Ṣari Saqaṭī. He studied jurisprudence under Abū Thawrī. In contrast to more extreme expressions of charismatic Sufism, Junayd advocated a 'sober' system of Sufism. He could speak with authority in the fields of theology, jurisprudence and ethics. He was known among his contemporaries as 'the Peacock of the Learned Men' and the Lord of the Sufi community. (Sulamī, pp. 153–163; Abū Nuʿaym, *Ḥilya*, x.255–287; *Tārīkh Baghdād*, vii.241–249; Qushayrī, i.105–108; Hujwīrī, pp. 128–130, 188–189; Ibn Khallikān, *Wafayāt*, i.338–340; Ṣafadī, xi.201–203; *EI*², ii.600, Abdel-Kader, *Life, Personality and Writings of al-Junayd*.)

KHABBĀB B. AL-ARATT, Abū ʿAbd Allāh (d. 37/657–658). A Companion of the Prophet, traditions do not agree about his origin. He is listed also among the People of the Veranda (Ahl al-Ṣuffa) during the post-Meccan period of the Prophet's life. A tradition of ʿAlī says he was the first of the Nabaṭ (Nabataeans) to become a Muslim. He transmitted thirty-two traditions of the Prophet, some of which were accepted in the canonical collections. ʿAlī prayed at his grave on returning from the Battle of Ṣiffīn. (Ibn Ḥanbal, *Musnad*, v.108–112; Abū Nuʿaym, *Ḥilya*, i.143–148; *Tārīkh Baghdād*, i.205–206; Nawawī, *Tahdhīb*, i.174–175; Ibn Khallikān, *Wafayāt*, ii.476; Ibn Ḥajar, *Iṣāba*, i.416; *EI*², iv.896–897.)

AL-KHAWWĀṢ, Ibrāhīm b. Aḥmad, Abū Isḥāq (d. 291/904). A companion of Junayd and other Sufi shaykhs of Baghdad, he was known for his affirmation of trust in God. He authored a number of works on Sufi ethics. He claimed to have made seventeen journeys to Mecca as well as other lone excursions into the desert. There are many stories about his encounters with lions. (Sulamī, pp. 284–287; Abū Nuʿaym, *Ḥilya*, x. 320–322; *Tārīkh Baghdād*, vi.7–10; Hujwīrī, pp. 153–541.)

MĀLIK B. ANAS al-Aṣbaḥī 'l-Madanī (d. 179/795–796). The foremost Muslim jurist of early Islam. His younger, contemporary historians Ibn Saʿd (d. 230/845) and Wāqidī (d. 207/822) placed him in the sixth class of Successors to the Companions of the Prophet. He founded the Māliki school of Islamic law and was Imam of Medina. Mālik's greatest work was the *Kitāb al-muwaṭṭā'*, the earliest surviving Muslim book of law, said to record 'the conventional consensus of opinion' in Medina. (*Mashāhīr*, p. 140; Abū Nuʿaym, *Ḥilya*, vi.316–355; Ibn Khallikān, *Wafayāt*, ii.545–549; Nawawī, *Tahdhīb*, i.757–79; *EI*², vi.262–265.)

AL-MA'MŪN, ʿAbd Allāh b. Rashīd (r. 198–218/813–833). The seventh ʿAbbāsid caliph, he was brought up by Zubayda, granddaughter of al-Manṣūr, the first ʿAbbāsid caliph. He was provided with the best of teachers in the Qur'ān, *ḥadīth*, jurisprudence, *adab* (manners and behaviour), music and poetry. On one of the fasts of Ramadan he was reputed to have read the Qur'ān thirty-three times. He was deeply embroiled in succession disputes in Khurāsān, and faced crises related to the unity of the empire, the challenge of the Byzantines, and the reconciliation of Sunnīs and Shīʿīs. Al-Ma'mūn pursued his passion for learning in the realm of Muʿtazilī theology and in the establishment of the House of Wisdom, which was recognised as a great achievement in the promotion of learning through the translation of Greek works into Arabic. Al-Ma'mūn passed away while on a military operation in Anatolia where he had had a number of successes. (Suyūṭī, *Tārīkh al-khulafā'*, trans. Jarrett, pp. 318–348; *EI*², VI.331–339.)

AL-RABĪʿ B. KHUTHAYM (or Khaytham), al-Thawrī (d. 63/682–683). Al-Rabīʿ belonged to the second generation of Muslims, the Followers, and lived in Kufa. He was one of eight early Muslim ascetics. He was exposed to the teachings of ʿAbd Allāh b. al-ʿAbbās. At some point in his adult life, he was struck with palsy and focused himself on bearing up patiently in suffering through discipline of worship and the fear of hell. (*Mashāhīr*, pp. 99–100; Abū Nuʿaym, *Ḥilya*, II.105–119.)

AL-RUMAYṢĀ', bint Milḥam (Umm Sulayn) (no dates). A celebrated female Companion of the Prophet. She was present with ʿĀ'isha at the Battle of Uḥud and again at Ḥunayn. She was know for her earnest faith. (Ibn Saʿd, *Ṭabaqāt al-kabīr*, VIII.310–318; Ibn Ḥibbān, *Tārīkh al-ṣaḥāba*, p. 103; Abū Nuʿaym, *Ḥilya*, II.57–61; Ibn Ḥajar, *Iṣāba*, IV.308.)

SAHL AL-TUSTARĪ, b. ʿAbd Allāh (d. 283/896). He as born in Tustar and received his early training in Islamic law under Ibn Sawwar. Sahl al-Tustarī blended two streams of early Sufism: the piety and disciplines of asceticism and the burgeoning mystical reflection. His legacy for future generations of Muslims lay in the pupils he trained, the aphorisms and maxims recorded by his biographers, and his short commentary on the Qur'ān, of which six known manuscripts are extant. (Sulamī, pp. 206–211; Abū Nuʿaym, *Ḥilya*, X.189–212; Qushayrī, I.83–85; Ḥujwīrī, pp. 139–140, 195–210; ʿAṭṭār, pp. 155–160; Ibn Khallikān, *Wafayāt*, II.429–430; Ṣafadī, XVI.16–17; *SEI*, pp. 488–489; Böwering, *Mystical Vision*.)

SĀLIM, MAWLA ABĪ HUDHAYFA, ʿUtba b. Rabīʿa (d. 12/633). A Companion of the Prophet, he was of Persian descent. As a poor emigrant, he was offered shelter in a corner of the mosque of Medina called the Ṣuffa. This area became known as the place of the People of the Veranda (Ahl al-Ṣuffa). (Abū Nuʿaym, *Ḥilya*, I.176–178; Ibn al-Athīr, *Usd al-ghāba*, II.307–309; Nawawī, *Tahdhīb*, I.206–207; Ibn Ḥajar, *Iṣāba*, II.6–8.)

SUMNŪN B. ḤAMZA al-Khawwāṣ al-Ṣūfī (d. 300/913). Samnūn was noted for his focus on love based on Qur'ānic passages. He called himself Samnūn the Liar for his concealment of his illness, for which he even pleaded with children to pray for his healing—a demonstration of humility and an endorsement of supplication (*duʿa'*). He had many friends among the Sufis, including Sarī 'l-Saqaṭī and he was a contemporary of Junayd (d. 298/910). His own experience of suffering made Samnūn sensitive to the suffering of others, thus bringing his faith to bear in concrete ways. (Sulamī, pp. 195–199; Abū Nuʿaym, *Ḥilya*, x.309–314; *Tārīkh Baghdād*, ix.234–237; Qushayrī, i.122–123; Hujwīrī, pp. 136–138; ʿAṭṭār, pp. 239–242.)

AL-SHĀFIʿĪ, Muḥammad b. Idrīs al-Qurashī (d. 204/820). Born in Gaza, Palestine and raised in Mecca, he became the founder of the Shāfiʿī school of law. His early life with the Bedouins gave him a solid grounding in Arabic language and poetry. He studied law under Sufyān b. ʿUyayna and Mālik b. Anas. His chief contribution was to make the Qur'ān, the Sunna and the *ḥadīth* the primary elements of jurisprudence (*usūl al-fiqh*), yet keep his theory of legal judgements from becoming too rigid for future development. (Abū Nuʿaym, *Ḥilya*, ix.63–161; *Tārīkh Baghdād*, ii.56–73; Ḥujwīrī, p. 116; Nawawī, *Tahdhīb*, i.44–67; *SEI*, pp. 512–515.)

AL-SHIBLĪ, Abū Bakr Dulaf b. Jaḥdar (d. 334/945–946). His family originated in Khurāsān. Though his *nisba*, Shiblī, refers to the town of Shibla in the vicinity of Samarqand, he was born in Samarra or Baghdad; his father was in the service of the caliph. Shiblī embraced Sufism and became a follower of Junayd (d. 298/910–911). He grew in faith and knowledge of jurisprudence, such that he became renowned for his devotion. (Sulamī, pp. 337–348; Abū Nuʿaym, *Ḥilya*, x.366–375; *Tārīkh Baghdād*, ix.389–397; Ḥujwīrī, pp. 155–156; Qushayrī, i.148–149; ʿAṭṭār, pp. 277–286.)

ʿUMAR B. ʿABD AL-ʿAZIZ b. Marwan (r. 99–101/717–720). The most pious of the Umayyad caliphs, ʿUmar was called the 'fifth rightly-guided' caliph. Born in Ḥulwan, an Egyptian village, and raised in Medina, he was brought up by the pious successors of the Prophet's Companions. Through his mother, he was descended from the Companion and Caliph ʿUmar b. al-Khaṭṭab. His grandfather served as a model of faith and discipline. He owned only one shirt, lived on a simple diet and passed his life in prayer. He had a scar on his forehead, the result of a kick from a horse he recieved as a boy. Caliph ʿUmar I once said, 'Of my posterity there shall be a man with a scar on his face who shall fill the earth with justice.' Caliph ʿAbd al-Mālik (d. 86/705) persuaded him to come to Damascus, where he was given the hand of the caliph's daughter in marriage. He returned to Medina as governor, and was later appointed caliph. ʿUmar II sought to ensure that justice was administered equally in all the provinces; he discouraged *jihād* wars as a pretext for plunder. At the same time, his programme to assimilate all Arabs and others into Islam continued during his regime. He was also noted for his sermons and counsels. (Abū Nuʿaym, *Ḥilya*, v.253–353; Suyūṭī, *Tārīkh al-khulafā'*, trans. Jarrett, pp. 233–248.)

ʿUMAR B. AL-KHAṬṬAB al-Qurayshī al-ʿAdawī (r. 13–23/634–644). A Companion of the Prophet and later caliph. The Prophet called him al-Fārūq (he who distinguishes truth from falsehood). In the Medinan period he took part in the battles of Badr, Uḥud and subsequent engagements. His closeness to the Prophet was evident. He became a father-in-law to Muḥammad by giving his daughter Ḥafṣa to him in marriage. ʿUmar became caliph with Abū Bakr's approval before the latter passed away. ʿUmar's ten-year reign as caliph was marked by many developments, both within and beyond the Islamic community. Muslim armies were victorious to the west, the north and the east, creating an empire far beyond the Arabian Peninsula. ʿUmar was the first to establish a public treasury, provide for military pensions, institute ordinances of Islamic law for public morals in punishments, define the status of non-Muslims and maintain a public register. (*Mashāhīr*, pp. 5–6; Ibn Ḥajar, *Iṣāba*, II.518–519; Suyūṭī, *Tārīkh al-khulafā'*, trans. Jarrett, pp. 112–152; *SEI*, pp. 600–601.)

ʿUQBA B. ʿĀMIR al-Juhanī (d. 58/677–678). A Companion of the Prophet, he was among the People of the Veranda (Ahl al-Ṣuffa). ʿUqba was a shepherd by occupation. He participated in the conquest of Damascus and fought with Muʿawiya against ʿAlī at Ṣiffīn (37/657). Muʿawiya appointed ʿUqba as the governor of Egypt. He collected fifty traditions of the Prophet (Ibn Ḥanbal, *Musnad*, I.143–159, 201) and was well versed in the recitation of the Qur'ān. (*Mashāhīr*, p. 55; Abū Nuʿaym, *Ḥilya*, II.8–9; Ibn al-Athīr, *Usd al-ghāba*, IV.53–54; Nawawī, *Tahdhīb*, I.336.)

BIBLIOGRAPHY

ʿAbd al-Bāqī, Muḥammad Fu'ād. *al-Muʿjam al-mufahras li-alfāẓ al-Qur'ān al-karīm*. 2 vols. Beirut: al-Khayyāt, n.d.

Abū Dāwūd, Sulaymān b. al-Ashʿath al-Sijistānī. *Sunan Abī Dāwūd* with the *Kitāb maʿālim sunan li'l-Khaṭṭābī*. Beirut: Dār al-Ḥadīth, 1394/1974.

Abū Nuʿaym, Aḥmad b. ʿAbd Allāh b. Aḥmad al-Iṣbahānī. *Ḥilyat al-awliyā' wa-ṭabaqāt al-aṣfiyā'*. 10 vols. Cairo: Maktabat al-Khānjī wa-Maṭbaʿat al-Saʿāda, 1351–1357/1932–1938.

Abū Yaʿlā al-Mawṣilī. *Musnad Abī Yaʿlā al-Mawṣilī*. 14 vols. Edited by ʿIzzat ʿUbayd al-Daʿās and ʿĀdil al-Sayyid. Beirut and Damascus: Dār al-Ma'mūn lil-Turāth, 1410/1990.

Aḥdab, Khaldūn al-. *Zawā'id Tārīkh Baghdād ʿalā al-kutub al-sitta*. 10 vols. Damascus: Dār al-Qalam, 1417/1996.

ʿAjlūnī, Ismāʿīl b. Muḥammad (al-Jarrāḥī) al-. *Kashf al-khafā' wa-muzīl al-ilbās ʿammā ishtahara min aḥādīth alsinat al-nās*. 2 vols. Beirut: Dār Iḥyā' al-Turāth al-ʿArabī, 1351/1932.

ʿAlī, ʿAbdullah Yūsuf. *The Meaning of the Holy Qur'ān, New Edition with Revised Translation and Commentary*. Brentwood, NJ: Amana Corporation, 1412/1992.

Ali, Muhammad. *The Holy Quran*. Lahore: Ahmadiyya Anjuman Ishaʿat Islam, 1963.

Arberry, Arthur J. *The Koran Interpreted: A Translation*. 2 vols. New York: Macmillan, 1955.

———. *Poems of al-Mutannabī: A Selection with Introduction, Translations and Notes*. Cambridge: Cambridge University Press, 1967.

———. *Revelation and Reason in Islam*. London: Allen and Unwin, 1957.

———. *Sufism: An Account of the Mystics of Islam*. London: George, Allen & Unwin Ltd., 1963.

ʿAṭṭār, Farīd al-Dīn. *Muslim Saints and Mystics*. Translated by Arthur J. Arberry. London: Routledge & Kegan Paul, 1966.

Baghawī, Ḥusayn b. Masʿūd al-. *Maṣābīḥ al-sunna*. Edited by Yūsuf ʿAbd al-Raḥmān al-Marʿashlī, Muḥammad Salīm Ibrāhīm Samāra, and Jamāl Ḥamdī al-Dhahabī. 4 vols. Beirut: Dār al-Maʿrifa, 1407/1987.

Bayhaqī, Aḥmad b. al-Ḥusayn al-. *Maʿrifat al-sunan wa'l-āthār*. 15 vols. Edited by ʿAbd al-Muʿṭī Amīn Qalʿajī. Aleppo and Cairo: Dār al-Wāfī, 1411/1991.

———. *al-Sunan al-ṣughrā*. 4 vols. Beirut: Dār al-Jīl, 1415/1995.

Bint al-Shāṭi', ʿĀ'isha ʿAbd al-Raḥmān. *Tarājim Sayyidāt Bayt al-Nubuwwa*. Beirut: Dār al-Kitāb al-ʿArabī, 1387/1967.

Böwering, Gerhard. *The Mystical Vision of Existence in Classical Islam: The Qur'ānic Hermeneutics of the Ṣufī Saḥl at-Tustarī (d. 283/896)*. Berlin and New York: Walter de Gruyter, 1980.

Brockelmann, Carl. *Geschichte der Arabischen Litteratur*. 2 vols. Weimar: Emil Felber, 1898/1902. *Supplementband*. 3 vols. Leiden: E. J. Brill, 1937–1942.

Buṣīrī, Aḥmad b. Abī Bakr, al-. *Misbāḥ al-zujāja fī zawā'id Ibn Māja*. Beirut: Dār al-Kitāb al-ʿArabī, 1406/1996.

Chittick, William C. *Faith and Practice: Three Thirteenth-Century Sufi Texts*. Albany: State University of New York Press, 1992.

———. *The Heart of Islamic Philosophy: The Quest for Self-knowledge in the Teaching of Afḍal al-Dīn Kashānī*. Oxford: Oxford University Press, 2001.

———. *The Sufi Path of Knowledge: Ibn al-ʿArabi's Metaphysics of Imagination*. Albany: State University of New York Press, 1989.

Corbin, Henry. *Creative Imagination in the Sufism of Ibn ʿArabī*. Translated by Ralph Manheim. Princeton, N.J.: Princeton University Press, 1969.

Dāraquṭnī, ʿAlī b. ʿUmar al-. *al-Mu'talif wa'l mukhtalif*. Edited by Mawfiq ʿAbd al-Qādir. 5 vols. Beirut: Dār al-Gharb al-Islāmī, 1406/1986.

Dārimī, Abū Muḥammad al-. *Sunan al-Dārimī*. Beirut: Dār al-Maʿrifa, 1406/1986.

Daylamī, Abū Shujāʿ, Shīrawayhi al-. *Kitāb firdaws al-akhbār bi-ma'thūr al-khiṭāb*. 5 vols. Beirut: Dār al-Kitāb al-ʿArabī, 1407/1987.

Donaldson, Dwight M. *Studies in Muslim Ethics*. London: S.P.C.K., 1953.

Encyclopaedia of Islam. Ed. J. H. Kramers, H. A. R. Gibb, et al. 2d edition. Leiden: E. J. Brill, 1954–2002.

Ghazālī, Abū Ḥāmid Muḥammad b. Muḥammad. *Bidāyat al-hidāya*. Cairo: al-Maṭbaʿa al-Khayriyya, 1330/1911.

———. *Iḥya' ʿulūm al-dīn*. 10 vols. Cairo: Maṭbaʿat Muṣṭafā al-Bābī al-Ḥalabī, 1358/ 1939.

———. *Iḥya' ʿulūm al-dīn*, books 31–36. Translated by Richard Gramlich as *Muḥammad al-Ġazzālīs Lehre von den Stufen zur Gottesliebe: Die Bücher 31-36 seines Hauptwerkes engeleitet, übersetzt und kommentiert*. Wiesbaden: Franz Steiner Verlag, 1984.

———. *Iḥyā' ʿulūm al-dīn*. Translated by Fazlul Karim as *Imam Gazzali's Ihya ulum id-Din*. Lahore: Sing Sagar Academy, n.d.

———. *Kitāb adāb al-maʿīsha wa-akhlāq al-nubuwwa*. Translated by Leon Zolondek as *Book XX of the Iḥyā' ʿulūm al-dīn*. Leiden: E. J. Brill, 1963.

———. *Kitāb ādāb al-nikāḥ*. Translated by Madelain Farah as *Marriage and Sexuality in Islam, al-Ġazālī's Book on the Etiquette of Marriage* (*Kitāb Ādāb al-Nikāḥ*). Salt Lake City: University of Utah Press, 1984.

———. *Kitāb asrār al-ṣalāh wa-muhimmātihā*. Translated by Edwin E. Calverley as *al-Ghazzālī's Book of the Iḥyā' on Worship*. London: Luzac and Co., 1925.

———. *Kitāb asrār al-ṣawm*. Translated by Nabih Amin Faris as *The Book of the Mysteries of Fasting*. Lahore: Sh. Muhammad Ashraf, 1992.

———. *Kitāb asrār al-ṭahāra*. Translated by Nabih Amin Faris as *The Mysteries of Purity*. Lahore: Sh. Muḥammad Ashraf, 1966.

———. *Kitāb asrār al-zakat*. Translated by Nabih Amin Faris as *The Mysteries of Almsgiving*. Beirut: Centennial Publications, 1966.

———. *Kitāb dhikr al-mawt wa-mā baʿdahu*. Translated by T. J. Winter as *The Remembrance of Death and the Afterlife. Book XL*. 2d ed. Cambridge: Islamic Texts Society, 1995.

———. *Kitāb al-faqr wa'l-zuhd*. Translated by A. F. Shaker as *On Poverty and Abstinence*. Cambridge: Islamic Texts Society, forthcoming.

———. *Kitāb al-ʿilm*. Translated by Nabih Amin Faris as *The Book of Knowledge*. Lahore: Sh. Muḥammad Ashraf, 1963.

———. *Kitāb al-khawf wa'l-rajā'*. Translated by William McKane as *al-Ghazali's Book of Fear and Hope*. Leiden: E. J. Brill, 1962.

———. *Kitāb al-maḥabba wa'l-shawq wa'l-uns wa'l-riḍā*. Translated by Eric Ormsby as *On Love, Longing, Intimacy and Contentment*. Cambridge: Islamic Texts Society, forthcoming.

———. *Kitāb qawāʿid al-ʿaqā'id*. Translated by Nabih Amin Faris as *Foundations of the Articles of Faith*. Lahore: Sh. Muḥammad Ashraf, 1963.

———. *Kitāb riyaḍāt al-nafs*. Translated by T. J. Winter as *On Disciplining the Soul*. Cambridge: Islamic Texts Society, 1995.

———. *al-Maqṣad al-asnā fī sharḥ maʿānī asmā' Allāh al-ḥusnā*. Edited by Fadlou A. Shehādī. Beirut: Dār al-Mashriq, 1971.

———. *al-Maqṣad al-asnā*. Translated by David Burrell and Nazih Daher as *The Ninety-Nine Beautiful Names of God*. Cambridge: Islamic Texts Society, 1992.

———. *Mishkāt al-anwār*. Edited by A. ʿAfīfī. Cairo: Dār al-Qawmiyya lil-Ṭibāʿa wa'l-Nashr, 1383/1963.

———. *Mishkāt al-anwār*. Translated by W. H. T. Gairdner as *The Niche for Lights*. Lahore: Kashmiri Baser, 1924.

———. *al-Munqidh min al-ḍalāl*. Edited by Jamīl Ṣalībā and Kāmil ʿIyād. Beirut: Dār al-Andalus, 1967.

———. *al-Munqidh min al-ḍalāl*. Translated by Richard Joseph McCarthy as *Freedom and Fulfillment*. Boston: Twayne Publishers, 1980.

———. *al-Munqidh min al-ḍalāl wa-bidāyat al-hidāya*. Translated by W. Montgomery Watt as *The Faith and Practice of al-Ghazālī*. London: George Allen and Unwin, 1963.

———. *Tahāfut al-falāsifa*. Edited by Sulaymān Dunyā. Cairo: Dār al-Maʿārif, 1374/1955.

Ghumārī, Aḥmad b. Muḥammad b. al-Ṣiddiq. *Fatḥ al-wahhāb bi-takhrīj aḥadīth al-shihāb*. Edited by Ḥamdī ʿAbd al-Majīd al-Salafī. 2 vols. Beirut: ʿĀlam al-Kutub, Maktabat al-Nahḍa al-ʿArabiyya, 1408/1985.

Guillaume, Alfred. *Ibn Isḥāq's Life of Muḥammad, A Translation of Ibn Isḥāq's Sīrat Rasūl Allāh*. Lahore: Oxford University Press, 1955.

Ḥākim al-Nīsābūrī al-. *al-Mustadrak ʿalā al-Ṣaḥīhayn*. 5 vols. Beirut: Dār al-Maʿrifa, 1406/1986.

Hitti, Philip K. *History of the Arabs from the Earliest Times to the Present*. 10th ed. New York: St. Martin's Press, 1970 (repr. 1991).

Hujwīrī, ʿAlī b. ʿUthmān al-Jullābī, al-. *Kashf al-maḥjūb li-arbāb al-qulūb*. Translated by R. A. Nicholson as *The Kashf al-mahjub: The Oldest Persian Treatise on Sufism*. London: Luzac and Co., 1936.

Ibn Abī Dunyā. *al-ʿAql wa'l-faḍl wa'l-yaqīn*. Edited by Majdī Ibrāhīm. Cairo: Maktabat al-Qur'ān, 1408/1988.

———. *Dhamm al-dunyā*. Edited by Majdī Ibrāhīm. Cairo: Maktabat al-Qur'ān, 1408/1988.

———. *Kitāb al-shukr*. Cairo: Maktabat al-Manār, 1349/1930.

———. *Makārim al-akhlāq*. Edited by James A. Bellamy. Wiesbaden: Franz Steiner Verlag, 1973.

———. *Muḥāsabat al-nafs*. Beirut: Dār al-Kutub al-ʿIlmiyya, 1406/1986.

Ibn al-ʿArabī. *Kitāb al-qabas fī sharḥ Muwaṭṭā' Mālik ibn Anas*. 3 vols. Edited by Muḥammad ʿAbd Allāh Wild Karīm. Beirut: Dār al-Gharb al-Islāmī, 1992.

Ibn al-Athīr, ʿIzz al-Dīn Muḥammad. *Usd al-ghāba fī maʿrifat al-ṣaḥāba*. 7 vols. Cairo: Dār al-Ḥadīth, 1390/1970.

Ibn al-Athīr, Majd al-Dīn, Abū al-Saʿadāt al-Mubārak b. Muḥammad al-Jazarī. *al-Nihāya fī gharīb al-ḥadīth wa'l-āthār*. 4 vols. Cairo: ʿĪsā al-Bābī al-Ḥalabī, 1383/1963.

Ibn Ḥajar al-ʿAsqalānī, Aḥmad b. ʿAlī. *al-Iṣāba fī tamyīz al-ṣaḥāba*. 4 vols. Cairo: Cairo: Maṭbaʿat al-Saʿāda, 1910.

———. *Kitāb lisān al-mīzān*. 7 vols. Hyderabad: Dā'irat al-Maʿārif, 1329–1331/1911–1913.

———. *Kitāb tahdhīb al-tahdhīb*. 12 vols. Hyderabad: Dā'irat al-Maʿārif, 1325–27/1907–9.

Ibn Ḥanbal, Aḥmad. *Musnad al-Imām Aḥmad b. Ḥanbal*. 5 vols. Beirut: al-Maktab al-Islāmī, Dār Ṣādir, 1389/1969.

Ibn Ḥibbān, Muḥammad, al-Bustī. *Kitāb mashāhīr ʿulamāʾ al-amṣār*. Edited by M. Fleischhammer. Cairo: Maṭbaʿat Lajnat al-Taʾlīf waʾl-Tarjama waʾl-Nashr, 1959.

———. *Ṣaḥīḥ*. Edited by Aḥmad Muḥammad Shākir. Cairo: Dār al-Maʿārif, 1952.

———. *Tārīkh al-ṣaḥāba alladhī ruwīya ʿanhum al-akhbār*. Edited by Būrān al-Ḍannāwī. Beirut: Dār al-Kutub al-ʿIlmiyya, 1408/1988. Ibn al-Jawzī, ʿAbd al-Raḥmān. *Zād al-masīr fī ʿilm al-tafsīr*. 9 vols. Damascus: al-Maktab al-Islāmī, 1384/1964.

Ibn al-Jawzī, Abū al-Faraj. *Ṣifat al-ṣafwā*. 4 vols. Hyderabad: Dāʾirat al-Maʿārif, 1355–1357/1936–1938.

———. *Talbīs Iblīs*. Beirut: Dār al-Waʿy al-ʿArabī, 1975.

Ibn Khallikān, Abū ʿl-ʿAbbās Shams al-Dīn Aḥmad b. Muḥammad b. Abī Bakr. *Wafayāt al-aʿyān wa-anbāʾ abnāʾ al-zamān*. 6 vols. Beirut: Dār Ṣādir, 1972.

Ibn Māja, Muḥammad b. Yazīd. *Ḍaʿīf sunan Ibn Māja*. Edited by Nāṣir al-Dīn al-Albānī. Beirut: al-Maktab al-Islāmī, 1408/1988.

Ibn Manẓūr, Muḥammad b. Mukarram. *Lisān al-ʿArab*. 7 vols. Cairo: Dār al-Maʿārif, n.d.

Ibn Qutayba, ʿAbd Allāh b. Muslim al-Dīnawarī. *al-Maʿārif li-Ibn Qutayba*. Edited by Tharwat ʿUkāshah. Cairo: Dār al-Maʿārif bi-Miṣr. 1389/1969.

Ibn Saʿd, Muḥammad b. Saʿd b. Manī al-Zuhrī. *Kitāb al-ṭabaqāt al-kabīr*. 9 vols. Edited by Edward Sachau. Leiden: E. J. Brill, 1917.

Ibn ʿUqayl, ʿAbd Allāh. *Sharḥ Ibn ʿUqayl ʿalā Alfiyya Ibn Mālik*. 4 vols. Cairo: Maṭbaʿat Muṣṭafā Muḥammad, n.d.

ʿIrāqī, ʿAbd al-Raḥīm al-. *al-Mughnī ʿan ḥaml al-aṣfār fī asfār fī-takhrīj ma fīʾl-Iḥyāʾ min al-akhbār*. 4 vols. Cairo: Maṭbaʿat al-Bābī al-Ḥalabī, 1358/1939.

———. *al-Mughnī ʿan ḥaml al-aṣfār fī asfār fī-takhrīj ma fīʾl-Iḥyāʾ min al-akhbār*. Edited by Ashraf b. ʿAbd al-Maqṣūd. Riyadh: Maktabat Ṭabariyya, 1995.

Izutsu, Toshihiko. *Ethico-religious Concepts in the Qurʾān*. Montreal: McGill University Press, 1966.

Jabre, Farīd. *Essai sur le lexique de Ghazali*. Beirut: Publications de l'Université Libanaise, 1970.

———. *La notion de certitude selon Ghazali*. Paris: J. Vrin, 1958.

Jīlānī, Faḍl Allāh. *Faḍl Allāh al-Ṣamad fī tawḍīḥ al-adab al-mufrad*. 2 vols. Homs: al-Maktaba al-Islāmiyya, 1389/1969.

Junayd b. Muḥammad, Abū al-Qāsim. *The Life, Personality and Writings of al-Junayd: A Study of a Third/Ninth-century Mystic.* Edited and translated by Ali Hassan Abdel-Kader. London: Luzac, 1962.

Kalābādhī, Abū Bakr Muḥammad b. Isḥāq al-. *The Doctrine of the Ṣūfīs: Kitāb al-Taʿarruf li-madhāhib ahl al-taṣawwuf.* Translated by Arthur J. Arberry. Cambridge: Cambridge University Press, 1935.

Khadduri, Majid. *Islamic Jurisprudence: Shāfiʿī's Risāla. Translated with an Introduction, Notes, and Appendices.* Baltimore: Johns Hopkins Press, 1961.

Khaṭīb al-Baghdādī, Aḥmad b. ʿAlī al-. *Tārīkh Baghdād aw Madīnat al-Salām.* 14 vols. Cairo: Maktabat al-Khānjī, 1931.

Lane, Edward W. *An Arabic-English Lexicon in Eight Parts.* London: Williams and Norgate, 1863 (repr. Beirut: Librairie du Liban, 1968).

Laoust, Henri. *La Politique de Gazali.* Paris: Librairie Orientaliste Paul Geuthner, 1970.

Le Strange, Guy. *Lands of the Eastern Caliphate.* Cambridge: Cambridge University Press, 1930.

Macdonald, Duncan B. *The Religious Attitude and Life in Islam.* Beirut: Khayat, 1965.

Maḥmaṣānī, Ṣubḥī Rajab. *Falsafat al-tashrīʿ fī'l-Islām: The Philosophy of Jurisprudence.* Translated by Farhat J. Ziadeh. Leiden: E. J. Brill, 1961.

Makkī, Abū Ṭālib Muḥammad b. ʿAlī al-. *Qūt al-qulūb fī muʿāmalāt al-maḥbūb wa-waṣf ṭarīq al-murīd ilā maqām al-tawḥīd.* 2 vols. Cairo: Maṭbaʿat Muṣṭafā al-Bābī al-Ḥalabī, 1961.

Mālik b. Anas. *Muwaṭṭā'.* Edited by Aḥmad Rātib ʿArmush. Beirut: Dār al-Nafā'is, 1397/1977.

Massignon, Louis. *Essai sur les origines du lexique technique de la mystique musulmane.* Paris: J. Vrin, 1954.

———. *The Passion of al-Hallāj Mystic and Martyr of Islam.* Translated by Herbert Mason. 4 vols. Princeton: Princeton University Press, 1982.

Massignon, Louis, and Paul Kraus. *Akbār al-Ḥallāj: Texte ancien relatif à la prédication et au supplice du mystique musulman al-Ḥosayn B. Manṣour al-Ḥallāj.* Paris: Larose, 1936.

Munāwī, Muḥammad ʿAbd al-Raʾūf al-. *Fayḍ al-qadīr: Sharḥ al-Jāmiʿ al-Ṣaghīr li'l-Suyūṭī.* 6 vols. Cairo: Maṭbaʿat Muṣṭafā Muḥammad, n.d.

Mundhirī, ʿAbd al-ʿAẓīm b. ʿAbd al-Qawī al-. *Kitāb al-targhīb wa'l-tarhīb.* 4 vols. Cairo: Muṣṭafā 'l-Bābī 'l-Ḥalabī, 1968–1969.

Mutanabbī, Aḥmad b. al-Ḥusayn al-. *Dīwān al-Mutanabbī.* Edited by ʿAbd al-Wahhāb ʿAzzām. Cairo: Lajnat al-Ta'līf wa'l-Tarjama wa'l-Nashr, 1944.

Nasā'ī, Aḥmad b. Shūʿayb al-. *Sunan al-Nasā'ī.* Edited by ʿAbd Allāh b. Ḥasan al-Shabrāwī. 5 vols. Cairo, Dār al-Hadith 1999.

Nawawī, Muḥyī al-Dīn b. Sharaf al-. *Tahdhīb al-asmā' wa'l-lughāt*. 3 vols. Beirut: Idārat al-Ṭibaʿa al-Munīriyya, 1977.

Nicholson, R. A. *The Mystics of Islam*. London: Routledge and Kegan Paul, 1914; New York: Schocken Books, 1975.

Othman, Ali I. *The Concept of Man in Islam in the Writings of al-Ghazali*. Cairo: Dār al-Maʿarif, 1960.

Padwick, Constance E. 'Al-Ghazālī and Arabic Versions of the Gospel, An Unsolved Problem.' *Moslem World*, Vol. xxix, no. 2 (April 1939).

Pickthall, Muḥammad Marmaduke. *The Meaning of the Glorious Koran*. London: A. A. Knopf, 1930.

Qushayrī, ʿAbd al-Karīm al-. *al-Risāla al-Qushayriyya*. 2 vols. Edited by ʿAbd al-Ḥalīm Maḥmūd and Maḥmūd b. al-Sharīf. Cairo: Dār al-Kutub al-Ḥadītha, 1385/1966.

Ṣafadī, Khalīl b. Aybak al-. *Kitāb al-wafī bi-wafayāt*. 29 vols. Edited by Helmut Ritter, et al. Wiesbaden: n.p, 1959.

Sarrāj, ʿAbd Allāh b. ʿAlī al-. *Kitāb al-lumaʿ fī 'l-taṣawwuf*. Translated by R. A. Nicholson. Leiden: E. J. Brill, 1914.

Shawkānī, Muḥammad b. ʿAlī al-. *al-Fawā'id al-majmūʿa fī al-aḥadīth al-mawḍūʿa*. Cairo: Maktabat al-Sunna al-Muḥammadiyya, 1389/1960.

Shehadi, Fadlou. *Ghazali's Unique Unknowable God*. Leiden: E. J. Brill, 1964.

Sherif, Mohamed Aḥmad. *Ghazali's Theory of Virtue*. Albany: State University of New York Press, 1975.

Shorter Encyclopaedia of Islam, edited by H. A. R. Gibb and J. H. Kramers. Ithaca, NY: Cornell University Press, 1953.

Smith, Margaret. *Al-Ghazālī the Mystic: A Study of the Life and Personality of Abū Ḥāmid Muḥammad al-Ṭūsī al-Ghazālī*. London: Luzac Company, 1944.

Subkī, ʿAbd al-Wahhāb b. ʿAlī al-. *Ṭabaqāt al-Shāfiʿiyya al-kubrā*. 6 vols. Edited by Maḥmūd Muḥammad al-Ṭanāḥī and ʿAbd al-Fattāḥ Muḥammad al-Ḥilw. 10 vols. Cairo: Maṭbaʿat ʿĪsā al-Bābī al-Ḥalabī, 1386/1967.

Sulamī, Muḥammad b. Mūsā. *Kitāb ṭabaqāt al-ṣūfiyya*. Edited by Johannes Pedersen. Leiden: E. J. Brill, 1960.

Suyūṭī, ʿAbd al-Raḥmān al-. *Jāmiʿ al-aḥādith li'l-masānīd wa'l-marāsīl*. 2 vols. Damascus: Maṭbaʿat Muḥammad Ḥāshimī al-Kutubī, 1400/1979.

———. *Tārīkh al-khulafā'*. Edited by Qāsim al-Shamāʿī al-Rifāʿī and Muḥammad ʿUthmānī. Beirut: Dār al-Arqam, n.d.

———. *Tārīkh al-khulafā'*. Translated by Henry Sullivan Jarrett as *History of the Caliphs*. Amsterdam: Oriental Press, 1970.

Ṭabarānī, Sulaymān b. Aḥmad al-. *Makārim al-akhlāq*. Edited by Fārūq Ḥamāda. Beirut: Dār al-Rashād al-Ḥadīth, 1400/1980.

———. *al-Muʿjam al-awsaṭ*. 10 vols. Edited by Abū Muʿādh Ṭāriq b. ʿAwaḍ Allāh b. Muḥammad and Abū al-Faḍl ʿAbd al-Muḥsin b. Ibrāhīm al-Ḥusaynī. Cairo: Dār al-Ḥaramayn, 1416/1995.

———. *Muʿjam al-ṣaghīr li'l-Ṭabarānī*. 2 vols. Edited by ʿAbd al-Raḥmān Muḥammad ʿUthmān. Medina: al-Maktaba al-Salafiyya, 1388/1968.

Ṭayālisī, Sulaymān b. Dāwūd al-. *al-Musnad*. Hyderabad: Maṭbaʿat Majlis Dā'irat al-Maʿārif al-Niẓāmiyya, 1321/1903.

Tirmidhī al-Ḥākim al-. *al-Nawādir al-uṣūl*. Beirut: Dār Ṣādir, 1972.

ʿUqaylī, Muḥammad b. ʿAmr al-. *Kitāb al-ḍuʿafā' al-kabīr*. 4 vols. Edited by ʿAbd al-Muʿṭī Amīn Qalʿajī. Beirut: Dār al-Kutub al-ʿIlmiyya, 1404/1984.

Vesey-Fitzgerald, S. G. "Nature and Sources of the Shariʿa." In *Law in the Middle East*, edited by Majid Khadduri and Herbert Lienbesny. Washington, D.C.: Middle East Institute, 1955.

Wāqidī, Muḥammad b. ʿUmar al-. *Kitāb al-maghāzī*. 3 vols. Edited by Marsden Jones. London: Oxford University Press, 1966.

Watt, W. Mongomery. *Companion to the Qur'ān, Based on the Arberry Translation*. London: George Allen and Unwin, 1967.

———. *The Faith and Practice of al-Ghazālī*. London: George Allen and Unwin, 1963.

———. *Muhammad at Medina*. Oxford: Clarendon Press, 1956 and Edinburgh: Edinburgh University Press, 1963.

———. *Muslim Intellectual: A Study of al-Ghazali*. Edinburgh: Edinburgh University Press, 1963.

Wehr, Hans. *A Dictionary of Modern Written Arabic*. Edited by J. Milton Cowan. Wiesbaden: Otto Harrassowitz, 1961.

Wensinck, Arent Jan. *Concordance et indices de la tradition musulmane*. 7 vols. Leiden: E. J. Brill, 1936.

Zabīdī, al-Sayyid Murtaḍā al-. *Itḥāf al-sāda al-muttaqīn bi-sharḥ asrār Iḥyā' ʿulūm al-dīn*. 9 vols. Beirut: Dār Iḥyā' al-Turāth al-ʿArabī, n.d.

Zamakhsharī, Muḥammad b. ʿUmar al-. *Tafsīr al-kashshāf*. 4 vols. Beirut Dār al-Kitāb al-ʿArabī, n.d.

Zwemer, Samuel M. *A Moslem Seeker After God: The Life and Teaching of Al-Ghazālī*. New York: Fleming H. Revell, 1921.

INDEX TO QUR'ĀNIC QUOTATIONS

Index to Qur'ānic Quotations

Index to Qur'ānic Quotations

Index to Qur'ānic Quotations

GENERAL INDEX

General Index